READINGS IN THE APPLIED ECONOMICS OF AFRICA

VOLUME 1: MICRO-ECONOMICS

READINGS IN THE APPLIED ECONOMICS OF AFRICA

Edited by
EDITH H. WHETHAM
Sometime Visiting Professor in Agricultural Economics
at Ahmadu Bello University Northern Nigeria

and
JEAN I. CURRIE
Sometime Lecturer in Economics at
Ahmadu Bello University

VOLUME I: MICRO-ECONOMICS

CAMBRIDGE
AT THE UNIVERSITY PRESS
1967

Published by the Syndics of the Cambridge University Press
Bentley House, 200 Euston Road, London, N.W.1
American Branch: 32 East 57th Street, New York, N.Y. 10022

Printed in Great Britain
by Billing & Sons Limited, Guildford and London

PREFACE

This two-volume collection of *Readings in the Applied Economics of Africa* is designed to supplement courses in economics given in African universities. The purpose of teaching economics is to help students to understand the working of the countries in which they will eventually become business men, lawyers, advisers, civil servants and politicians. But the ' principles of economics ' are too often memorized for reproduction at examinations, and are too seldom used to illuminate the current problems of rapid change, which are discussed mainly in journals and official reports. Students in the early stages of university courses cannot be expected to consult a variety of journals, even if available in their libraries, which may not be the case in new universities; further, librarians are finding difficulty in obtaining information about other African countries. There is therefore a need for a selection of papers illustrating the economy of African countries, papers which can be used in conjunction with standard text-books.

In Volume 1—Micro-economics, the use of resources is considered from the angle of the firm or the farm. Parts I and II deal respectively with agriculture and with industry, and Part III considers prices and markets, through which goods and services are exchanged and incomes are earned.

Volume 2—Macro-economics, contains papers concerned with the framing and implementation of economic policy. Part IV illustrates the problems encountered in compiling and using the national accounts of African countries. Part V is devoted to public finance, banking and the balance of payments; Part VI, dealing with economic development, includes papers on population, export trades and import-saving industries, employment and inflation.

The selection made by the editors from the mass of material now published has been determined by many factors, including topic, length, suitability for student discussion, geographical coverage and ease of access; they express their thanks to those authors who have allowed their work to be reprinted here, and to the editors of the journals concerned. For each paper, only those references have been included which are mentioned in the extracts printed. It has not been thought necessary to provide an index, but the scope of each paper has been indicated briefly in the List of Contents.

The editors have in preparation a companion text-book which

will be published shortly by the Cambridge University Press under the title *The Economics of African Countries*.

E. H. W.

December 1966   J. I. C.

AKNOWLEDGEMENTS

We should like to thank the following for their permission to reproduce copyright material: the author and the F.A.O. for K. C. Abercrombie's article; the authors and the Agricultural Economics Society for the articles by E. S. Clayton and H. A. Oluwasanmi; the University of Chicago Press for C. Davis Fogg's article; the authors and the East African Institute of Social Research for the articles by P. H. Gulliver and W. Elkan; the Food Research Institute of Stanford University and the Trustees of the Leland Stanford Junior University for G. B. Masefield's article; the author and the *Journal of Overseas Administration* for G. J. W. Pedraza's article; the author and the *Scottish Journal of Political Economy* for R. S. May's article; the author and *Oxford Economic Papers* for S. P. Schatz's article; the authors and the Editor of *Nigerian Journal of Economic and Social Studies* for the articles by S. U. Ugoh, S. Williams, T. M. Yesufu and O. Olakanpo; the author and the International Economic Association for G. Blau's article; the author, the Editor of *Africa* and the International African Institute for A. Cohen's article; the author and the Hoover Institution for P. Kilby's article; the author and the Economic Society of Ghana for R. L. Lawson's article.

Precise details of the original form of publication are to be found in the List of Contents.

CONTENTS

vii

Contents

Contents

CONTENTS OF VOLUME 2

PART I

USE OF RESOURCES—AGRICULTURE

---

1. THE TRANSITION FROM SUBSISTENCE TO MARKET AGRICULTURE IN AFRICA SOUTH OF THE SAHARA*

K. C. ABERCROMBIE

Characteristics of subsistence agriculture

Subsistence production may be defined as that part of their production which is used directly by the producers and their families. Marketed production is that which is sold or bartered for either domestic consumption or export.

Areas where production is used entirely for subsistence, and which are therefore completely self-contained and cut off from the rest of the economy, are of course already very rare in Africa, if indeed any remain at all. There are still, however, many communities where, although some sales or barter transactions take place, the production of a small surplus above immediate subsistence requirements is largely unintentional and the result of an occasional particularly favourable season. A third stage in the transition from subsistence to market agriculture is where the regular production of a marketable surplus is deliberately aimed at, but the main emphasis is still on subsistence production. In the final stage, production for the market predominates over subsistence.†

Some of the principal characteristics that result when production is mainly for subsistence must be briefly sketched, together with certain of the tribal institutions usually associated with this type of agriculture in Africa South of the Sahara. Many of these features will persist in some degree for a long time to come, and their impli-

---

* Some parts of this article are adapted from a study prepared by FAO for the United Nations Committee on Information from Non-Self-Governing Territories. See United Nations, *Special Study on Economic Conditions in Non-Self-Governing Territories*, New York, 1960, pp. 39–42.

† This useful division of the transition to market agriculture into four stages is developed by M. Yudelman and S. M. Makings in *A Note on the Economics of African Development in Southern Rhodesia, with Special Reference to Agriculture* (unpublished mimeograph).

1

cations should be carefully studied by those concerned with measures to promote the economic development of the region.

A main feature of communities where agricultural production is very largely for subsistence is their comparative isolation from the economic and other influences of the outside world. If there is hardly any exchange of goods and services with other areas, not only the influence of the price mechanism but also the inflow of innovations and ideas are bound to be extremely limited. Although the conservatism of African farmers may often be somewhat overstressed,* there is no doubt that the lack of familiarity with change resulting from this isolation powerfully reinforces certain features of the traditional tribal economy that tend to discourage innovation and initiative. This economy, at least in its most primitive form, aims only at the provision of subsistence for all members of the tribe, to the realization of which relatively limited aim it is quite well adapted so long as land remains abundant in relation to population.

The actions of the members of the tribe are to a great extent regulated by customs designed to avoid any individual initiative that might endanger the precarious equilibrium that has been achieved with the environment. The land belongs to the tribe. Its use is generally allotted to individuals or families on the basis of their subsistence needs, and it is rarely possible for the more able or energetic to enlarge their share. Especially where it is periodically reallotted, or in the many areas where shifting cultivation is still practised, there is little incentive to make improvements that would lead to greater production. In most parts of Africa the individual has responsibilities to a very numerous 'extended family' group, and this too discourages production for the market, since the proceeds must be so widely shared, while it also tends to swallow up any small surplus that he may occasionally produce.

Specialization can develop only to the extent that exchange takes place, and its almost complete absence is therefore a major characteristic where agricultural production is largely for subsistence. Even the

* Certainly some very substantial changes must have been accepted by most African communities at some time in the past, judging by the present importance in the region of maize, cassava and sweet potatoes, which were originally introduced from the American continent and in many areas have largely replaced indigenous crops as staple foods. It is estimated that these products now account for more than half of the total calories derived from starchy staple crops in Africa South of the Sahara. See FAO, *The State of Food and Agriculture 1958*, Rome, 1958, p. 106.

use of the land is to a great extent unspecialized and many different crops are often grown in association on the same plot. Food consumption is limited to little more than what the producer can grow himself on the particular type of land to which he has access, and its range is therefore usually small. As a varied diet provides the best chance of obtaining adequate quantities of all the nutrients essential for health, this limitation may have serious nutritional consequences.

When there is little deliberate production for sale, plantings will be enlarged only as the number of people to be fed increases, and the size of any marketable surplus will depend almost entirely on the weather and hardly at all on the price. Even where the production of a small surplus is specifically aimed at, the reaction to price changes may sometimes be abnormal. For one thing, the 'involuntary' element looms large in the small total surplus. In addition, where money is little used the demand for it appears to be mainly a 'target demand'* for the quantity needed to purchase certain specific goods and services not produced within the community. Thus, when prices are high producers may need to sell less in order to obtain their target of cash and will be able to retain more for their own subsistence. Conversely, when prices are low they may actually have to sell more, at the expense of their own consumption levels, to satisfy their minimum needs for cash.

Relative importance of subsistence and marketed production

While fairly adequate statistics of exports are usually available in Africa, those of the quantities used for subsistence or sold for domestic consumption (especially on village rather than urban markets) are both incomplete and unreliable for most agricultural products. Only very approximate estimates can therefore be made of the relative importance of the different categories of production. Even allowing for a wide margin of error in the statistics, however, it is clear that, in all except a few areas where export production is very highly developed, well over half of the total agricultural production does not enter the market.

A United Nations study provides the only estimate covering more

* S. Daniel Neumark, 'Economic development and economic incentives', *South African J. of Economics*, vol. 26, 1, March 1958, pp. 61–2.

than one country,* and calculates that around 1950 subsistence production accounted for an average of 65 to 75 per cent of the total crop area cultivated by the indigenous population in tropical Africa.† This is probably a more reliable indication than the estimates for single countries included in the study, though it is noteworthy that the proportion devoted to subsistence was put at considerably more than half for all areas except Ghana, where it was estimated to be as low as 20 to 30 per cent, reflecting the predominance of cocoa production for export. Production for export was estimated to account for 45 per cent of the crop area in Ghana, compared with 15 per cent in tropical Africa as a whole.

Crop area data indicate that some of the smaller territories not included in this study, notably Gambia, Mauritius, Réunion, the Seychelles and Zanzibar, are also exceptions. Crops mainly for export occupy a greater area than those for domestic consumption, so that production for subsistence accounts for less than half the total. The extreme case is probably Mauritius, where sugar cane alone takes up more than four-fifths of the arable land, and the area devoted to subsistence production must be very small indeed.

Some further indications of the relative importance of subsistence production are provided by estimates of agricultural income or of the value of agricultural production, as shown in Table 1. These, however, are very far from being calculated on a uniform basis. The production of European farmers, for example, is included for Kenya and Tanganyika but not for the Federation of Rhodesia and Nyasaland or the Union of South Africa. While some of the estimates are confined to the gross value of crop and livestock production, others cover the total contribution (including various non-farming activities) of the agricultural sector to the gross domestic product. There are many possible differences also in the concept and especially the methods of valuation of subsistence production itself.‡ The basis of the estimates is not described in detail in the table, so as not to complicate it unnecessarily, but it must be emphasized that because of

---

* Congo (former Belgian), former French Equatorial Africa, former French West Africa, Ghana, Kenya, Nigeria, S Rhodesia, Tanganyika, and Uganda.

† United Nations, *Enlargement of the Exchange Economy in Tropical Africa*, New York, 1954, pp. 8–14.

‡ For a discussion of the problems involved, see United Nations, Economic Commission for Africa, *Report of the Working Group on the Treatment of Non-monetary (Subsistence) Transactions within the Framework of National Accounts*, Addis Ababa, July 1960.

Table 1. *Estimates of Percentage of Subsistence Production in Total Value of Agricultural Production*

Country	Period	Percentage	Source
Cameroun	1956	[1]69	
Former French Equatorial Africa	1956	[2,3]77	Service des statistiques d'outremer, *Outre-mer 1958*, Paris, 1959, pp. 651, 655, 662, 677.
Former French West Africa	1956	[2]55	
Guinea	1956	[2]75	
Ethiopia	1954	[4]82	*First Five-Year Plan* (quoted in *Ethiopia Observer*, Vol. III, No. 4, May 1959, p. 108).
Kenya	1955–9	[5]60	East African Statistical Department, *Quarterly Economic and Statistical Bulletin*, No. 48, June 1960, pp. 70–1.
Tanganyika	1956–9	[5]59	
Uganda	1955–9	[6]741	
Federation of Rhodesia and Nyasaland	1954–8	[7]86	Central African Statistical Office, *Monthly Digest of Statistics*, Vol. VI, No. 8, November 1959, pp. iii–vii.
Northern Rhodesia	1954–8	[7]92	
Nyasaland	1954–8	[8]89	
Southern Rhodesia	1954–8	[7]79	
Union of South Africa	—	[9]75	*Summary of the report of the Commission for the socio-economic development of the Bantu areas within the Union of South Africa*, Pretoria, 1955, p. 86.

NOTE: In addition to the differences pointed out in the footnotes, there is also substantial variation in the concepts on which these estimates are based. They should therefore not be used for inter-country comparisons but only as approximate indications of the order of magnitude of subsistence production.

[1] Excluding livestock.
[2] Including forestry and fishing.
[3] Traditional enterprises only.
[4] Including forestry.
[5] Including forestry, fishing and hunting.
[6] Including fishing.
[7] African enterprises only.
[8] African Trust land only.
[9] African Reserves only.

lack of uniformity these figures should not be used for inter-country comparisons.

Taken as a whole, however, they appear to confirm the large proportion of subsistence in the regions' production suggested by the estimates of the area. Uganda, where the production of coffee and cotton for export is highly developed, is the only country for which data are available where subsistence is estimated as less than half of the total value of agricultural production. Subsistence may be expected to account for a somewhat smaller percentage of the value of production than of the land area, since products that are mainly exported generally have a higher value per unit than those mainly consumed locally, while, as discussed later, for many parts of the region the inclusion of livestock products also tends to lower the proportion of subsistence.

All of these estimates, whether in terms of land area or of value, are of course averages for whole countries, made up of all possible gradations, both of individual farmers and of communities or areas, from those producing solely for subsistence to those whose output is all marketed. Some data are also available which indicate the degree to which production for the market has been developed in certain more limited areas. For the Bongouanou area in the Ivory Coast, where substantial quantities of coffee and cocoa are produced for export, it can be calculated from household survey data that the imputed value of subsistence production accounted for 41 per cent of total income (almost entirely agricultural) in 1955–6.* In the cocoa-growing areas of the Western Region of Nigeria, subsistence was found in 1951–2 to be as little as 17 per cent of the total disposable income from farming of a sample of cocoa farmers, most of whom also sold large quantities of food products†. . . .

Preconditions for the transition to market agriculture

If, as is suggested by the estimates quoted earlier, more than half of the total agricultural production of Africa South of the Sahara is for subsistence, then the average farm family in the region feeds less than one non-farm family, in addition to providing for its own subsistence. In some of the more developed agricultural countries, on the other hand, the average farm family may produce enough to feed itself and some ten to twenty non-farm families as well.

This comparison illustrates very clearly the extremely low level of agricultural productivity in Africa. But it also indicates that, for productivity to reach the levels current in more developed countries and for the transition to market agriculture to go as far as it has in these countries, there must be a large number of non-farm families, either at home or abroad, for each African farm family to supply. Thus,

* Territoire de la Côte d'Ivoire, *Enquête nutrition-niveau de vie, subdivision de Bongouanou, 1955–1956*, Paris, 1958, pp. 124–30.
† R. Galletti, K. D. S. Baldwin and I. O. Dina, *Nigerian Cocoa Farmers*, London, 1956, p. 443.

while the present heavy preponderance of subsistence production in Africa is partly a reflection of the low yields resulting from primitive agricultural techniques, it can only be reduced and the level of productivity substantially raised if domestic and export markets are expanded. In a region where an average of more than two-thirds of the population are agricultural (in some countries as much as 90 per cent), the domestic market for agricultural products is obviously still very limited. For reasons discussed below, however, it is likely to expand more rapidly in the immediate future than the export market.

In many parts of Africa the initial impetus for the transition to market agriculture has come from the development of production for export, and in those areas where the process has gone furthest, export production is as a rule highly developed. The growth of production for export has a double effect on the rate of the transition because of the tendency for export producers, especially those growing tree crops, to purchase some if not all of their food. However, although for some countries and some commodities quite rapid changes are still possible, FAO studies indicate that in general the further expansion of exports seems likely to be rather slow. In recent years the volume of world trade in agricultural products has been increasing only slowly, largely because of developments in the industrialized importing countries, where substitutes for agricultural raw materials are increasingly in use, domestic output of some commodities has been sharply expanded, and the income elasticity of demand for most foodstuffs is low. This does not mean, of course, that additional production for export will fail to find markets. Nevertheless, although export opportunities will continue to expand, it seems fairly certain that there is no question in the near future of a rapidly and steadily rising export demand that could act as the principal magnet for drawing producers into the money economy.

Hence, the transition from a predominantly subsistence agriculture must depend mainly on the growth of domestic markets. This in turn is largely tied to industrialization and the growth of non-agricultural, generally urban, occupations, though it would seem that there are also considerable possibilities for greater sales among the agricultural population itself. Urbanization is already proceeding quite rapidly in some parts of the region. It enables a much steadier expansion of the commercialized sector of agriculture than does the fluctuating export market. Rapid urbanization implies that the marketed surplus must increase at a proportionately faster rate than subsistence production, which tends to expand in line with the slower growth of the farm population. Rising urban incomes also mean that demand increases even faster than the growth of urban population, and in addition they provide the opportunity for producers to diversify their production by turning to more expensive commodities such as fruit, vegetables, and dairy products.

Role of government

While the existence of a growing market is the chief precondition for the development of commercial agriculture, it is not always sufficient by itself to stimulate the production of a marketable surplus to meet the demand, and a good deal of government assistance may be necessary to help put the producer in touch with the market and encourage and assist him to produce for it. In some parts of Africa, particularly where large numbers of people have left the rural areas to seek wage employment, the expansion of the marketed surplus is already tending to lag behind the growth of urban demand and imports of certain food products have sometimes increased quite sharply. Especially in such areas, there is much scope for expanded domestic sales of agricultural products, and indeed they are essential if urban food supplies are to be assured without further increases in foreign exchange expenditure on food imports.

Transport and marketing facilities are obviously the basic requisites for linking the remoter areas with markets for their produce and thus for drawing them into the money economy. Transport has, in fact, received the major emphasis in most of the postwar development plans in Africa South of the Sahara. Where there are still large areas where production is almost entirely for subsistence, this is chiefly due to the absence, inadequacy or high cost of transport links with the rest of the economy. It is often said that the only commodity that can readily be exported from such areas is the labour of the inhabitants. Local feeder roads, such as have formed a large part of the development expenditure of the statutory marketing boards in some parts of the region, are of special importance in enlarging the area covered by the exchange economy. In the Northern Region of Nigeria, for example, the postwar building of feeder roads has resulted in higher prices to producers in the more remote areas, making it worth while for them to produce surpluses for sale, so that there has been a sharp increase in the movement of foodstuffs and a substantial reduction in the danger of localized shortages.* In a coastal area of East Africa, it was found when a new road was finished in 1953 that land had already been cleared and planted in anticipation of its completion.†

While the provision of the transport network must almost always depend largely on government action, governments may also have to assume themselves the responsibility for furnishing a large variety of marketing services, including the organization of processing, grading and handling and the construction of buying points and storage facilities. Better marketing arrangements are required in Africa especially for local food products, the marketing of which is generally much less well organized than export marketing. The establishment of facilities for regular sales has also proved the best method of accustoming Africans to treat their cattle as a marketable resource.

Economic incentives for subsistence producers require careful attention. In the early days of the development of production for the market in Africa South of the Sahara, while in some areas the production of certain crops for export was made obligatory, the desire for money appears to have been induced mainly by the imposition of direct taxes payable in cash, and by the activities of traders who penetrated deep into the bush with their wares. Later, large firms, combining the buying of produce for export with the merchandising of goods the farmers could not produce for themselves, have played an important part in encouraging the development of a commercial instinct. The necessity for a wide range of suitable goods to be available for purchase by producers was clearly demonstrated by the dislocation of production that resulted in some areas when imports of consumer goods were in short supply during the war. Although the supply of these goods is not the province of government, it is necessary for governments to encourage and sometimes help traders to operate in the remote areas that have to be opened up, or at least to remove any unnecessary obstacles to their activities.

The wider the range of goods that are accessible to the producers, the more quickly will their attitude to money change from 'the target demand' described earlier. Once this has occurred, the need for reasonably remunerative and stable farm prices becomes a very import-

* Northern Region of Nigeria, Ministry of Agriculture, *Movement of Local Foodstuffs, Northern Region, Nigeria*, Kaduna, 1958, p. 29.
† *East Africa Royal Commission 1953-1955 Report*, Cmd. 9475, London, 1955, p. 120.

ant aspect of incentives. Unless farmers have some confidence that prices will be remunerative, they will hesitate to incur the additional work or expense entailed in the regular production of a surplus for sale. Government price policies designed to give the farmer a reasonable return for his crop are therefore of considerable importance, though they must often be combined with marketing improvements to ensure that the price is actually effective at the farm level. The effect of taxation policies on the incentive to produce a marketable surplus must also be carefully considered.

Price stability is not in itself an incentive to produce for the market, but unstable prices may act as a significant disincentive. Although subsistence farmers have a low standard of living and are probably more liable to periodic food shortages than those who buy and sell on the market, there is an apparent stability and security in the subsistence economy that contrasts sharply with the fluctuations of the money economy. Price instability may be especially great in areas where a large proportion of production is for subsistence. For, as indicated earlier, when prices are low producers may have to sell more, so that the downward pressure on prices is intensified, and when they are high they may need to sell less, thus increasing the shortage on urban markets and forcing prices still higher. It should be emphasized, however, that this reaction to price changes appears to occur only when sales are very small in relation to total production, and that otherwise the response of African producers to price incentives appears to be no different from that encountered in more developed parts of the world.

Government action is also often needed in respect of traditional land tenure systems. As pointed out at the beginning of this article, the tribal systems found in most parts of Africa may often act as an obstacle to the improvement of techniques and the production of a surplus. Where production for the market has become highly developed, especially with permanent tree crops, economic pressures have generally caused some evolution of land tenures toward an individualization of rights. Direct action in this sphere is difficult, however, and governments have so far usually attempted to assist and systematize such spontaneous changes, mainly through land surveys and the registration of titles, rather than to initiate them.

Further important aspects of government assistance include the provision of credit facilities and of production requisites such as fertilizers, implements and improved seeds, the organization of co-

10

operatives, and extension work for the introduction of new crops and for the improvement of techniques and yields. Most of these activities assume greater importance in the next stage of development, when the farmer is already producing regularly for the market and requires guidance and assistance in order to improve his efficiency. Extension work, however, is also needed among communities producing almost entirely for their own subsistence, especially in the fields of home economics and nutrition education.

In addition, of course, the growth of non-agricultural activities, which is the key determinant of the expansion of domestic markets for agricultural products, also depends to a great extent on government action, through measures to promote industrialization and general economic development.

It is also desirable for governments to keep a close watch on the effects of their policies to stimulate the development of market agriculture and to apply such safeguards as are needed. Various dangers, including the subdivision of holdings on inheritance, the concentration of ownership, and chronic indebtedness, have to be guarded against in connection with changes in land tenure systems. If the tribal system of social security is allowed to disintegrate, something must be found to replace it. Careful attention must also be paid to soil fertility, as intensive production for the market, particularly under conditions of monoculture, has often been a major cause of erosion.

The commercialization of agriculture may easily be carried too far, so that the food supplies of the farmer and his family are jeopardized. It is noteworthy that the preharvest 'hungry season' that characterizes some of the drier areas of Africa is not confined to largely self-contained subsistence economies, but also sometimes occurs near large centres of population as a result of excessive sales. In a few areas export production has been developed to such a degree that the producers' food supplies depend entirely on purchases out of their highly fluctuating export earnings. While such specialization has well-known economic advantages, it may also have its dangers during the early stages of economic development.

Finally, it seems necessary to recognize more clearly that the transition from subsistence to market agriculture is one of the most basic aspects of economic development in Africa. Further information is needed on both the nature and progress of this evolution so that government policies can be oriented more specifically toward its promotion.

11

2. ECONOMIC AND TECHNICAL OPTIMA IN PEASANT AGRICULTURE*

E. S. CLAYTON

The much-publicized agrarian reforms now taking place in Kenya rest on twin pillars—the consolidation and enclosure of scattered fragments and the introduction of sound farming systems on to these consolidated holdings.† Farm plans have been devised for the various ecological zones, their prime purposes being the maintenance of soil fertility and the provision of a cash income of at least £100 over and above subsistence. The former is achieved by alternate husbandry and the integration of livestock into the system and the latter by the inclusion of a high-value cash crop—coffee, tea, pyrethrum, etc. The plans also include other subsidiary requirements such as a small famine crop area and a tree lot for family fuel needs.

Both the theory and practice of farm planning in Kenya have been developed in the department of agriculture and they have, not unnaturally, a heavy technical bias. The plans have a target cash income and the main source of this income is the cash crop; if this is removed what remains is largely a rotational, technical device for maintaining soil fertility. It seems fair for the economist to ask whether policy should not seek to maximize returns to the available resources of a holding within certain rotational and political limits instead of postulating a target income.

It would of course be pedantic to assert that optimal resource use is vital for the successful carrying through of Kenya's agrarian reforms. Certainly, the original policy-makers never conceived that it was necessary. After all, if coffee or tea could be included in the plan then, at prevailing prices, incomes would inevitably be sharply raised from their original abysmally low level. That would meet the

* I am grateful to Mr. G. Tyler for helpful comments on the programming aspect of this paper.
† See E. S. Clayton, 'Safeguarding Agrarian Development in Kenya', *J. of African Administration*, vol. 11, 3, July 1959, for further details.

political requirements of planning and the rotational requirement could be dealt with by normal technical considerations without particular regard to the nice adjustment of remaining resources from the economic point of view. This does not mean that ways of *increasing* income from the arable acreage have been ignored. In particular, the upgrading of stock is being undertaken to increase returns from grassland products. But this is not the same thing as consciously seeking to *maximize* returns.

As the reforms proceed, African agriculture will become increasingly commercialized and the efficiency of resource use may then assume some importance. In those conditions, farm planning (in theory and in practice) will need to pay more attention to economic resource allocation. With the data now available, it is possible to programme optimal solutions for certain ecological situations, as the following examples show.

The farm selected for this exercise is an actual holding situated in the Kagere sub-location of Othaya Division, Nyeri District, Central Province. This area lies in the Star/Kikuya grass ecological zone. The holding comprises 10·57 acres, which is somewhat bigger than the average. A detailed plan has been devised for it by the agriculturists, the details of which are as follows:

Some 3·78 acres are given over to rotational cropping on which is practised the following seven-year rotation:

	L.R.*	S.R.*
1st year	Grass	Roots (break ley)
2nd year	Legumes	Cereals
3rd year	Roots	Legumes
4th year	Cereals	Roots
5th year	Cereals	Grass
6th year	Grass	Grass
7th year	Grass	Grass

The land is thus cropped for four years and rested under pasture for three years. The remaining acreage is taken up by: homestead 0·59 acres, coffee 1·0 acre, napier grass (mulch) 1·05 acres, cassava 0·64 acres, permanent grass and trees 1·5 acres, napier grass (fodder) 0·9 acres, vegetables 0·51 acres, bananas 0·51 acres. The remaining 0·09 is taken up by paths. The stocking density is an adult beast to

* L.R. and S.R.=long and short rain seasons.

the acre, therefore, the holding carries four stock units. The labour available to this holding is not known but, on the basis of the known labour requirements,* the above plan requires three full-time adults if oxen are used for seed-bed cultivations. Assuming 300 working days annually, these men supply, on an eight-hour day basis, 600 man-hours a month, and although in no month do the needs of the plan exceed this, they do approach this total in eight of the twelve months. For subsequent exercises, therefore, it will be assumed that the same labour force is available.

The above plan is a typical one and observes the usual technical and political requirements. The fertility requirement is met by resting the land for three in seven years and the level of stocking ensures adequate manuring. The political requirement of £100 cash income plus family subsistence is easily achieved as a visual inspection will reveal. For example, one acre of coffee alone produces a net income of almost £200. Other departmental requirements include an area of 'famine crop' (cassava) as an insurance against crop failures and an area of trees (in the permanent pasture) to provide for family fuel needs.

As a first step in the exercise, all the above restrictions will be ignored and the sole aim will be to secure the maximum return to the available resources of land and labour. It is necessary, however, to qualify this, on common-sense grounds, by stating that some of the land will be retained in its present use. The vegetable and banana acreage is retained because they were included, in the first place, to give the family diet a necessary variety. In many areas these products (which will perhaps include fruit and tobacco as well as vegetables) cannot be bought and must therefore be home grown. But these areas will be looked on as a private garden and, therefore, as spare-time activities—unconnected with the 'farm business'. The tree area (and therefore the permanent pasture and 1·5 cows) will also be retained since in any case they are planted and fuel is not normally available by purchase. But, in this case, labour needs and revenue will be taken into account. Finally, for obvious reasons, the home-stead area remains unchanged. Thus, of the 10·48 acres of crop land some 7·37 acres will enter the programme.

Since an income maximizing procedure has not previously been

---

* Details of these will be found in E. S. Clayton, ' Labour Use and Farm Planning in Kenya ', *Emp. J. of Exp. Agric.*, vol. 28, 110, which is also the source for Table 1.

applied to Kenya conditions it seems logical to determine, as a first step, the optimal resource use without any departmental restrictions. If the optimal solution is found to be consistent with the restrictions then so much the better. But if the more important restrictions are violated the plan can be modified accordingly, whereupon the fall in income will measure the 'cost' of the adjustment. Which are the 'more important restrictions' is a matter for discussion, but the interpretation made here will differ from official policy. For example, *ex post facto* adjustments to meet any violation of the subsistence postulate are considered inadmissible as basic foodstuffs are normally readily available by purchase. To insist that the family subsistence must be 'home grown' would make the family poorer. Again, the growing of cassava as a famine crop is considered an inadmissible restriction on the grounds that the government's own grain storage is normally an adequate insurance against crop failures. On the other

Table 1. *Monthly labour needs (man-hours) and returns per acre*

Month	E. Potatoes¹ L.R.	S.R.	Maize L.R.	S.R.	Beans L.R.	S.R.	Millet² S.R.	Milk³	Coffee⁴ and mulch	Tea⁵
Mar.	89	—	73	—	101	—	—	17	135	85
Apr.	76	—	55	—	39	—	—	18	175	85
May	100	—	50	—	30	—	—	17	32	85
June	—	—	50	—	30	—	—	34	57	85
July	189	—	—	—	41	—	—	34	32	98
Aug.	—	—	—	—	—	—	—	34	32	—
Sept.	—	—	95	—	—	—	—	17	91	92
Oct.	—	89	—	73	—	101	57	17	110	85
Nov.	—	76	—	85	—	50	47	17	143	85
Dec.	—	100	—	70	—	49	—	17	142	177
Jan.	—	89	—	—	—	41	100	32	169	85
Feb.	—	100	—	95	—	—	79	31	189	85
Return	442s.		247s.	197s.	251s.		106s.	250s.	£95	£100

¹ Assume no spraying.   ² Seed broadcast.
³ Stocking is assumed at the rate of one cow an acre, hence labour needs relate to one cow and one acre of ley. All herd replacements are assumed to be bought in.
⁴ Coffee requires an equal acreage of mulch (napier grass) and they are, therefore, treated as one activity (i.e. ½ acre coffee and ½ acre mulch). Picking time relates to a parchment/cherry ratio of 1:6·9, the Nyeri average. No manuring is carried out since this is no longer departmental policy. Experiments have shown that bearing coffee does not respond to F.Y.M. See Department of Agriculture's Monthly Newsletter, July–September 1953. Spraying is taken at 100 hr/acre.
⁵ Tea data from private correspondence with the African Grown Tea Marketing Boards of Nyanza and Central Province.

hand, violation of fertility postulates would necessitate modification.

The basic data are set out in Table 1 which shows the monthly man-hours needed to grow one acre of certain crops, assuming oxen cultivation and the acreage returns (net of variable costs including seed, livestock depreciation, sprays, etc.). Further data are shown in the Annex to this paper. In this first programme, one livestock and five crop activities will be considered. These embrace the range of ecological possibilities as far as arable crops are concerned except for wheat, for which labour data is not available, and peas which have labour requirements similar to beans but a lower return per acre. On the livestock side, the lack of data prevents the inclusion of other livestock activities, e.g. pigs. Only one 'cash' crop is considered, in this case coffee, which is the usual departmental practice though of course its acreage is not restricted. But in the next programme, this restriction will be discarded. Double cropping is normal practice in Kenya and the arable crops considered can be grown in both the ' long ' and 'short' rain periods. But millet is normally only grown in this area during the short rain season. The yield data shows that only maize produces a different yield for each season. As its name implies, the short rain season is of shorter duration with a lower rainfall.

The final solution which yields a return of £322 is shown in Table 2. If the income from 1½ acres of pasture (£19) and the cost of oxen hire (at 30s. an acre equals £7½) are taken into account, the total net return is £334. If the same prices and yields used in the programme are applied to the original farm plan it would give a net return of £301, viz.:

	Acres	Return/acre	Total return
Maize	1·08	247s.	373s.
—	0·54	197s.	—
Beans	1·08	251s.	271s.
Potatoes	1·62	442s.	716s.
Milk	4·0	250s.	1000s.
Coffee	1·0	£190	£190
		Total	£308

Net of oxen hire equals £301. Thus the net gain of reorganization would be £33 or a 10 per cent increase.

The income from the programmed solution derives from the following pattern of cropping:

	Maize	Beans	Potatoes	Coffee and mulch	Fallow		acres
L.R.	—	1·71	0·52	2·68	2·46	=	7·37
S.R.	0·50	2·41	—	2·68	1·78	=	7·37

All the labour available is used up in March, April, October, January and February. But there is more than enough between May and September to absorb the 500-odd man-hours required for maintenance work on this holding and which has not been included in the programme. However, a most interesting feature of the solution is the relatively large amount of unused land—2·46 acres in the long-rain and 1·78 acres in the short-rain growing seasons. This emphasizes most clearly how labour can be a critically restricting factor, in a hand-labour farm economy, when it is associated with high labour-demanding cash crops. If this solution was feasible on all counts, it might be difficult to persuade an agriculturist that returns, on this holding, would be maximized only if some of the land was left idle (or rented out).

Table 2

Productive Activities			Z–C £
L.R. Potatoes	0·52 acres		0
S.R. Potatoes	0	,,	3·7
L.R. Maize	0	,,	3·8
S.R. Maize	0·50	,,	0
L.R. Beans	1·71	,,	0
S.R. Beans	2·41	,,	0
S.R. Millet	0	,,	18·4
Grass Ley	0	,,	3·2
Coffee and mulch	2·68	,,	0
Disposal Activities			
L.R. Fallow	2·46	,,	0
S.R. Fallow	1·78	,,	0
March Labour	0 hours		0·021
April ,,	0	,,	0·265
May ,,	386	,,	0
June ,,	344	,,	0
July ,,	295	,,	0
August ,,	463	,,	0
September ,,	331	,,	0
October ,,	0	,,	0·058
November ,,	28	,,	0
December ,,	41	,,	0
January ,,	0	,,	0·16
February ,,	0	,,	0·062

However, the solution infringes one if not two restrictions. It does not include any resting pasture but, on the other hand, the relatively considerable area of unused land could be brought into the rotation as fallow. This would not significantly alter labour requirements and may well afford adequate resting time for the tillage area to maintain fertility. But even if this were technically acceptable, the programmed solution does not provide sufficient F.Y.M. to achieve a level of manuring up to that of the original plan. This would ensure the application of F.Y.M. each year to 4 acres comprising:

1 acre arable crop land
1 acre napier grass (mulch)
1 acre napier grass (fodder)
½ acre pasture
½ acre vegetables

which more or less accords with departmental policy.* Each acre receives 5 tons of manure at each dressing and an adult animal will produce 5 tons F.Y.M. annually. Hence, the holding has to support four beasts which, at one to the acre, will require four acres of grass. Including fodder, this is what the plan provides. On the same basis, the programmed solution requires rather more than 3 acres of grassland ($\times$ 3 beasts) to supply manure at a similar level.

Since grass leys (in association with milk production) are unlikely to enter a programme on their own merits, in competition with perennial cash crops, and since they are a vital restriction from the rotation and F.Y.M. point of view, at the next stage an acceptable crop/ley ratio will have to be built into the programme to ensure non-violation of the fertility postulates.

For this purpose, the arable/ley ratio used in the original plan will be assumed, that is, four years cropping and three years grass. The grass will be stocked by milk cows at one to the acre. The same amount of land and labour is available. The same range of arable crops will be considered except for millet. Tea as well as coffee will enter the programme as cash crops and no restriction will be put on their acreage. Tea is included because this particular holding is so situated that both crops are ecologically feasible, and it will be interesting to see the results of a competition between the two.

The final solution is shown in Table 3. In this case, optimal

* Department of Agriculture, 'Fertility Maintenance of African Smallholdings', Departmental paper, May 1959.

18

resource allocation gives a net return of £389. When income from 1½ acres of pasture and the cost of oxen hire are taken into account the total return is £404. In comparison with the last solution, the inclusion of a ley/milk activity will reduce income whereas the inclusion of tea clearly increases it. In fact, the net increase is no less than £70.

The optimal cropping pattern is as follows:

	Maize	Beans	Potatoes	Ley	Coffee and mulch	Tea		Total
L.R.	0·65	0·45	1·21	1·73	1·26	2·07	=	7·37
		Fallow						
S.R.		2·31		1·73	1·26	2·07	=	7·37

which, it will be seen, incorporates a 4:3 arable/ley ratio.

All the labour available is used up in March, April, July and December, but there is enough labour available in the slack months to cope with the maintenance work which requires rather more than 500 man-hours. Pen manure is required for 3 acres annually, viz. 2 acres arable and mulch, ½ acre pasture and ½ acre vegetables. In practice, the holding will carry 3 cows (obviously not 3·23 and so income will be somewhat lower) which will provide the requisite amount of manure. The solution, therefore, violates neither the labour nor fertility restrictions.

As far as the land availability is concerned, the building in of a ley activity and/or the addition of tea results in a fuller use of land. It is completely used up in the long rain season; on the other hand, it is interesting to note that the arable acreage is entirely given over to fallow during the short rain period.

As a final example, it may be of interest to consider the effect of mechanization on this holding. In this instance, mechanization will mean the ' tractorization' of seed bed preparations only. Data are not available for other operations and, in any case, in the context of peasant agriculture, mechanization rarely means more than this. There are, furthermore, no cost data of tractors maintained by peasant farmers in Kenya and so the going contract rate will be charged. It should be added that tractor hiring for ploughing and cultivations is common in Kericho where these services are provided by African contractors. In the Central Province, however, contract work is in its early stages of development and this service is mainly provided by government tractor units. There is, however, increasing enthusiasm for tractor cultivations and several Africans have recently set up in the tractor contracting business.

The data and assumptions in this exercise were identical to those used in the last one, save for the use of tractors instead of oxen.

Table 3

Productive Activities			Z–C £
L.R. Potatoes	1·21	acres	0
S.R. Potatoes	0	,,	25·1
L.R. Maize	0·65	,,	0
S.R. Maize	0	,,	22·2
L.R. Beans	0·45	,,	0
S.R. Beans	0	,,	11·1
Grass ley	1·73	,,	0
Coffee and mulch	1·26	,,	0
Tea	2·07	,,	0
Disposal Activities			
L.R. Fallow	0	acres	2·0
S.R. Fallow	2·31	,,	0
March	Labour	0 hours	0·03
April	,,	0 ,,	0·12
July	,,	0 ,,	0·04
October	,,	200 ,,	0
November	,,	190 ,,	0
December	,,	0 ,,	0·45
January	,,	108 ,,	0
February	,,	87 ,,	0

The cost of tractor hire was taken as 55s. an acre. Its rate of work is 15 hours an acre as against oxen preparations of 38 hours or 93 hours an acre depending on whether a ley is being turned in. The final solution is shown in Table 4, which reveals the following cropping plan:

	Potatoes	Beans	Ley	Coffee and mulch	Tea	=	Total
L.R.	1·08	1·21	1·72	1·41	1·95	=	7·37
	Fallow						
S.R.	2·29		1·72	1·41	1·95	=	7·37

It will be seen that it differs little from the last solution. The tillage, ley and cash crop acreages are about the same. The labour needs are also similar. More significantly the net return is almost the same, £383 as against £388. In this particular circumstance, therefore,

20

Table 4

Productive Activities			Z–C £
L.R. Potatoes	1·08 acres		0
S.R. Potatoes	0	,,	27·4
L.R. Maize	0	,,	1·4
S.R. Maize	0	,,	25·6
L.R. Beans	1·21	,,	0
S.R. Beans	0	,,	13·1
Grass Ley	1·72	,,	0
Coffee and mulch	1·41	,,	0
Tea	1·95	,,	0
Disposal Activities			
L.R. Fallow	0	,,	2·1
S.R. Fallow	2·29	,,	0
March Labour	53 hours		0
April ,,	0	,,	0·15
July ,,	0	,,	0·03
October ,,	195	,,	0
November ,,	179	,,	0
December ,,	0	,,	0·47
January ,,	93	,,	0
February ,,	69	,,	0

mechanization at this level brings about no financial and very little cropping adjustment. A 'higher' level of mechanization, say for the weeding operation, may well give a very different result, although Raeburn found, under very different conditions, that 'full-scale mechanization' of peasant holdings was not economic.*

The original purpose of this paper was to determine the level of returns which optimal resource allocation would provide on a particular holding under different sets of assumptions. It is of some interest and importance to know the income potential of new farming systems—in this case, one of intensive cash crop production. It is also of particular interest to compare the financial returns of plans based on economic as opposed to purely technical considerations.

To make this comparison, it was clear that linear programming should be used since it is the most suitable technique for solving problems of maximization. It would, in addition, provide unique information on the opportunity cost of using resources to make

* J. R. Raeburn *et al.*, *Report of a Survey of Problems in the Mechanisation of Native Agriculture in Tropical African Colonies*, Colonial Office, H.M.S.O., 1951.

marginal adjustments to an optimal solution. And, moreover, the device would show how sensitive an optimal solution would be to price changes. This would be a particularly useful feature where an important part of farm production was sold on world markets.

However, in the process of applying this technique, certain interesting relationships were thrown up which cast new light on some of the peasant farming problems of Kenya. These relationships may well prove more important than the computation of optimal farm plans.

To go into more detail, an inspection of the foregoing programmes reveals the following points: Given the assumptions relating to production and price data, a grass ley producing milk will not enter an optimal solution on its own merits in competition with the ecological alternatives. However, the opportunity cost of producing milk from an acre of ley is given as £3·2, that is, the inclusion of grass in the programme would reduce net income from its optimal level of £322 by £3·2 for every acre of grass included. This is a modest price to pay to ensure fertility maintenance and, on economic grounds, would appear to justify the agriculturists' insistence on resting pasture and the application of pen manure.

Also worth noting is the considerable acreage of fallow required by optimal resource allocation. Where a grass ley competes freely in the programme almost one-third of the arable acreage is given over to fallow. But where a ley is built into the programme a different relationship arises. Here, fallow only occurs in the short-rain period, but of some significance is the fact that it occupies the *entire* short-rain acreage. The implication is, of course, that short-rain cropping, in association with intensive cash-crop farming, is uneconomic. This not only goes against the universal practice of the Kenya peasant farmer but contradicts the teaching of the agriculturists as embodied in their farm plans. Here is a not uncommon example of the divergence between technical and economic efficiency. There is a further implication arising from the high proportion of fallow required by optimal resource use. It is that under some circumstances of intensive farming in Kenya, labour and *not* land is the scarce or limiting factor of production. Whereas the reverse of this relationship is the common one in most settled peasant farming communities. It follows that where labour is limiting, the maximization of returns to this factor should be the prime economic consideration.

Another interesting feature is the acreage of cash crops to which optimal resource use gives rise. It is greater than that found on most holdings, though less than that which many agriculturists consider the most profitable, which is usually taken to be 100 per cent of the arable area. Of course, the cash crops do not occupy the entire acreage because a situation is being analysed where labour is limiting. However, this may well be the usual position where intensive cash-crop farming takes place on the family holding or where casual labour is not readily available. For example, the planting season is the invariable seasonal 'bottleneck' in peasant farming; but when coffee and tea are grown, seasonal labour peaks are increased and do not coincide with planting. In passing, an obvious point in relation to cash cropping should perhaps be made. It is simply that at prevailing prices and yields the gross acreage return from coffee is about twice that from tea. But the departmental postulate requiring an equal acreage of coffee and napier mulch (and mulch is essential for high yields) *halves* the gross acreage return from coffee and mulch, and is roughly the same as that from tea.

Some comments have been made on the effects of mechanizing seed-bed preparations. The hiring of a tractor for this task is not a profitable proposition. However, the use of tractor power lightens considerably the burden of the farmer who, for this reason, can be reckoned to increase his demand for tractor-hire even though it brings him no financial benefit. But, from a broader point of view, the absence of economic gain from tractor hire, as shown by the third programme, does call into question the wisdom of using public funds to set up government tractor units as a means of encouraging private African contracting. Of course, these points are no more than suggestive. The substitution of hand by tractor power would almost certainly be economic, whilst it remains to be seen what economic advantage, if any, arises from a higher level of mechanization and from the use of personally owned tractors.

Without linear programming most of the foregoing relationships could not have been discerned. And, although the above discussion relates to one situation and one holding only, nevertheless, it is a precise and quantitative discussion upon which policy decisions may be more soundly based. For this reason, programming appears as the most useful research tool to apply to peasant farming. The input-output data should be extended and improved and modal situations discovered relating to holding and family sizes in the different ecological zones. The application of programming to these modal situations will then throw up conclusions and relationships which will have some general applicability. But this is solely a matter of time and money. The important fact is that a tool exists to tackle the problem.

Annex 1. *Prices, yields and returns/acre of various farm products*

Crops		Yield per acre	Price per Unit to grower	Return per acre
English potatoes		40 bags	13s.	442s.
Maize	L.R.	10 ,,	25s.	247s.
	S.R.	8 ,,	25s.	197s.
Beans		6 ,,	43/25	251s.
Millet	S.R.	6 ,,	17/55	106s.
Coffee		10 cwt (parchment)	50 cents/lb cherry 1:6·9 ratio	£190
Tea (Green leaf)		5000 lb	40 cents/lb	£100
Stock		Yield	Price	Return
1 cow		200 gals	1/50 a gal.	250s.

Return per cow takes account of stock depreciation, the annual sale of a calf and spraying costs. Return from coffee takes account of the costs of spray material.

Sources: Departmental manuscripts by L. H. Brown and R. J. M. Swynnerton *et al.* Tea data from private communication from the African Grown Tea Marketing Board.

Annex 2. *Planting and harvesting times for certain crops in Central Province*

Crop		Planted	Harvested
Maize	L.R.	March–April	September–October
	Gathano	July–August	February–March
	S.R.	October–November	February–March
Beans	L.R.	March–April	June–July
	S.R.	October–November	December–January
E. Potatoes	L.R.	March–April	June–July
	S.R.	October–November	January–February
Millet	S.R.	October–November	February–March
Cow peas	L.R.	March–April	June–July
	S.R.	October–November	January–February
Coffee	—	—	June–February
Tea	—	—	October–May

Source: Department of Agriculture, P.A.O. Report, Central Province, 1950.

All other information on the timing of operations in the programmes are based on observations relating to a Labour Recording Scheme discussed in the article referred to in the footnote on p.14.

3. ECONOMIC AND SOCIAL FACTORS AFFECTING THE DEVELOPMENT OF SMALLHOLDER AGRICULTURE IN EASTERN NIGERIA

C. DAVIS FOGG

Approaches to agricultural development

There are five basic approaches to agricultural development being tried or considered in Eastern Nigeria. They are: (1) commercial plantations; (2) nucleus plantations; (3) settlement schemes; (4) smallholder 'investment' schemes; (5) smallholder 'improvement' schemes.

Commercial plantations involve large-scale planting (a minimum of 5,000 to 10,000 acres) and processing of export crops such as cocoa, oil palm, and rubber. Plantations usually use mechanized planting, maintenance, and harvesting where possible.

A nucleus plantation combines a commercial plantation and a settlement scheme. The 'nucleus' contains processing facilities and a commercial plantation run with paid labour. Smallholders are given small plots around the nucleus on which to build a house, grow subsistence crops, and grow the cash crop being produced by the central plantation. The nucleus plantation as planned in Eastern Nigeria and as operated in Uganda and Kenya either processes and markets the smallholder's produce for a fee or contracts to buy the produce at a fixed price.

Settlement schemes involve the resettling of a large number of farmers into one consolidated planting area. Each farmer is allocated land for housing, subsistence crops, and a commercial crop. Each settlement has centralized processing facilities for the commercial crop. In Eastern Nigeria the government provides the social services. The settlers are given a loan for their house, and living expenses, which must be repaid after their crops come into bearing.

Smallholder schemes do not attempt large-scale land consolidation, but work with the land that the individual or community al-

25

ready has. Investment type schemes try to persuade the farmer to plant commercial crops that take more than a year to mature. Thus, rubber, cocoa, and oil palm, which require five to seven years to come into production, are typical investment crops. In Eastern Nigeria the farmer is paid a subsidy in the form of planting materials, fertilizers, and cash. The subsidy is intended partially as (1) an inducement, (2) compensation for loss of income from land temporarily taken out of production, and (3) a contribution toward the cost of planting and maintaining the new acres. The farmer is usually required to plant a minimum number of acres (five in Eastern Nigeria), and he forfeits his subsidy if his acreage is not maintained to the instructions of the government.

Improvement schemes attempt to improve existing acreages through the introduction of more of the following: (1) improved planting materials, (2) improved cropping practices, or (3) fertilizers. For purposes of definition in this paper, I will assume that improvement schemes apply only to crops having a maturity cycle of less than twelve months, such as yam, cassava, and cocoa yam. Since the pay-back period is usually less than a year, cash subsidies to the farmer are not required.

Economics of agricultural development schemes

Table 1 gives output/input ratios for plantation, settlement, smallholder investment, and smallholder improvement schemes under conditions operating or contemplated in Eastern Nigeria. The output/input ratios for nucleus plantations are about the same as those of regular plantations and are not therefore listed separately.

Column 1 of Table 1 gives output/input ratios calculated for the economy as a whole. The output is priced at the world price (for export crops) or market price (for local crops), and the inputs include all costs to the market (or port), including the imputed cost of the farmer's labour and the cost of government extension services.

Column 2 gives the output/government input for each type of scheme. Output is priced at world or market price, and government input includes all costs to government. In the case of the smallholder schemes, this includes the costs of subsidies and agricultural extension services.

Examination of Table 1 shows that smallholder investment and smallholder improvement schemes offer the greatest economic return

Table 1. *Output/input ratios for plantations, settlement,
smallholder (investment) and smallholder (improvement) schemes*

Type	Output/ Input (1)	Output/ Govt. input (2)	Cash income of farmer/ cash outlay by farmer (3)
1. Plantations			
oil palm	2·3:1	2·3:1	—
cocoa	1·7:1	1·7:1	—
rubber	1·4:1	2·8:1	—
2. Settlement schemes			
oil palm, rubber	2·3:1	4 to 6:1	5 to 6:1
3. Smallholder (investment) schemes			
oil palm	7:1	26:1	5·5:1
cocoa	2:1	27:1	n.a.
rubber	3:1	37:1	6·0:1
4. Smallholder (improvement) schemes			
yams	2·9:1	6·4:1	5·3:1
cassava	3·8:1	8·4:1	6·9:1
cocoa	2·9:1	6·4:1	3·8:1

n.a. = not available

Column 1. Output/input ratio for the economy. The output/input ratio as defined below gives us some measure of the benefit of a scheme to the economy as a whole. Output/input ratios such as these can be used in evaluating alternative investment possibilities. The output/input ratio was calculated by valuing output at world prices (for export crops) or average market prices (for subsistence crops) and dividing by the total costs of all factors of production and marketing. The input figure includes (1) all production and maintenance costs including paid labour or the imputed cost of the smallholder's labour; (2) transport and handling cost to market or port; (3) cost of processing (if any); (4) depreciation of the estimated value of the land for investment crops. No attempt was made to discount the income and expenditure streams to take account of the time value of money.

Column 2. Output/government input ratio. Output was calculated as described above with the exception noted in (d) below. The ratio essentially measures the addition to G.N.P. (gross national product) per unit of government expenditure on a given scheme. Government inputs include the following:

(a) *Plantation schemes*: The government 'share' of expenses in plantations is assumed to be the product of the plantation expenses and the percentage government ownership. For oil palm and cocoa plantations, the government of Eastern Nigeria would be forced to subscribe 100 per cent of the capital because of artificially low Marketing Board prices. The return to the economy as a whole for oil and rubber plantations is attractive. The profit, however, is taken by the Marketing Board which maintains a large differential between the f.o.b. world price and the price paid to producers. The crops are therefore unattractive to private investors. Rubber is not under the control of the Marketing Board, and the government might therefore be able to attract 50 per cent private participation in rubber plantations. In this case, only 50 per cent of the cost and depreciation inputs are attributed to government input.

27

C. Davis Fogg

(b) *Settlement schemes*: Although settlers on the Eastern Nigeria Farm Settlements will have to pay back money advanced to them for subsistence, housing, land, and land development, the government will still have to bear the cost of agricultural extension services, administrative staff, schools, hospitals, roads, water supply, and other amenities. Government input includes the estimated cost of these amenities and services.

(c) *Smallholder (investment) schemes*: Eastern Nigeria is currently operating investment type planting schemes for oil palm, cocoa, and rubber. The government input for all three schemes includes the cost of extension services, planting stock, subsidized chemicals and fertilizers, and cash compensation. With the exceptions of extension services and subsidies on cocoa spraying chemicals, the government contribution ends before the crops come into full bearing. The out-of-pocket cost of the schemes to the government runs from £13 to £18 per acre planted (excluding the cost of extension services and administration).

(d) *Smallholder (improvement) schemes*: Improvement schemes assume that the crop to be improved is already being planted by the farmer. The output figure under this type of scheme is therefore incremental output, that is, the value of the additional produce obtained by adopting new methods. For cocoa, this entails spraying against fungus and pests. For yam and cassava, the improvement is the use of simple fertilizers. None of the improvement schemes cited here involves the introduction of new varieties of plant.

Eastern Nigeria currently is operating a cocoa improvement scheme. The government, at present, does not have a scheme to improve subsistence crops such as yam and cassava. The cost data for the latter came from Ministry of Agriculture field trial data and not from actual experience with an improvement scheme. It is assumed that the government subsidizes fertilizers and chemicals to the extent of $33\frac{1}{3}$ per cent.

Column 3. Cash Income to Farmer/Cash Outlay by Farmer. This ratio is useful in determining whether or not the scheme will be economically attractive to the farmer. Cash income is calculated using the price that the farmer is likely to receive for his produce. In the case of Marketing Board crops, this is substantially less than the world or market price. In the case of subsistence crops, the price received by the farmer would be the local market price less transport costs and middleman's profit. As the latter costs are unknown, the average market prices were used for calculating the farmer's income from rubber, yam and cassava. The cash outlay by the farmer includes nominal labour costs, cost of fertilizers and implements, and processing charges.

References and Accuracy of the Data

(a) *Plantation schemes*: The figures are based on the operating experience of the Eastern Nigeria Development Corporation and are therefore reliable. Marketing costs were obtained from the annual reports of the Eastern Nigeria Marketing Board.

(b) *Settlement schemes*: The data for settlement schemes were taken from a project description and costing provided by the Eastern Nigeria Ministry of Agriculture. The Ministry had not fully costed the farm settlement schemes, nor has the government yet decided precisely which cost is to be borne by the government and which by the settlers themselves. The output/input ratios are therefore educated guesses.

(c) *Smallholder (investment) schemes*: The figures are based on excellent project descriptions and costings prepared by the Eastern Nigeria Ministry of Agri-

28

culture and should therefore be accurate. An additional reference was 'Economic Analysis of Tree Crops Schemes (Oil Palm, Cocoa and Rubber)', prepared by the Ministry of Economic Planning, Enugu.

(d) *Smallholder (improvement) schemes*: The figures for the cocoa improvement scheme were obtained from the references cited in (c) above. The data for the yam and cassava improvement schemes were taken from *Fertiliser Use in Eastern Nigeria*, by Dr. W. S. Mann, Ministry of Agriculture, Enugu, March 1963.

(e) *General references included*:
  (1) Eastern Nigeria Marketing Board Reports, 1959–62.
  (2) Tables of costs of establishment, maintenance and harvesting of cocoa, rubber, and oil palm prepared by the Eastern Nigeria Ministry of Agriculture.
  (3) Costs of cocoa production in West Africa distributed by Cadbury Fry Ltd.
  (4) P. N. C. Okigbo, *Nigerian National Accounts, 1957* (Enugu: Government Printer, 1962).
  (5) Agriculture, *Sample Survey, 1959* (Lagos: Federal Office of Statistics, 1961).
  (6) Draft copy of a paper on the pattern of food consumption in an Eastern Nigerian village, by Dr. W. S. Mann, Ministry of Agriculture, Enugu.

(f) It should be emphasized that the costs for the smallholder (investment) and the settlement schemes are based on government projections rather than actual operating experience. The schemes began operating in mid-1962 and it is too early to tell if the cost projections are accurate and the incentives given to farmers sufficient to make the schemes a complete success.

to the economy as a whole. Settlement schemes run close a second, according to the costings provided by the government of Eastern Nigeria. I should note, however, that settlement schemes in Africa have been generally unsuccessful, and costs are usually far greater than anticipated by the sponsoring government. The most important conclusion derived from Table 1 is that smallholder schemes (particularly the investment type) show the highest economic output per unit of government input—an extremely important consideration in under-developed countries where government capital is so limited. The smallholder schemes, of course, show a high output to government input because: (1) they mobilize resources not otherwise available for productive investment, that is, farm labour, peasant savings, inefficiently used land, etc.; (2) the productivity of peasant land can be vastly improved by application of a few simple, proven agricultural techniques, as mentioned above; (3) there is an absence of the large overhead investment in housing, social amenities, transport facilities, and administrative staff found in the plantation and settlement-type schemes.

29

C. Davis Fogg

One can argue that the productivity of peasant holdings can be even further improved by land consolidation that allows more economical use of labour and elementary mechanized planting and harvesting. While this is true, the gains to be had by mechanization and—in many instances— consolidation can be considered at a later stage of agricultural development when marginal increases (10 to 15 per cent) in food and export crop production become important.

While risking over-simplification, we might postulate that agricultural development in areas similar to Eastern Nigeria should be divided into the following stages:

Stage 1: Smallholder Development. Primary emphasis would be on the introduction of elementary agricultural techniques to peasant farmers, village co-operatives, and community agricultural efforts. The increase in productivity and attending increase in G.N.P. will generate capital that can be used to (1) diversify the agricultural sector, (2) finance the initial development of industry, and (3) lift agricultural production to a level where larger scale efforts described under Stage 2 can be started.

The gains possible under smallholder development can be seen from the following example. Assume that country X has a G.N.P. of £1,000,000,000, 70 per cent of which can be attributed to the agriculture sector. If we assume that an average increase in production of 100 per cent is possible and that 30 per cent of the agricultural sector can be improved in the first ten years of development, the annual addition to G.N.P. at the end of ten years will be £210,000,000. This is approximately equivalent to a growth in G.N.P. of 2 per cent per year.

Stage 2: Continuation of Smallholder Development and Introduction of Larger Production Units. As smallholder productivity improves and when the majority of the willing or physically accessible peasant farmers have been approached, the government might shift its emphasis to the encouragement of larger consolidated production units. This, however, is not to say that plantation development and development of consolidated holdings should be neglected during the early stages of a country's agricultural development. On the contrary, plantations are often useful in attracting foreign capital, securing export earnings, providing research and nursery facilities, and providing training grounds for agricultural extension staff. Trial consolidation schemes are useful for demonstration purposes and for building up a reservoir of knowledge that can be applied on a mass

30

scale at a later stage of development. Development of peasant holdings is difficult because of the attitude changes necessary in the farmer if he is to accept agricultural methods deviating from time-honoured practices.

Economic incentives

Empirical evidence shows a fairly high degree of economic motivation among the various tribes in Eastern Nigeria. For example, in the early 1950s, when commodity prices were high, farmers planted about 20,000 acres of cocoa. Cocoa was not a crop that was traditionally planted or one which had been introduced previously, and the acreages were planted with little promotion on the government's part. Much the same was true of cashew in the late 1950s, and more recently of poultry production. Where the promise of economic return was high enough, farmers tried new and unproven crops. . . .

Given the fact that people react positively to economic incentives and are willing to accept change when the incentive is high enough, we can postulate that the degree of acceptance of new agrarian techniques partially depends on (1) the magnitude of monetary return, and (2) the timing of the return.

Judging from interest rates in the local money market, we can infer that the average peasant farmer would require a 70 to 100 per cent return to his cash capital input to induce him to use changed agricultural techniques. His cash output/input would have to be at least 2:1. In improvement schemes, I would estimate that the average farmer would have to expect a doubling in output before he could be induced to try new techniques. Referring back to column 3 of Table 1, we can see that the smallholder and settlement schemes would seem to offer sufficient cash return to induce the farmer to change his ways.

The timing of the return is also important. The more rapid the return, the more likely the farmer is to change his ways. While investment schemes pay off more handsomely in the long run, the improvement schemes usually pay off during one planting-harvesting season. The improvement schemes would therefore have more appeal to the illiterate with limited land and capital to invest. . . .

31

4· LABOUR MIGRATION IN A RURAL ECONOMY

P. H. GULLIVER

. . . To recapitulate very briefly: about one-third of all Ngoni males are away at work abroad at any one time, but up to 50 per cent in some areas; some one-tenth are more or less permanently absent. The average period of absence is between nine and eighteen months, and bachelors and those under thirty years old form the chief category of migrants. The majority of married migrants do not take their wives and children with them. Only about one-tenth of adult men do not migrate at least once; most men make two labour journeys, and only a few make more than three journeys. Speaking very broadly, the average migrant is able to bring back with him about 75 shillings in cash and another 50 shillings' worth of clothing. Labour migration has a history of about fifty years in Ungoni and the present annual exodus has been more or less maintained throughout the period of British rule in Tanganyika.*

The Tribal Economy

(a) *Agriculture and Food Production.* In Ungoni the women take the main share of the work of food production and cultivation. The men undertake the heavier parts of this work which involves the clearing and preparation of the new fields, and the hoeing up and ridging of fields for planting. Women also assist in this work, particularly in hoeing, and they carry out weeding and general maintenance (if any) and harvesting. Considering the peasant family as an independent farming unit, there is therefore a serious labour deficiency at home when the husband and head of the family goes off to the Coast. However a very great deal of heavy cultivation work, clearing and hoeing, is performed by community working parties who forgather after the work is done to drink beer at the expense of the

* Now Tanzania (Editors).

32

owner of the field. Thus even when the husband is away, the wife continues to make her beer and (perhaps with the help of a local kinsman) to summon a local working party to work in her fields. On the whole a migrant's wife can maintain almost as large an acreage as when her husband is at home. Apart from these working parties,and other people's working parties too, a man at home generally helps his wife to hoe up and plant additional land, and this latter is likely to be reduced considerably during his absence. Yet whilst he is away there is one less person to be fed from the wife's fields and consequently a smaller acreage than usual will suffice.

It has been noted already that most migrants go away after the planting season is over, and commonly a man will have completed the preparation of any new fields required for the following season.* Although the average migrant is away throughout the next wet (i.e., planting) season, he will normally return in time to work in the family fields the following season. Only where a migrant is away for two or more consecutive seasons does the wife at home experience serious difficulty; but even then the woman is able to obtain the assistance of her husband's brothers or her own kinsmen. She may, of course, have to expend more of her food store for beer for working parties.

There are naturally individual exceptions where the migrant's wife is unable to gain the assistance of kinsmen, but such cases are few. For the most part the average absence of a labour migrant scarcely affects the local production of food crops for home consumption. It should be remembered also that about half of the annual number of migrants are unmarried and do not therefore leave a wife behind to manage on her own. Some bachelors have been wholly or partly the chief male cultivator for their mothers, though this is not normally the case; a widow-mother of a migrant has the same recourse open to her as the wife of a migrant.

The principal role of local agriculture—the provision of the family food supply—is thus only slightly affected by the temporary absence of the average migrant. In addition, as normally, the wife is able to sell surplus produce to missions, local stores, etc., and to obtain ready cash. Even when the husband is at home a substantial minority of women earn much of their money with which to buy their own chief necessity—clothing. Cassava, beans, bananas,

---

* Bushland is cut and cleared and piled for burning between April and August. A fallow field is often given a preliminary hoeing at about this time to prepare it for re-use in the next wet season.

squashes, and also eggs and chickens are commonly sold in this way by the women.

(b) *Money Incomes and Cash Crops.* Few women continue the cultivation of cash crops, particularly of tobacco, whilst the husband is away. Although women generally help their husbands with such agricultural work, it is normally taken to be the sphere of the man himself, who likewise takes and controls the money so earned. Thus for the period of the migrant's absence the cash income of the family is reduced; and the overall production of these crops falls for the country as a whole because of the continual absence of so many men.

From the family point of view the loss of income is generally not serious because (i) it is temporary only, and (ii) the migrant brings back cash and goods when he returns home. Many Ngoni say that family income is increased by labour migration, since in a year or so a man can earn more money as a wage-labourer than as a cash crop producer. We saw that the total profit of an average spell abroad is in the region of 185 shillings (over two years' cash income for most Ngoni at home), and that the returning migrant brings back about 125 shillings in cash and goods. Of course many individuals bring back less than this amount and their families do suffer from lower incomes; nevertheless, speaking of the average, the ordinary family is no worse off financially and may be rather better off—at least from the short term point of view. On the other hand, labour migration does little or nothing to stimulate the returned man's efforts thereafter to grow cash crops and to increase his family's income; it may well reduce his efforts since he finds that cultivation at home is more difficult than wage-labour abroad.

From the wider and tribal point of view the inroads into cash crop production caused by the continual absence of so large a proportion of men are serious. The more crops that are produced for sale in the tribal area, the greater the general prosperity of the country—and prosperity feeds on prosperity. For example, a higher total of tobacco production in Ungoni would lower the proportion of overhead costs in the co-operative movement and the factory processing system, and thus it would increase the individual returns. Again there would be more money in circulation in the country with a larger crop and thus more trade and general enterprise.

The very fact that a man can go abroad to work and earn money thereby lessens his desire and efforts at home. It so happens that the earnings by migrant labour are as high as, or higher than, the earnings by agriculture eked out by local labour in the Songea District. Although men much prefer to stay at home if they can, yet this alternative source of money is a constant counter-attraction, especially if an agricultural season has been poor or techniques or judgement have deteriorated. Further, this alternative source of money is generally felt to be an easier way of earning, and more reliable since it is not affected (as far as the individual migrant is concerned) by poor rains or other uncertainties. Were there a high earning crop in Ungoni of the calibre of coffee in Umatengo, the alternative source of cash would be far less attractive; indeed, as with the Matengo themselves, it would hold little or no attraction at all. When a man begins to tire and lose heart in his tobacco, sunflower, or rice cultivation he tends to turn therefore to work abroad rather than to renewed and increased effort in his fields at home. He begrudges the extra effort in comparison with the relative ease of work abroad. It is true that with increased efforts at home an Ungoni could so increase his income from cash crops that the alternative of labour migration would then begin to lose its attraction because of its comparatively low return; as far as the Ngoni himself is concerned, such increased efforts do not yet appear to him either worth while or even possible. There is therefore a general depressing effect on the tribal economy and the tribal standard of living. Men are sapped of a certain self-responsibility to work and earn at home. Were they compelled through lack of the alternative of labour migration to rely on their own efforts in their own fields to maintain their incomes and their standards of living, there would of necessity have to be greater application and persistence of effort and a learning of the idea of being a whole-time farmer. Such increased efforts would not only bring their own direct and immediate reward, but might well teach men the meaning of farming and give them success and experience with which to develop their agriculture further.

A further depressing effect of labour migration which I have noticed quite frequently lies in the fact that the returned labourer with his stock of money savings and clothing tends to feel that there is no compulsion for him to work immediately after getting back home. He has perhaps enough clothing to last nearly a year and cash to buy further clothes and pay his tax in the following year. A month's work for P.W.D. or a mission, or a surplus of food crops will probably enable him to avoid the work and effort of growing tobacco or rice until the third year. Thus many men merely help in normal food production and leave cash crops until savings are considerably reduced or entirely spent. This is not an inevitable reaction but it is common enough to deserve mention.

On the other hand, it cannot be said that labour migration is solely responsible for the depressed and backward rural economy of Ungoni, for this is clearly not true. One of the most important factors is the relative isolation of the country and its long distance from the Coast, with heavy transport costs to reduce the returns from exported produce. Another set of factors lies in the level of agricultural conditions and the comparative failure so far to discover a cash crop producing a good return which can stand the long and expensive journey to the Coast or other markets. Tobacco is the main cash crop, but it is by no means well established outside the eastern region of the country and it appears to the peasant a difficult one to grow with its novelties and perplexities of seed-beds, regular watering, planting out, weeding, pruning and curing. There exists also the background difficulties of a somewhat inactive, tradition-bound native administration in which there has appeared very little notion of responsibility for and initiative in the development of the tribal economy. In addition the people live scattered fairly thinly over an extensive area in which communications have been poor, and this has impeded the efficiency of the Administration and technical services.

It is not possible or necessary in this report to go deeply into these causes of economic backwardness in Ungoni; the immediate point to be made is that labour migration tends to have a depressing effect on the tribal economy, but that it is only one of several factors amongst which it is not perhaps the most important. It is the experience of the present writer that high and continual labour migration results from general poverty and backwardness in a tribe, but that once established it does little to assist and even further depresses the economic condition of the people.

One particular and important depressing feature of labour migration which appears to the Administration is the loss of tax revenue and the reduction of Local Treasury funds and thus the reduction of Local Authority expenditure and enterprise. Where migrants leave the Territory to work there is, of course, a loss even to the Central Government revenue; but 99 per cent of Ngoni migrants go to other parts of the Territory. Although a migrant's tax is supposed to be passed on by the Local Authority of the labour area to the Local Treasury of his own home area for at least two years, this is by no means always carried out. The large majority of migrants go off without paying their tax at home, for they wait until they begin earning wages and then pay in the labour area. They also endeavour to pay their next tax before returning home. I have no figures for the revenue losses involved, but I am informed both by the Local Authorities and by Administrative officers that they are substantial.

If labour migration has a general effect of reducing local efforts in agricultural development and of maintaining a relatively low economic *status quo*, on the other hand it does provide a source of money income which in the short-term view, and until agricultural production improves, is necessary to the tribal economy. If we reckon an annual return of about 3,000 migrants who on the average bring back 120 shillings in cash and kind, there is an annual inflow of 360,000 shillings amongst a home population (1948) of 105,000 people or approximately 25,000 families.* This therefore amounts to an income of 14 shillings per family or about one-fifth of the annual cash requirements of a family at the minimum standard. This is not a negligible proportion and its cessation would mean a considerable fall in standards of living were there no increase in home production. It is, of course, merely suppositional to consider any such sudden cessation of migration, and even its gradual elimination (if that does occur in the future) will most probably follow a gradual increase in incomes earned at home. Nevertheless with this proportion of one-fifth in mind, we cannot assert that labour migration is wholly disadvantageous. In the past when agricultural export production was far lower than nowadays, labour migration made, in fact, a quite vital contribution to the economy of Ungoni, and enabled local standards of living to be raised.

It must be remembered also that most migrants do not remain away for lengthy periods nor do they go away frequently; and those most commonly involved are bachelors and men under thirty years of age. Whilst I certainly do not wish to suggest that labour migration has a general advantage for the tribe, especially one in which agricultural production has every chance of being increased, yet at the same time it does allow the young men to earn for themselves and to bring into their tribe valuable money income.

* Assuming the statistically average family to be four people—man, wife and two children.

37

5. AGRICULTURAL CHANGE IN UGANDA

Organization of production

. . . At this early stage in our inquiry we are faced, as we shall be repeatedly, by the inadequacy of the statistics. This is not due to the inefficiency of the Uganda government, which indeed has taken far more trouble than many tropical governments in this respect, but to the impossibility of obtaining reliable data about a peasant agriculture of tiny farms with the staff and funds that could be afforded.

Area farmed

The Department of Agriculture publishes each year with its annual report an estimate of acreage planted to crops. This estimate is prepared on two systems. Outside Buganda, chiefs' monthly returns of the number of plots planted to each crop are multiplied by a mean plot size for that crop determined by sample measurements. In Buganda, a mean crop acreage per taxpayer is determined annually by sample measurements and multiplied by the Buganda government's return of taxpayers. Both methods are admittedly inaccurate. Even in the case of the cotton estimate, over which the greatest care is taken, sample checks by the Department itself have shown the estimates to be at times as much as 60 per cent in error in districts outside Buganda. An investigation into the accuracy of these statistics has been published (*19*);* and revised crop acreage estimates for 1945 to 1956 which superseded earlier official figures were also computed (*22*). In any case, what these figures show is the acreage *planted to crops* and not the total *land used*. Since double cropping is practised, as noted above, in much of the Protectorate, many of the acres planted to maize may appear again as acres planted to cotton

* Numbers in brackets refer to sources listed at end of the article on page 57.

later in the same year, and similarly with other crops. Acreages of crops grown on non-African estates are obtained by asking the proprietors to fill in an annual form, and there is no check on the accuracy of most of them. Finally, the heads under which crops, or groups of crops, are listed in these tables have varied over the years.

Nevertheless, with all their defects, these tables are the only annual estimate we have of crop plantings, and, for what they are worth, the figures for 1945 and 1960 are given in Table 1.* This table shows an apparent increase in acreage planted to crops from 6,085,600 to 8,588,900 acres between these dates, or an increase of 41·1 per cent.

Table 1. *Estimate of acreage under crops in Uganda, 1945 and 1960*[1]
(Thousand acres)

Crop	1945	1960	Crop	1945	1960
Food crops:			Cash crops:		
Finger millet	1,090·5	1,161·8	Cotton	1,153·0	1,516·2
Plantains	836·7	1,545·9	Coffee (*Robusta*)	138·1	528·0
Sweet potatoes	482·8	598·7	Coffee (*Arabica*)	17·2	37·9
Manioc	476·7	605·8	Soybeans	33·9	5·1
Sorghum	390·8	678·3	Sugar cane	32·0	37·0
Beans	373·9	583·1[2]	Chillies	17·4	—
Peanuts	356·9	427·7	Sisal	9·4	6·0
Sesame	242·3	243·6	Tobacco	8·0	10·9
Maize	157·7	349·3	Rubber	7·6	—
Pigeon peas	126·4	181·1	Tea	4·5	16·8
Rice	62·3	4·4	Flax	1·5	—
Field peas	31·5	30·6	Pyrethrum	1·3	—
Potatoes	1·5	11·3	Cocoa	—	0·1
Wheat	1·2	—	Miscellaneous	29·3	—
Onions	1·0	3·3	All crops	6,085·6	8,588·9
Bulrush millet	—	6·0			

[1] Data from Uganda Protectorate, Dept. Agr., *Annual Report . . . 1945–46*, and *1960*, pp. 36, 45.
[2] Including cowpeas and gram.

* The revised acreage figures in the publication mentioned earlier (22) have not been used in this table because (*a*) they do not cover all crops and do not have a heading for 'other crops', so that no total can be derived from them; (*b*) though there is strong internal evidence that they do not include acreages grown by non-Africans, this is nowhere stated in the publication, so that their coverage is doubtful; (*c*) the figures for 1945 in this publication are stated to be less reliable than the others. However, the discrepancy with Table 1 is small (0·05 per cent on finger millet, 0·04 per cent on plantains, 0·5 per cent on cotton).

What is more easily established, because it is open to visual observation, is the location of all this new cultivation. It developed in three main ways. The first was by infilling between old-established cultivation in the more populous districts; and the extent to which many districts filled up with farms in this period, reaching an extreme in parts of Bugisu and Mengo, was striking to the eye. It must be supposed that this previously uncultivated land had been left so either because it was relatively inconveniently situated, e.g., far from water or a road, or was on less fertile soil. For these reasons it must be concluded that production from these new farms was likely to require more labour or to show lower yields than from the old ones.

The second process was a wholesale movement of population into large areas previously left unfarmed because of lower rainfall or poorer soils (the two usually go together in Uganda) than the old settled areas. Here, too, it must be expected that the national average of crop yields would be decreased by the inclusion of these inferior areas. This process has typically gone on in western and northern Buganda, where there was still much uncultivated country in 1945.

The third process has been dependent on special government activity. It includes the resettlement of farmers from overcrowded and exhausted areas in Kigezi on new areas in that district and in Ankole and Toro, an operation which began during World War II. By the end of 1949, 14,000 people had been resettled, and the process went on steadily with a variation between about 1,000 and 4,000 settlers a year. In the South Busoga resettlement area, 1,587 families had been established by 1960; and in the Kigumba resettlement scheme in Bunyoro, 360 holdings were occupied, largely by Kenya people, by the same date. More important than any of these schemes was the near elimination by insecticides of the 'mbwa' fly (*Simulium damnosum*) in the Nile River which had previously kept some very fertile riparian areas in Buganda and Busoga unpopulated. The result of this work was very heavy settlement from about 1952 and large new production in Bugerere county of Buganda and Bugabula county of Busoga. All the areas referred to in this paragraph were more productive than those from which most of the settlers came, and were thus a factor tending to raise national average yields of crops.

Livestock population

The livestock census figures published in each annual report of the Veterinary Department* are again admittedly inexact and will tend to be an under-estimate because of the well-known tendency of African stockowners to conceal their animals from enumerators or to understate their numbers. The figures for 1945 and 1959, the latest year for which a report is available at the time of writing, are given in Table 2.

Table 2. *Livestock numbers in Uganda, 1945 and 1959*[1]

Animals	1945	1959	Per cent increase or decrease
Cattle	2,293,740	3,590,335	+56·5
Sheep	995,321	959,324	−3·6
Goats	2,143,533	2,764,635	+29·0
Pigs	23,158	15,668	−32·3

[1] Data from Uganda Protectorate, Veterinary Dept., *Annual Report, 1945*, and Dept. Veterinary Services and Animal Industry, *Annual Report, 1959*.

From this table it will be seen that cattle have increased by a larger percentage than crop acreages; the increase in goats is somewhat smaller. Sheep numbers have slightly declined, probably because they are the domestic animals least esteemed by Uganda stockowners, who, as the pressure on pasture land increased, would be least inclined to devote valuable grazing to sheep. The decline in the number of pigs is probably due to the 1945 figure representing a peak population in Buganda at the end of the war when meat was acutely short and the demand for it greatly increased by returned soldiers who had acquired a taste for meat from army rations. Poultry figures are not available, but visual observation suggests that during this period they increased by at least the same ratio as the human population. This development would have been helped by the increasing numbers of pure-bred poultry distributed by the Veterinary Department, which in 1959 issued 22,210 Rhode Island Red and Australorp day-old chicks from Entebbe, together with 5,400 other birds; in the same year 23,500 day-old chicks were imported from the United Kingdom.

* Department of Veterinary Services and Animal Industry from 1952; the designation 'Veterinary Department' has been retained in this report for consistency and brevity.

Apart from these poultry, there was little change in the types of animals kept during these years. A few grade cattle with exotic blood were introduced immediately after the war, and a large number from 1957, by commercial enterprises; and by 1960 one or two African stockowners were beginning to purchase grade Guernseys or Jerseys from Kenya. By this year the Veterinary Department itself had decided to encourage limited keeping of Jersey crosses on tick-free farms, and its artificial insemination service which began in 1959 had Jersey semen on offer.

The ever-increasing numbers of cattle and goats during this period were, of course, owing to the extension of cultivation, kept on an ever-decreasing area of pasture. By 1960, pressure on grazing land had not yet become acute, though an increased worm burden in cattle which was noticed in some districts may perhaps be attributed to it.

As regards changes in the location of the cattle populations mentioned, the chief factor was reclamation of land infested by the tsetse fly. For some ten years before 1945, this fly had been spreading into some of the best grazing lands of Uganda. Between 1947 (when it was established) and 1960, the Tsetse Control Department succeeded in freeing about 6,000 square miles in Buganda and the Northern Province, with a resultant resurgence of cattle in these areas which may be exemplified by a single instance: Buruli county in Buganda held 144 cattle in 1945 and 46,000 in 1961.

Farm organization practices

Traditionally, the farming system of the Uganda peasant has involved an alternation of cropping periods on any piece of land with resting periods under a regenerating natural cover. As population density has increased, the proportion of land that could be left to rest has naturally declined—in a few congested areas almost to the vanishing point. In this respect the period 1945–60 is only one part of a long progression. In one small area in Teso which was subject to intensive agricultural surveys in 1937 and 1953 (26), the ratio of resting to cropped land had dropped between these two dates from 1·5 to 1·2. These figures may be very typical of the fairly densely populated districts. But for the country as a whole, the annual reports of the Agricultural Department give a ratio of available to cultivated land of 7·0 in 1952 and 6·8 in 1960. Within the cropping period, rotations in Uganda have always been irregular, but either cotton or a cereal was usually taken as an opening crop. Between 1945 and 1960 the use of cotton as an opening crop declined, owing to the successful propaganda of the Agricultural Department for earlier planting of cotton, which left less time to break the ground before this crop was planted.

The size of farms is said to have declined during this period in some densely populated districts, but it is difficult to obtain adequate data to assess this. In the Teso surveys mentioned, the area of crops planted per family fell from 9·3 acres in 1937 to 7·8 in 1953.

A tractor-hire programme operated by the Agricultural Department from 1948 made only a slow impact. In 1957, when it was well established, 6,172 acres were mechanically cultivated by the service, but in 1960 the total was only 5,739 acres. On the other hand, the number of ox-drawn ploughs increased very considerably. No complete figures are available, but in 1960 there were 83,707 ploughs in the whole country; in Lango district, there were 5,722 in 1947 and 14,484 in 1960; in the Teso area quoted above (*26*), the percentage of arable land opened by plough was 70.7 in 1937 and 95.0 in 1953. Fencing of grazing land was just beginning to make some headway at the end of the period. In 1957, a few fenced paddocks were reported to have been made by Africans in Buganda and Lango, and more people were encouraged to do so by the Farm Planning Unit of the Agricultural Department which started work in that year. In 1960, perhaps 100 farmers in Buganda had fenced paddocks.

The most outstanding progress in agricultural practice between 1945 and 1960 was undoubtedly in soil conservation. Here two main methods were used: in the perennial crop areas around Lake Victoria, 'bunds' (narrow-base terraces) planted with *Paspalum* grass, and in the drier areas of the country, buffer strips of grass left uncleared between cultivated plots. The Deputy Agricultural Adviser at the Colonial Office stated in 1950 that he considered the work in Kigezi to be the 'the most spectacular work on soil conservation anywhere in the British Empire'. In 1952, the Agricultural Department was able to report that 'in Buganda, it is now unusual to find holdings which are not provided with some form of erosion control'. These measures were still far from perfect in 1960; but in the preceding fifteen years, soil erosion in Uganda had been reduced from a major menace to quite a minor threat.

The position of estate production, as compared with peasant farms, changed in two respects during these years. First, there were in 1945 only a handful of Africans, all in Buganda, who could be described as coming into the class of estate producers. But in 1960, the annual report of the Department of Agriculture classified 4,582 acres, or 15 per cent, of the estate acreage of coffee as being on African-owned estates. Africans operating on this scale were almost all in Buganda, though in the same year an African in Teso farmed 350 acres by tractor, and in Bugisu a group of Africans had set up a company which ran a wheat farm with tractors, drills, and combine harvesters. The second tendency was for non-African estates to change hands. A number of European planters during these years sold out to Asians; but more important was the trend for individual planters of either race to sell out to companies which operated a large number of estates. The government, too, became indirectly an owner of agricultural estates. In 1952 the Uganda Development Corporation Ltd., which it had set up, purchased a large group of estates in Buganda which were being sold by a British firm, Buchanans. The motives for this transaction are somewhat obscure, but it would appear that the government wished to take the opportunity of bringing this large block of land back into national ownership rather than let it continue in alien hands.

During this period estate owners continued to recruit their labour as they could, from local or immigrant workers, the activities of recruiters being under the control of the Labour Department. Many African farmers continued to employ immigrant labourers, especially Banyaruanda in Buganda; Wrigley estimated that perhaps nearly half the income received by Baganda farmers was paid out to hired labour (*28*). An increasing number of Kenya immigrants sought employment in the Eastern Province. Within the peasant family itself, there were signs that the old distinction of work between the sexes was beginning to break down, and in the Eastern Province women could be found ploughing and men weeding, which was a reversal of the old order of things. Some small farmers, to an increasing extent, were undertaking a 'task' or 'ticket' of work (also locally known as 'leja-leja') for part of the day on the farms of wealthier neighbours. In the Northern Province, the old system of a group of some fifteen to twenty neighbours joining together for communal work in opening land, harvesting, and sometimes in weeding their plots is described as continuing in full force in Lango and Acholi districts by Parsons (*10*). As ploughs became commoner, this system was supplemented by a practice of those who owned no plough hiring from those who did, at a cost of about Sh. 40 per acre. A point to be noted is the loss of juvenile labour from farms as more children attended school. This was particularly felt in the herding of cattle, which by 1960 were on some farms not taken out to graze until 11 a.m. when an adult man had finished field work, and of goats, many more of which were tethered, rather than herded, in 1960 than in 1945.

Purchased current inputs

The articles most universally bought by African cultivators are hoes. In 1945, by which date almost all hoes were imported rather than locally made, 702,592 hoes to a value of £66,911 were imported; in the same year imports of 'shovels, spades, axes, and matchets' (not all for agricultural use) were worth £6,224 (*17*). In later years these items were differently classified in the trade reports; but in 1959 the total import of 'agricultural hand tools and implements' was worth £197,000 (*24*).

Animal feedstuffs were little bought during this period in Uganda. In 1945, a few African milk producers around Kampala had already been persuaded by veterinary officers to buy oil cake (peanut and sesame) from local mills; by 1960, they had advanced to the purchase of compounded feedstuffs from Kenya. By this latter date, a considerable number of poultry-keepers were also buying grain to feed their birds. Veterinary drugs to the value of £33,154 were purchased by stockowners in 1959 from African local governments under schemes supervised by the Veterinary Department.

Expenditure on seed was also minimal, though many peasants had the deplorable habit of overselling their crops at harvest and then having to buy seed back from traders at enhanced prices at planting time. Cotton seed was distributed free by the government, its cost being allowed for in the price structure of the industry. Maize seed was imported by the government from Kenya for distribution to growers in each year from 1945 to 1949.

Imports of fertilizers from overseas are not separately stated in the trade figures for earlier years, but in 1955 they amounted to 4,000 tons worth £102,000, and in 1959 to 9,407 tons worth £250,000. Imports from Kenya were insignificant, amounting to only £80 in 1960. These fertilizers were almost entirely used on non-African

45

estates, the sugar estates being the largest single users (the one in Buganda was stated to have spent about £150,000 on fertilizers in 1960). The use of fertilizers by African farmers was negligible.

There was, however, some use made by Africans of two other kinds of manure. Township-waste compost had been distributed from Kampala for some years before 1945; in 1948 this practice was extended to Entebbe, and 1,700 tons were distributed from the two places, but the scheme had been dropped by 1960. Distribution of coffee husks from the curing works, which were used as a mulch by farmers, had begun during World War II. At first, the husks were given free to encourage their use; later the recipient had to pay enough to cover the cost of transport. In 1948, 2,300 tons were distributed, and the quantity grew with the coffee crop, but annual figures are not available. A certain amount of sewage sludge from the Kampala sewage works was sold to the sugar estates. In parts of the country, farmyard manure had, by 1960, acquired a saleable value —a development in which Uganda was behind some other African countries.

An interesting new feature, though still on a small scale, was the purchase of insecticides by African farmers. From 1956 they were encouraged to buy knapsack sprayers and insecticide for spraying cotton, and from 1957 dieldrin for the control of the banana weevil. In 1958, in Teso 1,157 sprayers and 3,109 cans of insecticide were sold (9). The government became a major purchaser of bactericide when it was decided to dress cotton seed against black-arm disease before planting. In 1951, this was done in Teso, and by 1956 the practice had been extended to all cotton zones.

Purchases of fuel for agricultural production were limited to supplies for the few tractors in the country, whose numbers will be discussed later. Growers of fire-cured tobacco collected their own firewood for curing purposes. However, the agricultural processing industries of cotton ginning and coffee curing were large consumers of fuel. By 1945, many gins had already gone over from burning firewood or cottonseed to fuel oil, and starting in 1954, when hydro-electric power became available from the Owen Falls dam, many were electrified as the power lines were extended.

Capital inputs

Neither irrigation nor drainage absorbed capital from African farmers. In 1949, following the visit of an irrigation expert from

Aden, four Aden Arabs were engaged by the government to start experimental irrigation in Karamoja, but this and some other experiments remained on a small scale. The country's two sugar estates obtained a large part of their increase in yield during this period from the adoption of overhead irrigation; this was pioneered by the estate in Busoga, which was estimated to have spent £500,000 on this work by the end of 1961. Work on swamp drainage, begun before 1945, was carried on in certain districts by the government; in 1958, for example, the Water Development Department carried out an active programme in Kigezi. The annual reports on the government accounts show statements between 1945 and 1951 of a total of £12,050 received from the United Kingdom's Colonial Development and Welfare Fund for swamp drainage.

Rural water supplies were a continuing item in government expenditure and were also supported by Colonial Development and Welfare funds. In 1947, it was reported that 200 reservoirs and 700 boreholes had been made during the previous ten years, and this work proceeded in subsequent years. In 1954, a grant from the African Development Fund of £500,000 over five years for rural water supplies quickened the pace of provision. By 1958 there were 2,700 boreholes, and in that year ten dams and fifty-four valley tanks were completed. Fisheries may not be considered as part of agriculture, but it should be noted that, while fishponds were unknown in 1945, over 4,500 had been constructed by 1960 and these were mostly stocked with *Tilapia*, of which free supplies of fry could be obtained from a government fish farm near Entebbe.

Surveying of farms continued on 'mailo' land in Buganda, where the original backlog of work has never quite been overtaken, owing to continuous subdivision of these lands by sale; this was largely an expense that fell on the private individual.

Expenditure on agricultural machinery was of small importance and is difficult to estimate. Imports of tractors, not separately designated in the trade figures for 1945, were 82 in 1948 and 92 in 1960, but these figures include non-agricultural tractors; of those that were used for farming, most were on the non-African estates. In 1960, there were thirty-eight tractors owned by African farmers in the whole country, the largest numbers being in Acholi and Buganda. Imports of other agricultural machinery and implements, classified under various heads but including ploughs, amounted to a value of £11,370 in 1945 (*17*) and £86,521 in 1960 (*1*). . . .

Agricultural productivity

Only for two or three crops can even a rough estimate be made of how yields per acre changed during the period since World War II. The first of these is cotton. Here a number of factors tended toward an increase in yield. A wholly new system of seed replacement was adopted during these years; instead of new waves of seed in districts at irregular intervals, annual replacement was achieved in the area growing BP52 cotton by 1954, and later in the S47 area. Already, between 1947 and 1950, the purity to variety in Buganda was reported to have been raised from 75 to 90 per cent. These new waves of seed were derived from multi-line strains bred at the Empire Cotton Growing Corporation's experiment station at Namulonge, and were estimated to give an annual increment of yield of 2·5 to 3·0 per cent. At the same time, the average ginning outturn went up between 1945 and 1960 from about 30 to 33 per cent. The planting of S47 seed in 1951 over the whole of the Northern and Eastern Provinces except Busoga was held largely responsible for a 60 per cent increase in yield in that year. The effect of dressing seed with a copper bactericide is shown in a report in 1954 that in an area where seed had been dressed for five years, the incidence of black-arm disease had been reduced from about 53 to 4 per cent. Finally, spraying with insecticide, earlier planting, and somewhat closer spacing all helped to raise potential yields.

As against these tendencies, overcropping probably led to greater soil exhaustion as the length of the resting period dropped with increasing population. Soil erosion continued, though on a much smaller scale than before. The extension of cotton cultivation to new areas of poorer soils and lower rainfall has already been mentioned. Over the whole period, cotton acreage decreased greatly in Buganda, an area of generally good soil, and increased in all the other provinces, whose soils were for the most part poorer.

Table 3 gives the official figures of national cotton yields for each year from 1945 to 1960. It does not disclose any steady tendency either to rise or to decline in yield, and it would be reasonable to conclude that the trends making for increase or decrease were very nearly in balance.

In the case of coffee, the records of acreage and exports show an apparent production of 2·5 cwt of clean coffee per acre in 1945, and 4·1 cwt in 1960. This is easily explicable, since in 1945 when prices were rising a much larger proportion of the acreage was young coffee not yet in full bearing than in 1960 when prices were dropping; furthermore, in 1945 some 10 per cent of the able-bodied males of the country were serving with the armed forces or in non-productive war work, and this undoubtedly told on the standard of cultivation of all crops. However, there was an undoubted real rise in yield per acre between these years, and this must largely be attributed to the improvement of standards of tree pruning from 1945 to 1960, in both Buganda and Bugisu.

Table 3.   *Yield of seed cotton per acre, Uganda average, 1945-60*[1]

Season	Pounds	Season	Pounds
1944–5	337	1952–3	290
1945–6	265	1953–4	325
1946–7	247	1954–5	227
1947–8	218	1955–6	305
1948–9	333	1956–7	313
1949–50	282	1957–8	288
1950–1	301	1958–9	263
1951–2	332	1959–60	300

[1] Data from Uganda Protectorate, Dept. Agr., *Annual Report*, successive issues.

A third crop for which we can make some assessment, though exact figures are not available, is sugar cane on the two large non-African estates. Their increasing expenditure on irrigation and fertilizers has already been mentioned, and there were also other technical advances; for example, in 1957 heat treatment of setts for ratoon-stunting disease is stated to have increased yield by 36 per cent. There is no doubt that there was a very great increase in yields, which by 1960 probably averaged about 50 tons of cane per acre. By contrast another estate-grown product for which figures are available, tea, showed little change in yield over the period.

No other crops provide sufficient data for a proper assessment of yield, but in general it is probable that the position is the same as for cotton—improvements in technique were about in balance with poorer conditions, and over-all yields appeared to change little during the period. If we reflect that the most crowded rural areas in Bugisu were by 1960 carrying a population of over 1,000 to the square mile, and that these people were still obtaining much the same amount of food and income that they had been used to, the achievement must be reckoned a considerable one.

49

Output per man-day is still more difficult to assess. One way to estimate it is to divide the population into the acreage of crops planted. For this purpose, 1945 is an unsuitable year because of wartime factors mentioned earlier and because the population estimate for that year is very unreliable since no census had been taken since 1931. It is best to compare the years 1948 and 1959, in both

Table 4. *Labour requirements for production of crops in Uganda, specified years, 1949-60*[1]

(Man-days per acre)

Item	1949		1950		1960	
	Ngetta	Uganda av.	Serere	Buganda	Teso	Serere
Crop:						
Finger millet	72	72	—	—	48	35
Sorghum	—	—	25	—	21	27
Maize	56	80	—	74	—	—
Peanuts	90	108	69	159	59	104
Beans	—	80	—	—	—	—
Cowpeas	—	—	—	—	33	—
Cotton	93	122	81	110	91	88
Sesame	60	75	—	—	—	—
Sweet potatoes	—	115	59	68	—	—
Manioc	—	100	—	116	—	—
Coffee	—	100	—	—	—	—
Method:	Hand, some ox work	Mainly hand work	Some ox work	Hand	Ox ploughing	Hand

[1] Data for 1949 by G. B. Masefield, for Ngetta from *The Uganda Farmer* (London, 1949), p. 155; for the Uganda average from *A Handbook of Tropical Agriculture* (Oxford, 1949), p. 22; for 1950 from Gr. Brit., Col. Off., *Report of a Survey of Problems in the Mechanization of Native Agriculture in Tropical African Colonies* (1950), p. 100; for 1960 from H. Doggett, *Food Crop Production in Uganda* (unpublished, Seventh Annual Meeting of the Uganda Agricultural Association, 1960).

of which a complete population census was taken. In 1948, a total population of 4,958,520 appears to have grown 1·31 acres of crops per head, and in 1959 a population of 6,536,616 (an increase of 31·8 per cent) grew 1·35 acres per head—if anything, a slight increase in productivity.

Some figures that are available for the labour requirements of various crops, in man-days per acre at different dates, are given in

Table 4. Insofar as they reveal any trend, it is toward an increase in productivity. They also show that ox ploughing has, for most crops at all dates, been more productive than hand labour; and it is probably the increased use of the plough that has been responsible for any increase of output such as is suggested in the previous paragraph.

The general opinion of agricultural officers during these years was that in farm families in Uganda a man worked an average for the year of about three hours per working day, and a woman much more, but not wholly on farm work. They considered that there was no noticeable change in output during the period; and the same general opinion was expressed by employers of estate labour, who expected to get about twenty-five hours' work per week from a labourer (*12*). These apparently low figures are mitigated by the fact that both farmers and labourers often undertook 'leja-leja' work outside their regular work.

Composition of output

Table 5 shows the chief overseas agricultural exports of Uganda in the years 1945 and 1960. Though this does not provide a perfect picture of production (e.g., in 1960 far more sugar and tobacco were exported to Kenya than in 1945), it illustrates the general increase that has taken place in export crops. By far the most important item in this increase is the enormous expansion of coffee production, while cotton has more than held its position.

The only available measure of total agricultural production, including food crops, is in figures given in the estimates of the gross domestic product of Uganda in 1954–9 (*26*). The value of the gross domestic product from agriculture at factor cost for these years is given as follows (in thousand pounds sterling):

1954	84,903
1955	88,792
1956	85,262
1957	88,253
1958	87,192
1959	87,138

These figures suggest little change in output during these years; but a real increase is hidden by a decline in money value. During this period, prices were dropping not only on world markets but internally in Uganda; the 'Index of Actual Prices in African Markets' (December 1956 = 100) stood at 93 in December 1957 as compared with 157 in 1953. There is no doubt at all that, as with export crops, the total output of food crops greatly increased between 1945 and 1960, for the steadily increasing population continued to enjoy much the same level of food consumption. . . .

Table 5. *Principal agricultural exports of Uganda (excluding exports to Kenya and Tanganyika), 1945 and 1960*[1]
(Long Tons)

Commodity	1945	1960
Cereals, including flour	2,259	5,048
Pulses, including flour	2,712	3,336
Oilseeds:		
Castor beans	171	1,684
Cottonseed	34,094	39
Peanuts	—	356
Sesame	—	9,507
Soybeans	—[2]	443
Sunflower seed	—	292
Animal feedstuffs:		
Cottonseed cake	661	71,643
Other oilseed cake	60	—
Bran, etc	—	118
Coffee, raw, hulled	19,675	115,879
Tea	908	3,861
Sugar, raw	11,067	—
Chillies	470	201
Tobacco, unmanufactured	11,761	86
Cotton, raw	47,224	58,933
Sisal, fibre and tow	998	621
Rubber	578	—
Hides	1,052	3,196
Skins	—[3]	764

[1] Data from Colony and Protectorate of Kenya and Uganda Protectorate, *Annual Trade Report of Kenya and Uganda, 1946* (Nairobi, 1947); and Br. E. Afr., E. Afr. High Commis., E. Afr. Customs and Excise Dept., *Annual Trade Report of Kenya, Uganda and Tanganyika for . . . 1960* (Mombasa, 1961).
[2] Not separately reported in 1945—possibly included with pulses.
[3] Reported in number of skins 475,068; compared with 1,177,251 in 1959, according to the *Annual Report* of the Veterinary Dept.

Transportation

Both railways and roads were extended and improved after World War II. The chief railway extension was from Kampala to Kasese in Toro, which was opened as far as Mityana in 1953 and to Kasese in 1956. Though primarily an ore-carrying line to serve the new copper mine at Kilembe, this extension was stated in 1956 to be 'already carrying substantial quantities of agricultural produce and general cargo and coffee'. In 1960 construction began of a railway extension from Soroti to Lira in the Northern Province, and work also began on shortening the main line in Busoga, which was estimated to reduce by about fifty miles the haul to the port of Mombasa through which most Uganda exports passed. In the same year, a new steamer was placed on the Lake Victoria services through which much of the produce of Masaka and Ankole was evacuated.

Roads were improved in both quantity and quality. Extensions in the two National Parks served tourism rather than agriculture; but extensions useful for produce evacuation were made in parts of Bugisu, Kigezi, and the Sese Islands which had had no roads before. For the first time in Uganda, roads outside the towns were paved, particularly those main roads which radiated from Kampala to the chief up-country centres. Many of these roads were also shortened, since steeper gradients than those originally admissible for the use of ox-or handcarts could now be accepted.

Apart from these developments opening up new areas to a slight extent as regards agriculture, it does not appear that there was much change in the distance commodities moved. The exception was the provision of foodstuffs for the few large towns, which because of their increasing populations had to draw on an ever wider area. Satisfactory figures for the town populations are not available from the 1948 census, owing to lack of definition of town boundaries; but Kampala at that time had a population of roughly 58,000. At the 1959 census, the populations of the four largest towns were: Kampala, 123,320; Jinja, 29,741; Mbale, 13,569; Entebbe, 10,941. Kampala drew an increased supply of foodstuffs from Bugerere county, which had been cleared of the 'mbwa' fly, and of cattle from Karamoja. The mountain area of Bugisu was beginning to supply large quantities of plantains to Busoga during dry weather. A supply of fresh vegetables to Kampala from the high-altitude district of Kigezi, organized and encouraged by government, first began on a large scale in 1952, but competition with Kenya supplies limited its expansion.

In fact, Buganda generally and Kampala in particular continued, and perhaps to an increasing extent, to draw on Kenya for supplies.

In 1958 Buganda imported 22,890 goats from Kenya, and 50,000 poultry carcases in the year and an average of 5,000 dozen eggs per week came to Kampala from Kenya; in 1960 Kampala imported about 6,000 gallons of fresh milk daily from Kenya (*11*). In 1952, a total of 4,660 Kenya cattle were sent to Kampala and 4,480 to Jinja. . . .

Incentives to change

The extent to which crop production changed in response to changing demand was limited by the fact that prices for the chief cash crops were fixed by government and not by the free play of supply and demand. Nevertheless the extent to which the demand could affect production is shown in the great fluctuation in sales of some minor crops already described. The effect of rises in price was undoubtedly also potent in increasing cattle sales over the period as a whole. Thus in 1950 it was reported that cattle prices in all districts had more than doubled since 1944; but from 1957 to 1960 the cattle prices were falling.

The availability and wages of labour, and the possibility of alternative economic employment, are also points to be considered. The wages of rural labour in Uganda were not controlled during this period, but a statutory minimum wage of Sh. 33 per month was enforced in Kampala and Jinja from 1950. By 1960, the level of wages in these places had risen to Sh. 80 per month. The annual reports of the Labour Department estimate an average wage for unskilled labour on non-African plantations of Sh. 14 per month in 1945, and Sh. 31 to 48 (according to province) in 1958. Verbal information given by Baganda was that in 1960 they were paying Sh. 35 to 40 per month to Banyaruanda farm labourers for a 'task' of only about two hours per day. Many of these men were, however, working two or three 'tasks' or 'tickets' a day, usually for different employers; it was common for them to work an evening shift, not for cash, but for their day's food.

Baganda farmers grumbled in both 1945 and 1960 that farm labour was difficult to get, but there is no evidence that this shortage was acute, and good employers seem to have had little real difficulty in attracting men. Partial counts by the Labour Department at the main entry points only on Uganda's international frontiers showed that 104,689 labourers entered Uganda from Ruanda, the Belgian Congo, and the Sudan, in 1945, while 40,176 left; and that 79,340 entered and 78,853 left in 1958. Immigrant labourers from Kenya and

Tanganyika were not recorded, but their number in the later years of the period certainly exceeded that in 1945.

As regards the pull of non-agricultural employment, industrialization was slowly increasing in Uganda during these years. The Labour Department's 'Enumeration of African Employees', which does not include labour employed by African farmers or by very small employers, gives a total of 158,557 in 1950 and 228,889 in 1960. However, much of the increased demand for labour was met by immigrants. At the textile factory near Jinja, for example, Tanganyikans came second only to natives of the West Nile district among employees grouped by origins in 1960.

From all these considerations, it does not seem that labour conditions changed to any extent that would substantially affect agricultural production during the period under review.

Consumer goods, an important incentive to agricultural production, were in very short supply in early postwar years, and it is believed that much money at this time was simply hoarded by African cultivators. The increasing availability of goods coincided with a rise in crop prices, especially marked during the Korean war, and standards of living rose rapidly. It is probable that during this period the desire to keep up with one's neighbours was a potent incentive to production. In some outlying districts such as West Nile, Karamoja, and Kigezi, many people in 1945 were still going naked or wearing only skins; by 1960, the use of clothes was much more widespread. In the more sophisticated areas, the use of footwear became commonplace; and purchases by Africans of corrugated iron roofs, bicycles, European-type bread and beer, and even cars, were no longer limited to a tiny wealthy class. Money was ardently desired to pay school fees for children. Thus during this period people in the remoter districts first felt a real desire for money on a large scale, while in the more developed areas they realized increasingly the benefits it could bring.

It must be remembered that, with falling crop prices in the later 1950s, greater production was needed for the cultivator to maintain the same income. It has been loosely said, but it is an approximation to the truth, that Uganda in 1960 produced twice the agricultural exports of 1950 but received only the same income from them.

G. B. Masefield

Governmental policies

Land tenure. Following the recommendations of the East African Royal Commission of 1953–5, the Uganda government in 1958 embarked for the first time (outside the 'mailo' lands) on the granting of registered land titles to Africans who were already occupying the land according to native custom. This beginning was made in Kigezi district; in 1959 the work was extended to Ankole, and in 1960 to Bugisu. By the end of 1960, a total of 6,287 such titles had been given and some owners had already begun to use these titles as security for obtaining loans from the African Credit and Savings Bank. But in several other districts the African local governments flatly refused to have anything to do with the scheme, and in these the Protectorate government did not press it. In 1955 the registration of land titles was decentralized with the establishment of four district Land Offices in Buganda.

While these were the main official changes in land-tenure policy, changes in practice which were taking place unofficially must not be overlooked. In several districts the customary system under which an African occupier enjoyed only the usufruct of the land by tribal permission was gradually giving way to a conception of individual tenure under which land was bought and sold under thin disguises or even openly. In some areas, what purported to be contracts of sale were drawn up by laymen, not lawyers, and signed before witnesses. How these gradual changes took place, and how they were partly accepted into the unwritten customary law, has been traced in detail by Fleming (5) for the district of Busoga. By 1960, prices of land in such transactions and in the sale of 'mailo' land in Buganda had reached very high figures in some areas. In some of the most crowded parts of Bugisu, prices as high as £100 per acre were mentiond by informants. In the immediate vicinity of Kampala, £300 per acre might be paid; but for Buganda as a whole, £5 an acre was probably an average price for ordinary agricultural land in 1960, as against perhaps £3 in 1945.

Fragmentation of agricultural holdings was not as acute a problem in Uganda as in some African countries, but did exist in the more densely populated districts such as Kigezi, Bugisu, Busoga, and parts of Buganda. A spot survey at Kisoro in Kigezi in 1958 showed that of three holdings selected at random one was made up of thirty-two separate parcels, one of twenty-three, and one of twenty-two. In such areas, where cultivation is really of the nature of horticulture and

56

the fragments are close together, no great agricultural ills result. So little study has been given to the problem that it is impossible to say how far it intensified during the period. . . .

References

1. E. Afr. High Commis., E. Afr. Customs and Excise Dept., *Annual Trade Report of Kenya, Uganda and Tanganyika for . . . 1960*, Mombasa, 1961.
4. 'Development of Mechanised Farming in Uganda', *Trop. Agr.*, vol. 31, 4, 1954.
5. J. T. Fleming, *Recent Developments in Customary Kisoga Land Tenure*, Entebbe, 1961.
9. D. J. Parsons, *Systems of Agriculture practised in Uganda*, No. 1: Introduction and Teso Systems, Uganda Prot., Dept. of Agr., Ser. 3, 1960.
10. *Ibid.*, No. 3: The Northern Systems.
11. *Ibid.*, No. 2: The Plantain-Robusta Coffee Systems.
12. G. P. Saben, *Saben's Commercial Directory and Handbook of Uganda*, Kampala, 1960.
17. Uganda Prot., Blue Book for 1945 (1947).
19. Uganda Prot., *Investigation into Acreage Statistics, 1959*.
22. Uganda, *Revised Crop Acreage Estimates, 1945–1956* (n.d.).
24. Uganda, Memorandum by Government on the Future Organisation of the Bugisu Coffee Industry, 1958, Sessional Paper No. 19 of 1958.
26. G. Watts Padwick, *Rice in Uganda*, Imp. Chemicals Industries Ltd., 1954.
28. C. C. Wrigley, *Crops and Wealth in Uganda, A Short Agrarian History*, E. Afr. Inst. Soc. Res., Kampala, 1959.

6. LAND CONSOLIDATION IN THE KIKUYU AREAS OF KENYA

G. J. W. PEDRAZA

Introduction: the obstacles

Land consolidation, farm planning and resettlement are being carried out in many of the tribal areas of Kenya. There are, however, considerable differences in the methods employed in the various regions, resulting from the various traditional systems of land tenure, the degree of co-operation of the people and from climatic and other conditions. This article sets out to describe the problem only as it affects the three Kikuyu districts in which there is a general similarity of procedure.

Before the advent of the European, and indeed for many years afterwards, there was no pressure on the land generally conceded to be the preserve of the Kikuyu. All land was held communally by the ten clans, whose elders had the power of allocation to clan members. Much of the land was under forest, which was, however, steadily destroyed as the people looked for more fertile areas to replace their exhausted patches of cultivation. The problem of an apparent land shortage emerged only with the rapid increase of population, resulting from the cessation of inter-tribal wars and the introduction of medical facilities and famine relief measures.

In the interval between the two world wars, and for some years afterwards, there were three major obstacles to be overcome before any real contribution to the problem could be made. The first, and probably the most difficult, was the suspicion with which the tribe looked upon any move by government affecting land. Land, to the Kikuyu, is a possession transcending in value even that of his wives and children. The process of conditioning the mind of the Kikuyu to the acceptance of better methods of agriculture, in its widest sense, was therefore long and tedious. It was aggravated for many years by opposition to progressive measures which emanated from political

58

agitators and by the shortage of trained staff. All these difficulties have now been overcome to a large extent.

The second major obstacle which had to be overcome was the inborn conservatism of the peasant farmer, who was accustomed to the traditional methods of agriculture which had remained unchanged for many years. This difficulty has almost been overcome and the farmer now accepts the fact that he has much to learn, even though he, or to be more accurate his wives, may not relish the additional work entailed.

The third obstacle to progressive farming has been the system of land tenure and inheritance. It is only in the last few years that the leading Kikuyu farmers have accepted the fact that their customary laws on these questions constitute the most formidable barrier to good farming practices. Intensive propaganda and demonstration, together with the removal of subversive influences during the emergency, have resulted in a widespread realization that the old customs must give way to modern methods. It is now probably true to say that a majority of the tribe wish to proceed as quickly as possible with land consolidation and to follow the advice which they receive on agricultural improvement.

The customary system of land tenure

It is perhaps best to look briefly at the customary system of land tenure and inheritance before describing the process of consolidation itself.

As stated above, all clan land is held in trust by the elders of the clan. They have the power to allocate any available land to a member of the clan if he is landless. In practice, however, there is now little land left for allocation. Land may also be inherited once it has been allocated. A third method of acquiring land is by purchase. Until recently, land which had been sold could be redeemed at will by the vendor, on repayment of the purchase price. It was, however, essential to abolish the right of redemption before consolidation could proceed and this has been done by the African district councils of the three districts, acting on the advice of their respective law panels.

The traditional laws of inheritance lead directly to rapid fragmentation and are primarily responsible for the present condition of agriculture in the reserve. A man may have the right to cultivate 12 acres of land, which, in most areas, would, if properly farmed, be an economic unit capable of supporting a wife and family at a good standard of living. He may well, however, have three wives, to each of whom he allots 4 acres to cultivate on his behalf. Moreover, under customary law the area cultivated by each wife is divided between her sons on the death of the father. The son of the first wife, being an only son, would receive the full 4 acres cultivated by his mother. The three sons of the second wife would receive 1⅓ acres each. None of these areas are economic units, but they will nevertheless be subdivided again on the death of the sons and as a result it is not uncommon for a man to inherit as little as one-quarter of an acre. Furthermore, as a result of other customary laws of inheritance, or through purchase, a man frequently finds that he has a number of fragments of land, often separated from each other by some miles, so that he cannot farm them properly however much he may wish to do so. Finally, insecurity of tenure, resulting from the great volume of litigation over land which was common before the declaration of the emergency, dissuades the farmer from improving his land. Of what use is it, he thinks, to improve my land when I may well lose it tomorrow before the courts?

The effort on the part of government officers to improve the standard of agriculture in the reserve has been going on for many years and has been attended by considerable success in many areas. It eventually became necessary, however, to attack the problems posed by the basic system of land tenure and inheritance before any further spectacular progress could be achieved. This called for agreement by the people to four major changes in custom. They were, respectively:

(a) the consolidation of widely separated fragments into one holding;

(b) the abolition of boundaries between different clan areas, where the requirements of consolidation make this desirable;

(c) the prohibition of the subdivision of land through inheritance below what is considered to be an economic holding; and

(d) the issue of individual titles, which are necessary to give security from litigation, but which will, in fact, also abolish the authority of the clan elders over land.

These principles have been accepted generally by the leading Kikuyu during the past few years. The majority of the population has also

60

accepted consolidation of the fragments as being desirable, but it is uncertain to what extent the people have appreciated the full implications of land consolidation on their customary systems of tenure and inheritance. It is, however, unlikely that they will sustain any objections which they may have when the great benefits to be derived from the process become apparent.

The method of consolidation

Consolidation is necessarily a lengthy process. At present no legal sanction exists to authorize either its implementation or its end product. It is based purely on the agreement of the people concerned and is not carried out in any area where there is opposition to its introduction.

Land consolidation teams have been formed in each division of the three Kikuyu districts. Their composition varies between the districts, but basically they consist of a team leader; a number of recorders, or measurers, whose main task is to measure up fragmented holdings and to compute the total acreage held by each individual; and a staff of farm planners, who lay out each consolidated holding on sound agricultural lines. All these are Africans who are specially trained for the work. Apart from their specialized knowledge they must be honest, since the opportunities for corruption are innumerable in an exercise of this kind.

Choice of a consolidation area depends on several factors. While the emergency continues, only those areas which are co-operative are likely to be selected. Subject to this condition, it is essential that the people themselves wish to have their land consolidated, since the whole scheme is based on agreement and consent. It is equally essential that the people are prepared to practise good husbandry after consolidation is completed, in order not to waste the time and effort involved. Amongst other considerations are the acreage of the areas selected and the desirability of building up blocks of sufficient size to justify aerial survey at a later date.

Consolidation is carried out area by area, and these areas may vary in size between 1,000 and 3,000 acres. Before measurement can begin, the team must effect exchanges of land, so that the fragments of each man who is to be settled in the area to be consolidated are concentrated in that area. This involves a long process of negotiation, but it is hoped that the people will eventually themselves carry out these exchanges in advance of the team, as the desire for consolidation increases. The recorders proceed to ascertain and measure the boundaries and extent of each fragment, and the approximate total acreage held by each man is then computed. No attempt is made to carry out an accurate survey, nor is this possible with the staff and the time available. Clan elders and local people are co-opted to assist in determining each man's boundaries and the team leader is responsible for settlement of the more difficult disputes which arise. Records are kept of the location and measurements of each fragment.

Whilst this work is going on a staff of plane tablers make a topographical map of the area. This shows sufficient local landmarks to enable individual boundaries, and a soil conservation plan, to be inserted later, and includes contours at 12-foot vertical intervals. Although a certain degree of precision is required in the compilation of this map there is no attempt at very great accuracy.

On the completion of these two concurrent stages, representatives of the administration, agricultural, health, education, police and of the other departments which have particular interests in the consolidation area, meet together to plan the future layout of the area. These officers are now in possession of a topographical map of the area, a record of the total acreage held by each man, information concerning the location of each of his fragments and the names of the landless persons.

The agricultural officer first draws in on the map the soil conservation plan for the area. This includes provision for the water consumption requirements of humans and stock, in the shape of dams and boreholes. The next phase consists of marking on the map the area to be occupied by the village. Choice of a suitable site depends on the availability of water, health requirements, accessibility and other factors. The size of the village is governed by the acreage required to house those who own 3 acres or less, together with the acreage required for a church, school, shops, recreation area, community hall, cemetery, medical centre and the police post. Further areas are also reserved on the map for tree nurseries, agricultural demonstration plots, coffee and tea factories and any other facilities which are likely to be required by any of the departments concerned. A road plan, designed to open up the area, is then superimposed. Finally, the total acreage required for all these public purposes is computed and is found by making a proportionate deduction from the total acreage held by each individual.

Representatives of the administration and agricultural department, together with the consolidation team and clan elders, are now in a position to put in the new boundaries of consolidated holdings, both on the ground and on the map. At this stage, close supervision is required to ensure that each individual receives land of agricultural value comparable to that which he has vacated. His consolidated holding must also contain a proportion of arable, cash crop and grazing land, to facilitate planning of an economic farm. As a general rule, allotments of under 3 acres are grouped round the village where the owners will have to live, and holdings of 3 to 6 acres are placed beyond these. Holdings of over 6 acres are placed still further away from the village. The object of this grouping is to encourage those with 3 to 6 acres to buy up the adjacent allotments in order to increase their holdings to an economic size. Those who own less than 3 acres contribute one-quarter of an acre to their housing plot in the village, whilst the landless are given a similar plot, for which they will pay rent to the African district council. The landless and the allotment holders will become the village artisans and shopkeepers of the future and will also be available to work as paid labourers on the larger holdings. In this way it is intended to absorb a large proportion of the surplus population in productive labour. When the allocations have been made the new boundaries are then agreed with clan elders and owners and marked in on the topographical map.

During the process of measuring up fragments, the team has already noted down the cash crops and other improvements for which compensation will be payable in the event of the owner being moved elsewhere on consolidation. A scale is laid down for all items which attract compensation. The rates given are not binding, but they nevertheless form a useful guide to all concerned. While they are seldom exceeded, they are frequently reduced, with the consent of the elders and the landowners concerned. Compensation is paid between landowners and the transactions are recorded at a specially convened meeting held after the consolidation has been carried out.

Enclosure and farm planning

Consolidation is followed as soon as possible by enclosure. Boundaries are fenced with the most suitable material at hand and, where necessary, are also planted up with seedlings, which will grow into permanent hedges. Immediate enclosure is necessary, both to give the owner an increased pride in his holding and to provide boundary marks which will show up on an air photograph. It is proposed that consolidated holdings should be surveyed by air at a later stage, preparatory to the issue of individual titles to land. Meanwhile, consolidation is followed up by a team who make an accurate survey of new boundaries. This forms the basis on which individual farm plans will be made.

Farm planning by the agricultural department also follows the completion of consolidation. In the early stages this planning consists of treating each feature as a whole. The general plan which has been adopted is that slopes of between 0° and 20° should become arable land; those between 20° and 35° should be bench-terraced and planted with cash crops, and slopes steeper than 35° should be put down to grass. This will suffice as an interim measure to raise agricultural production without delay. As soon afterwards as the staff position permits, individual and detailed farm plans are made in order to show the farmer the best division of his land between the various food and cash crops and grazing; the cycle of rotation for each portion and the ideal layout for the homestead area with adequate paths of access, paddocks and other improvements.

It is at this stage also that an assessment is made of the need of each individual for a loan to assist him in developing his land. Loans of up to £125 may be paid from African district council or government development funds and these are repayable over five years at $4\frac{1}{2}\%$ interest. The form of loan agreement contains, amongst other conditions, a declaration by the landowner and his heirs that the consolidated holding will not be subdivided below what is considered to be an economic size.

Soil conservation works are carried out as soon as possible after consolidation, since it is essential to follow up this initial work with measures to raise production and to show visible results to the people. Bush and unwanted trees are cleared and bench-terraces, 'cut-off' drains, spillways and narrow-base terraces are constructed, either by the people themselves or by paid gangs. The newly made terraces are then prepared for planting by the application of manure from village cattle sheds and compost which is made on the spot. A proportion of the wages of the paid gangs is paid from development funds and the balance is debited to the loan which the smallholder will receive. This is done in order to extend the life of development funds and of the available loan capital, and also to ensure that the individual makes some contribution towards the work done on his behalf.

It is hoped that it will be possible to arrange for two aerial surveys of the consolidation areas. The first of these would give the consolidation teams a map of the present fragmented holdings, with contours at 12-foot vertical intervals, which would be used for planning purposes. This would replace the production of a topographical map by the ground survey methods which are described above and would thereby release staff and so speed up the issue of detailed farm plans. The second survey would provide a map showing the boundaries of the consolidated holdings and would form the basis for the issue of individual titles to land.

The significance of consolidation

There is no doubt that land consolidation and farm planning is of primary importance and urgency in the post-emergency reconstruction policy. It will, in addition, make a major contribution towards the resettlement of the Kikuyu because it results in the increased capacity of the land to carry the population and provides employment, as farm labourers, for a large number of those with little or no land, on the holdings of their more fortunate neighbours. Consideration is, therefore, being given to the staff and finance required to increase the rate of progress, so that consolidation and farm planning of the three Kikuyu districts may be completed within the next five years. Experiments designed to streamline the methods employed are also under way and these indicate good prospects of success. Additional funds required will probably be found by African district councils. Although the cost will be heavy, it would be inequitable and unwise to increase government contributions to this work without making even greater contributions to the agricultural progress of those other tribes which have remained loyal during the emergency. Financial considerations preclude such a policy. In order to lighten the burden, it has been proposed that fees should be charged for preparation of the farm plan and for registration of individual titles. This has yet to be approved and will require enabling legislation.

Considerable discussion has already taken place on the legislation required to give legal authority to the consolidation of holdings and to cover the issue of individual titles. At present, as has been shown above, the whole process is based only on agreement. Although local customary law gives some protection, through the power of the clan elders to re-allocate land amongst members of the clan, it is undesirable that this should continue to be the only safeguard. This power does not, for instance, extend to land which has been purchased. It would, therefore, be possible for a man whose consolidated holding did not include land which he had previously bought to demand that the latter be restored to him. This would lead to a series of similar demands, which would produce chaos in the entire scheme.

It is clear that some form of interim title will be required to give landowners reasonable security of tenure pending the issue of a valid title. Without such security there will be no incentive to develop holdings during the interval which inevitably intervenes between consolidation and final registration. It is also probable that it will be necessary to limit the period during which the work of the consolidation teams can be challenged after the new holdings have been demarcated. Legislation will, in addition, be required to prevent subdivision below what is considered to be an economic unit.

Land consolidation constitutes an agricultural revolution in the Kikuyu Land Unit and it will have the most profound effect on the lives of the people. The increased prosperity and purchasing power of the individual will lead to a higher standard of living and to a greater demand for goods of all kinds. The effect of this, and of other similar schemes elsewhere, which are aimed at improving the productive capacity of the land will, in turn, have a profound effect on the economy of a country the prosperity of which will inevitably be based on agriculture for many years to come.

PART II

USE OF RESOURCES—INDUSTRY

---

7. AN AFRICAN LABOUR FORCE

W. ELKAN

Labour turnover

. . . The Kampala factory of the East African Tobacco Company was built in 1937 and acquired by its present owners in 1948. It has in the past employed as many as 900 men. Since 1948, however, the number of employees has been gradually reduced to about 600 whilst at the same time output has increased.

This has been brought about principally by introducing more machines, but the contribution of careful labour management has not been insignificant. In some ways it is no doubt true that mechanization facilitates good labour management, but conversely, unless attention had been paid to it, the introduction of the new machines might have proved disappointing in its results.

Employers in East Africa face two major problems: how to reduce labour turnover and how to improve the efficiency of their labour force. The two problems are of course related. Workers do not reach their maximum efficiency until they have done a job for some time and to some extent the problem of how to improve efficiency resolves itself into one of getting people to stay longer in one job. In this chapter we shall be concerned with the first of these problems. We shall analyse the nature and extent of turnover and attempt to discuss some of its causes.

The tobacco factory did not begin to collect monthly figures until 1952, and it was not until October 1953 that a distinction began to be made between men discharged in the ordinary sense and men who failed to turn up again although they had given no notice of their intention to leave. We cannot therefore estimate with any accuracy the success of different attempts to reduce labour turnover, but only outline the situation at the present time.

If we exclude men dismissed for major breaches of discipline, the average rate of turnover for the months of October 1953 to May

67

1954 was 7·6 per cent. Every month, in other words, seven or eight men in every 100 employed had left the factory either because they wanted to or, in a very few cases, because they had exhausted the patience of their supervisors by being continuously absent. This figure in itself, however, conceals a multitude of possibilities. It matters very much who are the ones who leave and to this an average of this sort provides no answer.

A study of the employment record cards of men who left the factory between September 1953 and June 1954 reveals two things of particular interest.

Table 1. *Resignations and voluntary discharges,*
September 1953–June 1954
(Kampala)

Length of service	Ganda	Ankole	Ruanda	Luo	12 other tribes	Total	
							%
Under 1 year	39	8	13	15	44	119	58
1 and under 2 years	8	10	11	2	9	40	20
2 and under 3 years	5	6	4	2	2	19	9
3 and under 5 years	8	3	—	—	3	14	7
5 years and over	13	—	—	—	—	13	6
	73	27	28	19	58	205	100

A very high proportion of those who left did so in their first two years. Even within the first two years, the rate of leaving is a rapidly decreasing one: 58 per cent left in their first year, 20 per cent in their second year. Further, of the 119 men who left in their first year, 80 did so within the first two months, and 101 within the first six months. When we come to consider whether the causes of turnover amongst newcomers differ from those amongst men with longer service, the importance emerges of the background from which a man comes. The labour force is drawn from regions differing widely in their economic structure, and the ambitions and attitudes of men from backward areas are distinct from those of men who have grown up in the economically more advanced parts of East Africa. The figures of the table confirm that we should try to relate turnover to men's geographical origin, or more simply, to their tribe . . .

The substantial number of Ganda who come to the factory seems at first sight to disprove the contention, which is often heard, that the Ganda will not enter unskilled employment; that so many leave so soon seems, on the contrary, to support it. The explanation to this apparent riddle may lie in the prospects which they find. A Ganda will stay if he sees before him a prospect of rapid increases in his earnings. Otherwise he leaves and goes from job to job. As I shall try to show later, the Ganda appear in increasing numbers to be accepting the status of permanent wage-earner (as opposed to independent farmer), and this is of course related to the keenness to get the best wage possible, even where this involves, as among the unskilled, frequent change of job.

Other causes of the heavy turnover among newcomers may be, first, the method of selecting employees; second, ignorance of the wages paid; and third, the method of payment.

A great deal of the turnover in the early stages can be attributed to the method of selection. Men are picked out from a crowd which assembles outside the factory on the first day of each month, according to the impression created by their appearance. No questions were asked until recently, when the firm decided to give preference to men with some education. But even now no proof of education is required, and it is luck alone if the firm in fact picks those with the longest spell at school. The result of this procedure is that men are frequently placed in jobs which they dislike or at which they are incompetent and being new in the factory they leave sooner than ask to be transferred to other work . . .

The fact of immigrant labour, which is perhaps the most striking feature of African industrial life, and which distinguishes it from European experience, is something over which the tobacco factory or any other firm has relatively little control. The habits and aspirations of the immigrant worker have, at least in the short run, to be taken as given, and are not likely to be modified by changes of labour policy on the part of individual employers. It is, nevertheless, possible to say something about the methods by which the firm seeks to persuade men to stay in their jobs. It is hard to know by what criteria their success might be judged, since there is no other factory here of comparable size or nature; my impression is, however, that the firm does achieve a very creditable degree of stability. After all, nearly a third of its employees have a record of three or more years' service . . .

The firm's policy appears to be to reduce turnover in three ways. First, it seeks to pay wages which compare favourably with those

69

paid elsewhere, and in addition men are given opportunities to increase their total earnings by working overtime and through production bonuses. In the month of June, only 57 men received the bare minimum wage. Secondly, it provides a number of welfare services such as free medical attention, a free snack in the canteen, overalls, and sick leave. Finally, it runs a Provident Fund to which the firm contributes on a 50–50 basis. . . .

Many causes contribute to the rather strained and dissatisfied condition of the immigrant factory worker, and prominent amongst these is the fact, generally overlooked by the men before they come to Kampala, that wages have to cover the cost of food. Few of those who come, attracted by seemingly high wages, have thought about the cost of food at all, for food is not something which one buys. Money one spends on tea and sugar perhaps, but not on flour or plantains. To 'eat one's wages' seems preposterous.

It is of course inevitable that industrial workers should pay for their food in cash. No English worker now resents it, though he may complain about the price of food. In Kampala men also complain about the price of food, but to imagine that they will be satisfied if prices of food could be reduced by simplifying the channels of distribution is to overlook the basic resentment against the very fact that food should have a price at all. This attitude towards food has an important bearing on efficiency. Since men resent having to spend money on food they may sometimes spend less than is necessary to maintain health and strength. The effect of diet on working efficiency can be exaggerated, but it cannot be ignored. It is doubtful whether undernourishment is such as to leave men actually hungry. But it is probable that they are ill-nourished, i.e. they spend their money on food that satisfies hunger, to the exclusion of things which in the long run maintain health and energy. This has three consequences. In the first place, men will not go on doing it indefinitely, and it may therefore be regarded as a contributory factor to labour turnover. One English-speaking Ankole clerk put it like this: 'A man comes to Kampala to earn cash. If his wages allow him to earn the things to which he is accustomed, he will stay for a long time. But most men in order to save have to accept poor food and within a year they go back—they will not punish themselves for longer'. In the second place, it makes men lethargic in their work, unable to summon the energy to work hard consistently or to make the occasional extra effort required to prevent some mishap or to do a job thoroughly. Even where industrial relations are at their best, one notices an atmosphere of 'I don't care', which may well be due more to the food in men's stomachs than to any native ill disposition in their minds. . . .

The difficulty of combating absenteeism is enhanced by the fact that absences are sometimes very profitable. Granted that much absenteeism is connected with intemperate living, there is yet a proportion of men who take days off because the loss in wages which it entails is more than counterbalanced by gains of trade, harvest, or inheritance. Kampala offers many opportunities to the occasional trader—to men who will peddle a load of fish sent them by relatives from across the lake or who have the occasional load of plantains for disposal. Men who have land nearby may gain more by taking days off during the planting and harvesting seasons than they lose in wages. Again, a man stands to gain more by being present at the division of a deceased relative's property than by being present at his place of work. Absenteeism due to these causes is naturally most common amongst those whose homes are nearby.

8. DIRECT OVERSEAS INVESTMENT IN NIGERIA, 1953–63: SOME ASPECTS OF ITS CONSTITUTION AND CONTRIBUTION TO NIGERIA'S ECONOMIC DEVELOPMENT

R. S. MAY

. . . Eighteen British companies with appreciable investments in Nigeria were interviewed and, in addition, questionnaires were sent to eighty-eight others out of which thirty-eight replied. On the basis of size of net assets this survey covered over 80 per cent of British investment and some 60 per cent of total investment from overseas.*

The background

Nigeria, throughout the period under consideration, which included the granting of full Independence in 1960, continued to adopt a liberal economic policy towards private enterprise. In order to encourage overseas investment, particularly in manufacturing, a system of tax incentives, tariff protection, customs duty drawbacks and 'pioneer certificates' was established.† Industrial estates were set up and investment opportunities investigated and publicized.

---

* (a) Official Statistics, also, were often unsatisfactory and although calculations have been made using such data in order to assess approximate magnitudes, too much reliance should not be placed on specific percentages and other computations.

(b) I should like to take this opportunity to thank those companies which helped me so very considerably in this project. It is unfortunate that, in the interests of secrecy, their names cannot be revealed here. Most of the thirty-eight questionnaires returned were fully completed, but in some cases particular questions were unanswered, which accounts for the variation in total coverage between Tables.

† (i) Industrial Development (Income Tax Relief) Ordinance 1958 liberalized and extended the former Aid to Pioneer Industries Ordinance 1952. The period of relief depends on the amount of capital expenditure up to the end of the first two years from the commencement of production. (ii) Industrial Development (Import Duties Relief) Ordinance 1957. (iii) The Drawback (Customs) Regulations 1959. (iv) The Dumped and Subsidised Goods Ordinance 1958. (v) Generous depreciation allowances on buildings and machinery are also given.

72

The Government has taken pains to reassure private overseas investors: 'capital will be secure against arbitrary interference . . . the Government will maintain the principle that foreign investors can transfer their emoluments to any place of their choice'.* The 1962–68 Development Plan also indicated the very definite role which private enterprise was to play. £389·5 millions out of 1183.3 millions gross capital formation was scheduled to come from private sources, of which private overseas investment was planned to contribute some £200 millions.

It has not been the case, however, that all foreign investment has been accepted and on any conditions. In order to qualify for tax and other reliefs, the investment has to be of an approved type and operations have to be conducted according to certain principles. Thus 'in order to qualify as a pioneer enterprise, a company must . . . be incorporated in Nigeria and be a public company with at least 10 per cent Nigerian share in the equity capital and . . . use 45 per cent Nigerian components'.* Pioneer status is important since tax holidays of up to five years, or beyond if losses are experienced, can be obtained. A share in the equity capital has meant in practice the right to nominate members of the Board of Directors. In this way a considerable amount of influence can be exerted on these companies' policies and operations. Even where no direct assistance is received, foreign companies are expected to conform to the general spirit of these requests. Although there is freedom to remit dividends, 'it is hoped that a reasonable percentage of all profits after taxes will be reinvested in the same or other enterprises in Nigeria'.* 'No precise limits will be laid down for the numbers of Africans to be employed in senior, managerial, technical and professional posts, but it will be expected that posts which can be efficiently filled by Africans should not be filled by non-Africans.'† In certain fields too, private overseas investment is not desired. 'The Federal Government, while recognizing the part played by expatriate enterprises in the commercial development of Nigeria to satisfy the needs of the Nigerian consumer, believes that, in the interests of the Nigerian people, Nigerian traders and businessmen should greatly increase their present share

---

* *Statement on Industrial Policy*, 1964. Federal Ministry of Information.
  Note: The 10 per cent Nigerian shareholding may be of a private or official nature.
† ' Opportunities for Overseas Investment in the Federation of Nigeria ', Nigerian Government Statement 1958.

of external and internal trade.'* Only in certain sectors are there continuing opportunities for the expatriate company—'department stores and other similar large-scale projects . . . and also commercial organizations distributing technical goods'.†

In agriculture, also, opportunities for overseas investment are limited.

In other words, while foreign capital is welcomed, it has to conform to the 'rules of the game'—and these 'rules' are designed to maximize the benefits to the local economy. But this, however, is the kind of atmosphere in which private enterprise has been used to working in advanced countries. Providing the 'rules' are known and 'fair' and are not arbitrarily changed at short notice, then private enterprise has shown it can flourish and, at the same time, make an important contribution to economic development.

Size and constitution

The net external liabilities (including foreign share capital, current accounts with parent company and suppliers' credits) were measured for the companies concerned in 1962 by the Central Bank of Nigeria. The total obtained was unsatisfactory for a number of reasons: insufficient coverage of the survey: exclusion of banks, insurance companies and certain transport companies; difficulties in distinguishing between short and long term capital. Nevertheless the figures do give a rough guide and the first available one, of the total stake of overseas investment in that territory.

'*Trading and services*' is quantitatively still the most important sector, although the indications are that it is declining in relative size. Profitable opportunities have been narrowed following the formation of the Marketing Boards in 1947 and 1949 and, more recently, government policies, which have had the effect of extending the operations of indigenous firms.

With the contraction of the range of profitable opportunities, plus the general advance of the economy, it was to be expected that the trading companies would become more involved in '*manufacturing and processing*'. Tax incentives, industrial estates, tariff protection, etc., encouraged this. It was a natural extension of activities to move from simple importation into import substitution. The market had

* Annual Report of the Ministry of Commerce and Industry 1960–1.
† Nigerian Government Statement 1956.

Table 1. *Foreign investment in Nigeria analysed by type of activity, 1962*

(£'s millions)

Sector	Paid up capital including reserves	Other liabilities (net)	Total	Percentage distribution
Mining and quarrying	15·2	65·4	80·6	36·9
Manufacturing and processing	20·1	16·7	36·8	16·8
Agriculture, forestry and fishing	3·6	0·7	4·3	1·9
Transport and communication	0·5	1·9	2·4	1·1
Building and construction	3·7	3·9	7·6	3·5
Trading and services	24·9	60·9	85·8	39·3
Other activities	1·2	−0·3	0·9	0·5
Total	69·2	149·2	218·4	100·0

Note: (1) The figures are as at end of 1962 or of nearest financial year and relate to companies wholly or in large part owned by foreign companies or non-residents.

(2) Most foreign investments are channelled through subsidiaries (81 per cent of total fixed assets), the remainder being about equally divided between branches and other forms of organization.

Source: *Central Bank of Nigeria, Economic and Financial Review*, June 1964, p. 11.

been established and the trading companies' knowledge about local conditions and requirements was invaluable. This was done either alone or with specialist manufacturing firms, the latter providing the technical 'know-how', the trading companies supplying general managerial services, and information on the local market as well as, in many cases, the marketing outlet itself. It was also a natural move to upgrade goods which had been hitherto exported in a raw or unfinished state. Local assembly or blending, too, was a popular starting-point. Concurrently companies which had hitherto only had sales outlets considered local manufacture.

The other major sector is '*mining and quarrying*'. Here the two main activities are, first, petroleum exploration and production, and secondly, tin mining. Overseas firms are dominant here. Both, and particularly the first, require large amounts of capital and a high degree of specialist knowledge. In the former, long pay-out periods and high risks are also characteristics. In the case of Shell-B.P., the pre-eminent oil company in Nigeria, full 'break-even' is not expected until 1968, some twenty years after the start of exploration activities, and after a cash deficit which in 1963 amounted to £65 millions.*

With regard to '*agriculture, forestry and fishing*' the amount of investment from overseas has been small. Expatriate plantations have not been very extensive. There are a number of reasons for this: unhealthy climate, difficulties, even before Independence, in securing land and official approval and an unfavourable Marketing Board price system. '*Building and construction*' is also a minor sector as is '*transport and communications*' which is for the most part in indigenous hands.

As regards the concentration of investment, the United Africa Company accounts for a good proportion of the total. In his report to the shareholders in 1961, the Chairman of Unilever stated that in Nigeria total investment of U.A.C. and other, minor, Unilever subsidiaries amounted to £48·5 millions. However, with the growth of the manufacturing sector there is increasing heterogeneity. Between 1956 and 1961, U.A.C.'s capital expenditure according to their Statistical and Economic Reviews (25 and 28) amounted to £15·2 millions. This compares with a total capital investment from overseas over the same period of £123·2 millions (see Table 2).

Direct investment in Nigeria from overseas increased considerably over the period.

There have been some variations, but a satisfactory upward trend was established up to 1962. In that year and the following sharply reduced figures were recorded. At first sight they appear most disappointing in view of the target of £200 millions for the period of the 1962–8 Development Plan. However there are special factors which account for this decline and the indications are that they are of short-term duration. These relate to the governmental policy of extending the participation of indigenous traders in the distribution field. This had been anticipated by expatriate companies and their reaction to it was quite swift. As a result this was soon reflected in the investment statistics as the companies affected ran down stocks and reduced their liabilities, particularly their external ones to head office.

What was more encouraging was the increase in investment in other sectors, particularly in manufacturing and processing and especially in later years.

* M. S. Robinson, ' Nigerian Oil: Prospects and Perspectives', *Nigerian J. of Social and Economic Studies*, July 1964.

Table 2. *Source of funds for investment*
(£'s million)

	1953-4	1954-5	1955-6	1956-7	1957-8	1958-9	1959-60	1960-1	1961-2	1962-3	1963-4 B
Private capital investment from overseas[1]	5·5	10·4	9·6	19·1	17·1	14·0	24·0	19·0	30·0	10·4	15·0
Official donations	3·5	3·2	3·9	2·6	3·4	3·9	3·5	4·9	2·0	9·8	7·6
Other capital inflow	−14·0	−38·6	−0·6	5·9	13·5	27·0	11·0	50·4	42·5	31·6	17·6
Sub-total	−5·0	−25·0	12·9	27·6	34·0	44·9	38·5	74·3	74·5	51·8	40·2
Personal savings of individuals and small enterprises	22·6	31·1	33·2	40·3	48·6	45·3	44·6	73·6	93·7	N.A.	N.A.
Government surplus and other national savings	37·1	60·8	32·2	29·4	24·5	29·9	50·4	6·6	3·9	N.A.	N.A.
Sub-total	59·7	91·9	65·4	69·7	73·1	75·2	95·0	80·2	97·6	N.A.	N.A.
Total investment funds	54·7	66·9	78·3	97·3	107·1	120·1	133·5	154·5	172·1	N.A.	N.A.
Overseas private capital investment as a percentage of total investment funds	10·1	15·5	12·3	19·6	16·0	11·7	18·0	12·3	17·4	N.A.	N.A.

B=Provisional.   N.A.=Not available.
[1] Including reinvested profits. *Note*: The estimates for personal savings and the investment by small enterprises are subject to a large margin of error.

Source: Columns 2-7: *Commonwealth Development and its Financing*, No. 5, *Nigeria*, H.M.S.O., 1963.
Source: Columns 1 and 8-11 calculated using same basis and derived from Federation of Nigeria Digest of Statistics.

Table 3. *Foreign business investment by type of activity,*
1950/1–1954/5, 1961, 1962
(£ millions)

Sector	Gross capital expenditure by major private companies[1]		Net flow of foreign business capital[2]			
	1950/1– 1954/5	%	1961	1962	Total	%
Agriculture, forestry and fishing	3·5	8·8	−0·9	−0·1	−1·0	−3·0
Mining	13·8	34·7	+5·8	+4·5	+10·3	30·8
Manufacturing and processing	3·4	8·5	+5·0	+12·0	+17·0	50·9
Transport and communications	4·7	11·8	+0·3	+0·1	+0·4	1·2
Trading and business services	12·2	30·6	+12·3	−9·1	+3·2	9·6
Building and construction	2·2	5·6	+0·5	+2·8	+3·3	9·9
Others	—	—	—	+0·2	+0·2	0·6
Total	39·8	100·0	+23·0	+10·4	+33·4	100·0

[1] *Source: Investment in Nigeria*, U.S. Department of Commerce, 1957, p. 162.
[2] Central Bank of Nigeria, *Economic and Financial Review*, June 1964.

Note: The above are not strictly comparable since the former (the only data of this type available for the period in question) relates only to major companies. However they do indicate a major change in direction of overseas investment.

As for the period after 1962, disinvestment still continues in distribution, but at a much reduced rate, and should soon be completed. A net British disinvestment of £13·6 millions in the distributive sector in 1962 was reduced to £0·1 million in 1963.* Concurrently, of course, new investment is taking place in this sector with the construction of department stores and other large-scale projects at present beyond the capabilities of most indigenous undertakings.

Certainly the coming of full political independence has had no adverse effects upon the inflow of foreign investment: even as regards the trading sector such disinvestment would probably still have taken place, but perhaps spread over a longer period. Indeed international business investment has shown a remarkable tendency to increase as Independence approached, especially in manufacturing. This is gratifying when one considers Nigeria's need for both capital and technological and managerial know-how.

* I should like to express my thanks to the Statistics Division of the Board of Trade for this, and other, information.

Table 2 also shows the relative contribution of direct investment from overseas to total investment funds. Over the period shown, it has averaged some 15 per cent and as such has been a very important incremental source of capital.

The effect of this investment from overseas on the national income taken as a whole has been hidden by the movements in the predominant agricultural sector. In the latest figures, for 1961–2, agriculture, livestock, fishing, forest products and land development taken together accounted for £654·0 millions or 62 per cent of a total national income, at 1957 prices, of £1046·8 millions. In these sectors, however, the extent of investment from overseas is minimal. On the other hand, as regards manufacturing where international business investment is predominant, although it as yet accounts for only a very small proportion of total national income (some 2 per cent) in real terms, its contribution increased fivefold over the decade 1950–60.

'Mining and oil' is the other sector which has received during the period a good deal of investment from overseas. Again it is very small—about 1 per cent of total national income—and during the period 1953/4–1961/2 has remained at about this size. However the prospects for a substantial increase in contribution are very bright. As for 'distribution and services' it is difficult to distinguish income generated by expatriate from that by indigenous investment, but it is much greater than the other sectors. Altogether one might say that total national income has been much more dependent upon indigenous enterprise and such factors as commodity prices than overseas investment, but in particular sectors its influence has been great. These are the sectors, also, that are likely to be growth points for future development as well as making significant contributions in other ways, such as through foreign exchange earnings and the diversification of the economy.

'It is not possible to discover from the published statistics exactly how the funds for the capital formation of private enterprises are derived. The greater part of the funds available seems to be the undistributed profits of the large concerns. . . . There were, however, substantial inflows of new capital for such enterprises as the cement factories.'* There is some evidence that new capital increased considerably in relative importance as the decade progressed, largely

---

* *Commonwealth Development and its Financing*, No. 5, *Nigeria*, H.M.S.O., 1963, p. 21.

because of the increasing size of expenditure in respect of manufacturing and the oil industry:

(a) Of the twenty-six manufacturing companies concerned in this
survey, the approximate relative size of the various sources of
finance, as at 1963–64, was: new capital 60 per cent; indigenous
sources 25 per cent; retained earnings (including profits made in
other projects and re-invested) 15 per cent.

(b) For 1958–60 and 1962–3 (the only years for which such
information is available) retained earnings of U.K. companies
amounted to only about a third of new investment.*

Reasons for investment

Why did foreign investment increase during the period? Heavy
expenditure on oil exploration and production facilities alone

Table 4. *Factors influencing investment—twenty-six manufacturing
companies*

Factor	Frequency of mention
To avoid being shut out by tariffs and other restrictions	15
Specific invitation of/Encouragement from the Nigerian Government	11
Long term prospects of Nigerian economy	9
To take advantage of increased demand	7
Activities of competitors	7
Request by/Encouragement from company already in Nigeria	5
Profits on supply of machinery	3
Presence of raw materials	2
Others	8
	67

Source: Questionnaires and Interviews.

accounts for about a third of the total. As for the other sectors fifty-
five companies gave information, through the medium of interviews
or answers to questionnaires, on the specific factors which made
them invest in Nigeria. In the case of companies engaged in marketing, distribution and construction, the fundamental factor appears
to have been to take advantage of the increase in effective demand.
Between 1950 and 1960 the Nigerian national income increased, in

* Derived from statistics supplied by the Statistics Division, Board of Trade:
these exclude oil investments and, except for 1963, insurance.

real terms, at about 4 per cent per annum, a rate which was exceeded in the earlier part of the decade when commodity prices were more favourable. The latter themselves encouraged investment in the primary sector. The increased government expenditure on infrastructure was also important. As regards manufacturing companies, however, the answers given were far more complex.

Nigerian governmental action and persuasion has been most important in influencing British manufacturing companies. The erection of tariff barriers to protect infant industries placed many U.K. companies in a dilemma. In most cases they would have preferred to have continued to supply goods manufactured in this country. Due to economies of scale this could be done in most cases more cheaply. This policy would also considerably reduce the amount of capital at risk overseas. However, the pressure to set up local manufacturing projects was strong. To opt out of local manufacture at this stage would not only mean an immediate loss of an export market but make it extraordinarily difficult to re-enter the field at a later stage.

A vital factor was the favourable assessment of the long-term outlook for the Nigerian economy. The large population (a disputed 55 millions) was a point which was mentioned by a number of companies. National income *per capita* was, it is true, still low, but prospects for further improvement were considered good by most companies. The activities of competitors, often European, also influenced a favourable investment decision. This helped to crystallize a decision which might otherwise have been postponed. Existing firms in Nigeria, too, played a significant part in attracting new investment, particularly from smaller and medium-sized companies which did not have the staff to maintain an adequate and continuous world-wide review of investment opportunities. Once confidence about long-term prospects, political stability and the like has been established a small number of large international companies can themselves attract a good deal of new investment.

The generous tax incentives given especially to manufacturing companies, however, appear to have had only a marginal effect. Only five out of the twenty-six manufacturing companies questioned stated that they were 'very important' (2) or 'important' (3) in influencing their investment decision. What appears to have happened is that while Nigerian Government invitation/encouragement—a specific one to individual companies—was important in first attracting interest, the actual investment decision was much more influenced by the longer term considerations rather than short term tax advantages. What was more eagerly sought after was tariff protection, without which many projects would not be able to face competition from imports. Import duty drawbacks were also important. Just as significant as the scale of allowances was their efficiency in operation. The difficulty in practice in securing import duty relief was frequently mentioned. However, the recently instituted 'approved user' system should improve the situation. Overall, the need seems to be to make the incentives work more effectively, rather than add to the already generous allowances.

Tax incentives given by developing countries are sometimes frustrated by the lack of appropriate complementary legislation in the advanced countries. This might at first sight appear to explain in part the marginal effect of Nigerian tax incentives. British companies which obtain relief from tax in Nigeria find themselves, due to an unsatisfactory double taxation agreement, subject to the full rate of United Kingdom tax when remitting dividends to their parent. There is no doubt that this situation is unsatisfactory and should be remedied as soon as possible. However, in practice, it does not appear to have had quite the negating effect which might have been expected since, in these circumstances, steps were taken to avoid paying U.K. tax.

One factor which was conspicuous by its absence among those inducing investment from overseas was 'lower labour costs'. It is true that wage rates in Nigeria are considerably below those in Europe. In that sense labour was indeed 'cheap', but indirect costs take away much of this advantage. Among these were: (a) The high cost of training, including the cost of low production rates in the initial years due to enforced 'training on the job'. (b) The high cost of supervision and administration. This was due both to the more intensive supervision required and the much higher cost of expatriate staff as compared to Europe. (c) The costs of welfare facilities provided for all employees.

'Joint' projects

In order to ensure that the country's manufacturing capacity is at least partially owned and controlled by Nigerians, an official policy has been adopted of reserving part of the equity of new projects for indigenous ownership. At the moment this is being done largely by government agencies, particularly the Development Corporations, although in a sizeable minority of cases the Regional or Federal Government hold shares. The underlying strategy is that these shares will be eventually released to the Nigerian public and the funds so liberated can be reinvested in new undertakings. In practice these funds have not been turned over in this way, and what has happened is that the total government investment has had to grow in size. Particularly at a time when capital is needed for the Development Plan, this has caused an added strain on scarce resources.

It has also been common for private companies themselves to form joint undertakings, to spread risks or to gain technological and marketing 'know-how'.

The expected pattern of equity holding is confirmed by an examination of the capital structure of the fifty-six companies surveyed.

In Nigeria joint undertakings have become much more prominent recently with the acceleration in the setting up of manufacturing projects; marketing companies, on the other hand, were in almost every case 100 per cent owned. Other companies demonstrated a pattern between the two but tending towards 100 per cent ownership.

Manufacturing companies exhibited much more diverse capital structures. One-quarter of them had four or more partners. Also prominent as partners were a number of institutions—the development associations of certain banks, quasi-official development companies incorporated in Nigeria, and private development bodies such as the Commonwealth Development Finance Corporation. Ownership patterns also tended to get more complex as size increased. 'Official' participation tended to be a minority one, although usually much greater than the 10 per cent now specifically required for a pioneer certificate. In only three of the fourteen companies concerned was it a majority one and in each of these cases there was agreement with the expatriate company for the sale of the remainder of the equity at independent valuation. The British companies involved did not regard their investments as being necessarily of a long term nature. This is an interesting development in direct investment and one which may well become more common in the future.

There was also a more tenuous government participation through such joint institutions as the Nigerian Industrial Development Bank, or Northern Nigeria Investments, the latter financed by both the Northern Nigeria Development Corporation and the Commonwealth Development Corporation. Out of the twelve manufacturing companies listed as having no direct official participation, four had indirect participation of this kind.

Government equity interest is therefore very extensive in the manufacturing and processing sector and particularly amongst recently established companies.

It could be argued that this would interfere with effective management. This aspect was pursued with the companies concerned. There was undoubtedly some pressure exerted on specific points, particularly recruitment, but it was asserted that in practice this did not affect the main stream of management decisions.

From the companies' viewpoint such government participation had advantages: (a) It was thought to be a protection against expropriation, at worst, or misunderstanding, at best. An 'open book' policy was invariably adopted by the expatriate company concerned: profits, business practices and policies were considered to be above reproach and it was better that they should also be seen to be so. Such a policy appears to have been successful in Nigeria in securing government/business co-operation. (b) The good offices of the government could also be useful in arranging expatriate staff quotas, import duty drawbacks and other matters requiring official approval. In practice, however, support of this type appears to have disappointed companies which had expected a greater degree of government assistance. (c) This helped to identify the company concerned with the economic development of Nigeria rather than with overseas business interests. (d) Among other reasons were—to help sales where the Government was a major customer; it also reduced the size of the initial capital at risk.

Another indication of the greater flexibility in general towards the capital structure of affiliates is given by the answers of the U.K. parent companies who were asked what kind of ownership pattern they preferred in their overseas operations. Naturally none desired a minority position, but only 44 per cent stated that they wished 100 per cent ownership: in 30 per cent of cases only over 50 per cent ownership was preferred: 20 per cent had no preference or predominant pattern and 6 per cent wished 50 : 50. Reaction to government participation in general was mixed, but here again flexibility was evident.

Some progress has also been made with regard to Nigerian public equity participation. By the end of 1963, six expatriate companies had offered for sale a proportion of their ordinary shares (four cases) or convertible debentures (three cases). The latter had the advantage of overcoming the problem of the lean years during which the company was being established. In order to attract as many small savers as possible the minimum amounts to be applied for were much reduced, only £10 in the case of ordinary shares. In addition ordinary and preference shares of an investment company were traded: this enabled the Nigerian investor to participate in seven other expatriate companies whose shares were not quoted on the Lagos Exchange.* Finally, a number of other companies, mainly engaged in tin mining, made some shares available for purchase in Nigeria.

The direct issues have been successful, in cases above the expectations of the company concerned. They show that even in an underdeveloped country it is still possible, with the right project, sufficient publicity and particular methods, to mobilize private local capital for industrial investment. They also demonstrate the greater willingness of some expatriate companies to have, indeed in cases to seek, local public equity participation. Due to the thinness of the market, however, such participation must perforce be limited at this stage.

Effect on Nigeria's balance of payments

Direct investment by overseas companies has helped Nigeria's balance of payments very considerably:

Exports: Tin (and columbite) and crude oil exports have made an important contribution. The former has averaged about 5 per cent of total exports and is expected to remain at that level over the next few years. Earnings from crude oil exports, on the other hand, have increased very spectacularly. Beginning in 1958, they had by 1961 already exceeded the former in value and by 1963 accounted for approximately 11 per cent of total exports. It was recently estimated† that they will at least equal £100 millions in 1970, or approximately 60 per cent of total non-oil exports in 1963—a fivefold increase over 1963 exports. Liquefied natural gas will also be exported.

The small foreign investment in the agricultural sector also contributes directly through the export of commodities.

---

* Participation as at 31 August 1963.
† *West Africa*, 27 February 1965, p. 233.

As regards manufacturing, however, there is little in the way of an export trade, nor are any significant exports anticipated over the next decade even to neighbouring territories, not only because of the political difficulties in arranging a West African Common Market, but because of the general popularity of import substitution carried on behind tariff barriers. Where progress has been much better is in the upgrading of commodity exports: tin smelting and plywood manufacture are two outstanding examples. Prospects for further advances in this sector are good, providing tariff barriers in the developed countries are favourable.

As an approximate calculation foreign business investment is directly responsible at present for some 20 per cent of Nigeria's foreign currency earnings: this proportion will grow significantly as crude oil exports increase.

Imports. During the decade under consideration there was a considerable increase in investment in manufacturing: most of this was for import substitution. In some cases the progress made has been excellent, e.g. cement, textiles. In addition to full manufacture, local assembly has accelerated, saving freight charges and stimulating local production of certain items. Nor is there any evidence for supposing that expatriate companies have done other than attempted to maximize the local input proportion. The system of official incentives, 'requirements', and persuasion also helps to ensure that the beneficial effects to the Nigerian balance of payments are maximized.

Major foreign exchange savings (net imports of oil products were £11 millions in 1963) will also be made by the new oil refinery, planned to come 'on stream' in 1965. The equity of this refinery will also be shared: 40 per cent Government; 40 per cent Shell and B.P.; 20 per cent Nigerian public. Meanwhile, natural gas is a useful source of energy for the Eastern Region.

Because of the large capital sums and the advanced level of technology required, plus the pressure on government funds from Development Plan projects, it is likely that import saving projects will be largely dependent upon private overseas investors at least for the foreseeable future.

Profit ratio on operations in Nigeria

The contribution of overseas investment to the economic development of backward countries may be significantly reduced if exorbitant profits are made and remitted. Earnings of British investment in Nigeria, however (excluding oil and except for 1963, insurance), averaged only 6·4 per cent on a total net asset value of investments over the period 1958–63.*

It is difficult to calculate with any degree of certainty the earnings percentage of total foreign investment, but the indications are that it is even less than this.

There are three reasons which can be put forward as at least a partial explanation of these low returns:

(i) A large proportion of investment is recent in origin and not showing much in the way of return.†
(ii) The disinvestment in the trading sector had a direct effect on the earnings percentage.
(iii) Delayed break-even in respect of the heavy oil investments.

As to anticipated returns, seventeen companies with mainly manufacturing interests gave information on this matter. The returns at which they aimed varied at between 10 and 20 per cent after tax on capital invested, with a concentration at the lower end of the scale. Ten out of the seventeen aimed at between 10 and 12½ per cent. The overall average was 12·9 per cent. These expected returns were in each case compared with the average return, after tax, on net assets employed, achieved by the group of companies to which the Nigerian subsidiary or affiliate belonged. Considering only those companies whose operations were conducted primarily in the United Kingdom, the average overseas return aimed at was 13·1 per cent or only 6 per cent above an average group return of 7·1 per cent. This extra return, however, was not only modest but often not achieved in practice.

Evidence from those concerns whose shares or debentures are quoted on the Lagos Stock Exchange—and hence whose published accounts are more readily available—points in the same direction of 'moderate profits'. Altogether there seems to be little evidence, at

---

* Derived from ' Investments and Earnings Overseas', *Board of Trade J.,* 7 August 1964, 19 April 1963. The 1963 figures were supplied by the Statistics Division.
† The progress of affiliates, however, appears to have been in most cases according to expectations. Of twenty-six parent companies whose subsidiary had commenced operations in Nigeria since 1958, sixteen said that growth had been about the same as expected, while in five cases it had been above and five below. There was no significant difference between manufacturing and other sectors.

least in Nigeria, to support the charge that expatriate concerns make 'exorbitant profits' to the detriment of the host economy. Indeed, it may well be that the profit rate achieved is too low, bearing in mind the uncertainties of operating in an underveloped country.

Dividend remittances

Not surprisingly in view of the moderate profit rate achieved, the size of current payments in respect of direct investment has not been a problem item in Nigeria's balance of payments:

Table 5. *Nigeria's balance of payments: payments in current transactions in respect of direct investment*
(£ millions)

Year	Current Payments A	Private capital[1] investment (net) B	A as a % of B	Merchandise exports C	A as a % of C
1953	7·5	5·5	136	124·2	6·0
1954	6·6	10·4	63	149·5	4·4
1955	6·7	9·6	70	132·5	5·1
1956	5·4	19·1	28	134·6	4·0
1957	3·4	17·1	20	127·5	2·7
1958	5·8	14·0	41	135·6	4·3
1959	8·5	24·0	35	162·1	5·2
1960	8·1	19·0	43	167·0	4·9
1961	6·5	30·0	22	170·9	3·8
1962	6·0	10·4	58	165·4	3·6
1963a	9·0	15·0	60	185·3	4·9
Total	73·5	174·1	42	1654·6	4·4

[1] Provisional.

Source: *Annual Abstract of Statistics*⎫ Federal Office of Statistics, Lagos.
Digest of Statistics ⎭

Note: ' The figure for private capital investment is not net of reinvested profits which are initially included as a current payment.'

It is unfortunate that the official statistics are unsatisfactory because of the treatment of reinvested profits. However it does mean that the size of dividend remittances is even less than indicated above.

In practice remittances have not been great from the newly established expatriate companies, largely due to unprofitable operations in early years and internal financing of expansion, particularly in manufacturing. The older established companies tended to remit a higher proportion of their profits. . . .

Direct overseas investment and Nigerian taxable capacity

The presence of international companies in Nigeria has benefited government revenue through the payment of direct taxes, offset to some extent by tax concessions. Such companies also play a significant part in collecting revenue, in the case of excise duties, particularly on tobacco, or paying import duties. In addition to the gross amounts involved, since undertakings in which overseas capital is involved are much larger than the average, there is the significant advantage that collection is much easier and cheaper, an important feature in Nigeria, where resources for such a task are limited. There are also many indirect benefits, such as the expenditure of expatriates on relatively highly taxed luxury goods, their own income tax and the greater ease in the collection of tax from all employees.

More specifically, there is the significant, and growing, contribution of the oil industry. Under the present legislation—the Petroleum Tax Ordinance 1959*—the Government takes 50 per cent of the profits, including such items as rents and royalties: the latter are paid during the period up to the 'break-even point', but in addition an important special feature in Nigeria is the provision for paying some profits tax earlier than would otherwise be the case by temporarily disregarding depreciation provisions in computing profits. Actual payments have been very substantial: it is estimated that up to 1964 government revenue had benefited by some £30 millions, and that this would rise by some £9 millions in 1965 and at least £12 millions in 1966.† All regions in Nigeria are helped by such payments. The revenue derived from the oil industry is increasing at a much faster rate than total government current revenue.‡ It will thus form a most useful additional income at a time when increasing development expenditure has to be met out of public funds.

Tin production and government revenue derived from it have, in contrast to crude oil, been relatively static between 1953 and 1963, moving in response to commodity prices for this metal. They have also been considerably surpassed in size. As to the future, in contrast

* This legislation is currently under review.
† *West Africa*, 27 February 1965, p. 233.
‡ £140 millions in 1963.

to oil, it is unlikely that tin production will grow to any appreciable extent, but it does provide a useful incremental income—£1·3 millions in 1962–3.

The question may be asked—is it not possible to raise the government 'take'? Unfortunately Nigeria is a high cost producer of both tin and oil when compared with other suppliers. She also produces only a small proportion of total world supplies—tin 6 per cent; oil 0·3 per cent—and is therefore unable to influence world prices.* In both cases she is a marginal producer and there is a very real danger that further impositions would price her out of the market, particularly in the case of oil which is already in over-supply. There is thus little scope, if any, for increasing still further the benefit to government revenues, achieved without any use of or risk to capital, by such a step.

The stimulation of indigenous enterprises

This has been promoted by 'official' means—45 per cent Nigerian components; 'persuasion' by Government appointed directors, etc., but it also appears that most expatriate companies have been more than willing to abide by such requests. To an extent this is a result of an awareness of the need to be *seen* to be helping Nigerian economic development: to a very much greater degree, however, it stems from a genuine desire to contribute. The fact that almost all expatriate companies look upon their investments as long term ones considerably reinforces this inclination. Where all other factors are the same or about the same, preference is definitely given to the Nigerian supplier or contractor. Even where costs are higher it is a common practice to give such preference provided the extra cost does not exceed 5 or 10 per cent.

Due to the underdeveloped nature of the economy expatriate companies often find that they have to undertake functions which they would normally expect to be provided externally in an advanced economy, e.g. transport, repair work. As the economy, local or national, advances these activities may be 'hived off' and performed by Nigerian firms. Such a policy has in fact been adopted by the more progressive companies, even to the extent of providing credit

* In the case of columbite Nigeria does produce 95 per cent of the total world supplies, but the market for columbium is weak at present and the outlook unpromising.

on the transfer of facilities. It is to be hoped that more firms will adopt this flexible attitude. However, the scope for indigenous enterprise must be limited at present by the low level of technological knowledge.

Conclusion

Well over half of the total foreign investment in Nigeria in 1963 originated during the previous decade, £175 millions being invested by international companies. The inflow of new capital, as distinct from retained profits, also increased in importance.

Operations have been carried out on terms which have been mutually acceptable. The Government has endeavoured to maximize the benefits to Nigerian economic development through 'requirements' tied to tax and other allowances and 'requests' the spirit of which all expatriate companies were expected to respect. An equity shareholding was also taken in the rapidly expanding manufacturing and processing sector; in the extractive sector, expatriate companies were required to provide government revenues with considerable sums. International businesses, on their side, have been anxious to secure a stake in the growing Nigerian economy at a time when tariff barriers were being constructed. Because of the concern with profits over the long term, rather than quick returns, investors have been more than willing to accede to these official requests, particularly since they often coincided with their own aims—the reduction in costs and favourable 'public relations'. There is also evidence of greater acceptance of local equity participation. Most expatriate companies and especially the larger do appear to show the required 'imaginative adaptability and sense of social purpose': besides, by conducting their affairs in this way they are ensuring, and therefore maximizing, their profits over a longer period.

Direct investment has been made in Nigeria on the basis of three freedoms—freedom from expropriation, freedom to remit, and freedom from arbitrary interference with management. These are fundamental if international business is to thrive and to continue to benefit the local economy. That it has done so very considerably there can be no shadow of doubt. Over the period 15 per cent of the total funds for investment have been provided from overseas business sources, with a consequent increase in the national income. In particular sectors the progress made has been very great: the manufacturing sector has increased considerably, while 'it is no exaggeration to say that for Nigeria the development of its oil resources has been the most important single economic development of the last ten years'.* The balance of payments, far from being weakened by remittances, has been considerably strengthened. Profit margins have been moderate.

One great advantage of investment from overseas is that it eases the strain on domestic sources of capital. By taking appreciable equity shareholding in manufacturing projects this advantage has been lessened. There would appear to be a case for a different approach in this matter, making more use of these intermediate institutions which are themselves financed both by private enterprise and Government, such as the Nigerian Industrial Development Bank. Such participation would not only ease the strain on government finance but would also be more widely acceptable to private enterprise.

Nigeria's wealth still depends primarily on her agriculture. The efficient development of this sector and such matters as the level of commodity prices are vital in determining her rate of growth. However, direct investment from overseas has made a major contribution to Nigeria's economic development over the past decade. Given the maintenance of liberal economic policies, political stability and unity, Nigeria should continue to benefit greatly from the presence of international companies.

* M. S. Robinson, ' Nigerian Oil: Prospects and Perspectives', *op. cit.*

9. THE CAPITAL SHORTAGE ILLUSION: GOVERNMENT LENDING IN NIGERIA*

S. P. SCHATZ

A shortage of capital is usually considered one of the most immediate and pressing as well as most fundamental obstacles to domestic private investment and thus to economic growth in the less developed economies. In Nigeria, the country which provides empirical support for the thesis presented here, this opinion is widely held and it is certainly the belief of the indigenous businessmen themselves. A survey of Nigerian businesses indicates that 'most Nigerian business-men believe that inadequate capital is their main or sole business handicap'.†

The thesis of this article is that frequently the belief that a capital shortage is the effective or operating impediment to indigenous private investment is mistaken, that it is an illusion created by a large false demand for capital, and that what really exists is not an immediate shortage of capital at all, but a shortage of viable projects, i.e. projects that, all things considered, promise to be sufficiently profitable to attract indigenous private investment. Let me point out that I use the term 'viability' in a broad sense here. When a project is considered unlikely to be commercially successful for any reason—whether the project itself is badly conceived, or because the applicant has insufficient entrepreneurial ability, or because conditions external to the enterprise are unfavourable—then the project is 'not viable'.‡

* The author is indebted to the Ford Foundation for a grant which made possible some of the research on which this article is based. He is grateful for helpful comments to O. Aboyade, S. A. Adu, H. M. A. Onitiri, and O. Sonubi of the University of Ibadan, and G. K. Helleiner of the Nigerian Institute of Social and Economic Research and Yale University.

† Sayre P. Schatz and S. I. Edokpayi, ' Economic Attitudes of Nigerian Business-men ', *Nigerian J. of Economic and Social Studies*, December 1962, vol. 4, 3, p. 266.

‡ I have argued elsewhere that the chief impediment to private investment in West Africa is not lack of entrepreneurial ability, but a wide range of factors that may be summed up as the economic environment. ' Economic Environ-ment and Private Enterprise in West Africa ', *Economic Bulletin* (Ghana), December 1963, vol. 7, 4.

S. P. Schatz

The chief source of evidence used in this article is the loans experience of Nigeria's Federal Loans Board (FLB) from its establishment in 1956 to December 1962.* The FLB is a development bank, operated by the Federal Government of Nigeria, which makes loans to indigenous entrepreneurs for undertakings in fields other than agriculture or trade.† The commercial viability of projects submitted to the FLB is rather carefully investigated by the Industries Division of the Federal Ministry of Commerce and Industry. This Division then presents its recommendations to the FLB, which generally accepts them. Approved loans are subject to the further requirement before they are finally sanctioned that the potential borrower must have adequate collateral to secure the loan. Security is investigated only after the project has passed the viability test.

Since some of the lending activities of the Regional Governments' Loans Boards in the Federation of Nigeria have been greatly influenced by political considerations, it is worth making the point at the outset that this has not been true of the Federal Loans Board. This is analytically important because it allows us to carry on an analysis of the *economics* of the Board's lending activities free from the complicating effects of political factors. The relative insulation of the FLB from political considerations is best shown by the fact that, for the period covered by my observations, the Board accepted the recommendations of the Industries Division officials in 96 per cent of the applications that came before it. All evidence indicates that the recommendations of these Industrial Officers, most of whom were non-Nigerian, were based on economic rather than political considerations. This is universally agreed upon by those who are familiar with the situation, Nigerians as well as Europeans.

False shortage of capital

We examine the thesis of this article by scrutinizing all applications first considered by the FLB by August 1961.‡ This cut-off date allows time to follow up on the eventual disposal of the applications.

* I am grateful to government officials connected with the Federal Loans Board for their unstinting co-operation. I have dealt more fully with this material in a forthcoming book, *Development Bank Lending in Nigeria: the Federal Loans Board*, to be published by Oxford University Press.
† Legal restrictions on the kinds of economic activities the FLB may finance were lifted in 1962.
‡ Except for a few applications considered during four early meetings of the FLB, the records for which were lost.

Two hundred and ninety applications were judged by the criterion of commercial viability.* Of these, 229 (79 per cent) were rejected ('viability rejectees') and sixty-one (21 per cent) were approved ('viability approvees'). Of the sixty-one viability approvees, fifty-four (89 per cent) had acceptable security while seven (11 per cent) were refused loans because of inadequate security.

Table 1. *Federal Loans Board action on loans applications*

Total number of applications judged on the basis of viability	290	
Rejected	229 (79%)	79%
Approved	61 (21%)	21% 100%
Of those whose viability was approved		
Security also approved	54 (89%)	19%
Security rejected	7 (11%)	2% 21%

We see a false demand for capital consisting of two parts. The apparent demand for FLB loans funds, or what may simply be called the apparent demand for capital, is represented by the 290 applications judged on the basis of viability.† The first and major segment of the false demand for capital comprises the 229 viability rejectees. They do not constitute part of the genuine demand for capital because, obviously, loans are not made simply on the basis of the aspiring borrowers' estimates of the prospects of their projects. Those with projects which the potential lenders have adjudged unworthy have a *desire* for capital but not an effective demand for capital. The seven security rejectees constitute the second and much smaller segment of the false demand for capital.‡ These are eliminated from the genuine demand for capital because would-be borrowers who cannot produce security acceptable to the lender

* There were 336 applications altogether. I have judged that forty-six of the rejected applications were not appraised on the basis of probable commercial viability, but were rejected on other grounds, for example, because they were for projects that were beyond the FLB jurisdiction.
† It could well be argued that the forty-six applications rejected on grounds other than viability, and perhaps other groups as well, should also be included in the apparent demand for capital. In order to avoid some rather esoteric discussions, I am omitting these; their inclusion, however, would strengthen my thesis.
‡ The relatively small number of security rejectees results partially from the FLB's application procedure. The FLB judges applications on a viability basis first, and then goes on to appraise the security offered by the viability approvees only.

will not be given loans. The security rejectees also have a desire but not an effective demand for capital.

Thus, taking the viability and the security rejectees together, 236 of the 290 applicants have a false demand for capital, while only fifty-four have a genuine demand. Assuming applications of equal size, 18 per cent of the demand for capital is genuine and 82 per cent is false. If we use the actual average sizes of applications, however, the false demand for capital is larger. The average loan requested by the viability rejectees was £16,648; the average loan requested by the viability approvees was £9,620. Using these figures, we find that 89 per cent of the capital demand was false while 11 per cent was genuine, i.e. the false demand for capital was eight times as large as the genuine.

These figures understate the relative magnitude of the false demand for capital in Nigeria in several ways. Many FLB applications fall by the wayside before they reach the Board because it is made clear in preliminary discussions that the applicant has no chance of success. Moreover, we will see that the FLB, under pressure to make loans, has sometimes gone to considerable lengths to find projects loanworthy. It is also willing to finance projects which are not quite promising enough to be accepted by commercial lenders. We will also see that the prospective viability of some marginal applications is enhanced and the appraisal made more sanguine than it would be if potential investments were considered purely on their own merits because various kinds of government assistance will be rendered to the applying firm. These factors tend to reduce the number of viability rejectees and/or increase the number of viability approvees that emerge from the FLB loan appraisal process.

The number of inadequate security cases is also understated. When a promising project is held up because of inadequate security, the FLB, reluctant to retard economic development, often waters down its security requirements substantially. Where there appeared to be no alternative other than rejection of a promising project, the FLB has sometimes simply approved loans with no security at all.

Real shortage of viable projects

We have said that Nigeria manifests a large false demand for and therefore a large false shortage of capital. In this section we discuss reasons for believing that what really exists in Nigeria is a shortage of viable projects.*

In terms of loans disbursed, FLB activity was quite limited. The FLB made only forty-four loans to the firms whose applications it first considered during its first five and a quarter years.† The aggregate amount of money lent was slightly more than £400,000.

The amount loaned was as small as this despite the fact that the FLB searched assiduously for viable projects. Responding to deep-seated popular desires for rapid development, the FLB frequently judged projects leniently in an effort to find some that could be considered loanworthy. The Board has sometimes gone to great lengths to carve a promising part out of a generally unacceptable application. A firm that engaged in sawmilling and hand production of furniture, for example, applied for a loan of more than £20,000 for log-handling equipment, furniture-making machinery, and the construction of a building. Investigation by an Industrial Officer indicated that the firm had incurred a net loss the previous year, that it had a substantial number of debts, that the proprietor had little or no knowledge of machine-produced furniture (which line of production was, in any case, overcrowded), and that the firm's hand-furniture business was not viable. The sawmilling project was much more promising, but the applicant was adamant about applying for the furniture business as well. The FLB nevertheless refrained from rejecting the application; it deferred its decision and informed the applicant that the Board would probably be favourably inclined to an application for the sawmilling project only. When the applicant acted upon this advice, he was approved for a loan of close to £9,000. The FLB will also sometimes disregard unfavourable factors for a particularly promising entrepreneur. For example, an application was submitted for a loan to enable completion of a partly

---

* Of course, *some* commercially viable investment projects are held up for lack of funds in all countries, but our concern here is with major obstacles. Perhaps it is worth mentioning that in view of the substantial divergences between private and social effects, a lack of profitable projects does not necessarily mean a lack of projects having a net social utility. I have discussed this issue in my articles, 'Underutilized Resources, " Directed Demand ", and Deficit Financing (Illustrated by Reference to Nigeria) ', *Quarterly J. of Economics*, vol. 73, 4, November 1959, and ' The American Approach to Foreign Aid and the Thesis of Low Absorptive Capacity ', *Quarterly Review of Economics and Business*, vol. 1, 4, November 1961.

† Ten of the fifty-four loans that were approved for both viability and security remain unissued for various reasons.

built hotel by an experienced and capable hotel manager, who also ran a successful enterprise of his own. The report on the application, however, stated that the hotel business was already well served in the area of the prospective enterprise, and any ordinary applicant would probably have been rejected. It was felt, however, that this man would be successful despite the competition, and the FLB approved the loan. The FLB will also pay less than full heed to its own policy rules of thumb for a promising entrepreneur. Thus, because the sawmilling industry was already well developed and competition in the industry was keen, the Board had expressed a reluctance to make loans for this purpose. Nevertheless, when a (different) sawmill proprietor who was already running his existing businesss successfully and whose prospects for successful expansion were good applied for a loan, his application was approved. The FLB's leniency with respect to security and its practice of taking into account the salutary effects of prospective government assistance to borrowers also increased the proportion of applicants who received loans.*

The shortage of viable projects is shown most clearly, perhaps, by the record of the loan recipients. I have examined the FLB progress reports and various other materials on the forty-four FLB borrowers in order to assess the success of their loan financed projects. The results are shown in Table 2.

For sixteen of the firms, mainly those which received their loans most recently, no assessment of business success can yet be made.† Of the remaining twenty-eight firms, ten (36 per cent) are proceeding successfully so far. Eleven (39 per cent) have proved unsuccessful. These are cases in which the loan approved project can be judged with confidence to have been unsuccessful. Many of these firms have been taken to court as loan defaulters. Seven (25 per cent) of the projects are shaky, i.e. they are having serious difficulties but may pull out of them.

There is a supplementary group of borrowers under FLB jurisdiction whose business performance we can also assess. This group

---

* It must be understood also that loan approvals were not held up for lack of funds. Because of a delay in government appropriations, a shortage of capital funds did appear toward the very end of the period studied, but the only effect was to delay somewhat the actual disbursal of the loan funds.

† There is one no-assessment case dating from 1957–8 because, as a result of special circumstances pertaining to land acquisition, the firm had not yet started the loan-approved project by the end of 1962.

consists of four FLB loan recipients approved at early meetings for which no records were available and seven other loan recipients which were transferred to the FLB jurisdiction after having received loans from the FLB's predecessor, the Colony Development Board.

The records of the supplementary group of loan recipients as well as the overall record of the two groups combined (omitting the no assessment cases) are shown in Table 3.

Table 2. *Success of projects*
Forty-four FLB loan recipients

Year loan was issued	Successful	Unsuccessful	Shaky	No assessment
1956–7	1	1	0	0
1957–8	6	4	2	1
1958–9	3	5	0	0
1959–60	0	0	3	1
1960–1	0	1	2	3
1961–2	0	0	0	8
1962–3	0	0	0	3
Total	10	11	7	16

This record is a poor one.

It may be countered that such a judgment is unduly harsh, for many small businesses fail in the highly developed economies also. But the loan recipients are not new businesses, which provide the bulk of the business failures in developed economies, for the FLB

Table 3. *Success of projects*
Enlarged group of FLB loan recipients

	Successful	Unsuccessful	Shaky
Basic group	10	11	7
Supplementary group	5	5	1
Overall record	15 (38%)	16 (41%)	8 (21%)

does not make loans to new firms. These were businesses that survived the high mortality rates of the first years. Moreover, this was not a random sample of Nigerian businesses. The loan recipients constituted a select group. They had gone through a selective process which eliminated 82 per cent of the applicants. Fragmentary evidence indicates that similar select groups have fared much better in other countries.* Third, the loan recipients have had their loans for only a short time. The median loan, in terms of date disbursed, was made in the 1958–9 fiscal year, about four and a half years before the data of this study were collected, and many of the firms experienced considerable delays in receiving equipment, etc., so that they were unable to start on their projects until many months after they received their loans. It must therefore be expected that not only many of the shaky firms but also some of those operating successfully so far will fail. Fourth, considerable government assistance has been provided to the loan recipients. The borrower is helped to spend his money wisely. For example, a furniture producer who planned to spend £2,500 for his machinery was steered to equipment that was not only more suitable, but which also cost about half as much. Technical advice and assistance have been given on such matters as the availability of servicing facilities, installation of equipment, and production techniques. Marketing assistance has also occasionally been provided. Loan recipients have sometimes been shielded from competition. While a continual shortage of staff has caused the flow of assistance to be much smaller than the FLB would have liked it to be, it was nevertheless far from negligible.

Thus, a highly selected group of indigenous firms—firms which had already been well established, which had projects that had been carefully reviewed and approved, which had, moreover, received special government assistance—have produced a most disappointing scorecard of success and failure, a record which, furthermore, is bound to deteriorate since many of the loan recipients have not yet had time to come to grief.

The facts that (1) so few of those who completed applications (after many of the weaker firms had been headed off during the preliminary stages) had acceptable projects, and (2) that such a large proportion of the acceptable projects failed despite efforts to help them, combine to indicate that the significant shortage in the indigenous sector of the Nigerian economy is one of profitable projects. The large false demand for capital creates the illusion that

* See Nathaniel H. Engle, *Industrial Development Banking in Action: A Study of Organisation, Operations, Procedure of Private Development Banks in India, Iran, Pakistan, Turkey,* mimeographed, Pakistan Industrial and Credit Corporation (?), 1962, pp. 275–8, 51, 16, and Shirley Boskey, *Problems and Practices of Development Banks,* published for the International Bank for Reconstruction and Development by the Johns Hopkins Press, Baltimore, 1959, p. 101.

there is a shortage of capital. But the record indicates that, *rather than a large number of viable projects vainly seeking capital, capital has been vainly seeking viable private projects.*

I suggest that this is true not only of Nigeria, but of many other of the more economically underdeveloped countries as well.

10. NIGERIAN CEMENT INDUSTRY

S. U. UGOH

Production costs

. . . Cement is a capital intensive industry. The industry has been developed in countries where labour costs have been high, and therefore most of the technological innovations in the cement industry have been labour saving. Moreover, other gadgets have been invented to improve the quality of cement and to minimize any variations from such quality.

The Nigerian Cement Company has adopted the techniques developed elsewhere and its ability to adapt this technique to suit the domestic resource endowment is seriously limited. We find then that although labour is comparatively cheaper in Nigeria than in Europe or North America, the technique of production used in cement manufacture in Nigeria is capital intensive rather than labour intensive. However, although wages are relatively low in this country, it is most unlikely that a technique that is labour intensive would have produced cement at a lower unit cost than what now obtains. This is another way of saying that cheap labour does not necessarily mean low unit cost of the output, especially if the efficiency of such labour is very low.

The proportion of the different components of total cost to the aggregate depends on various factors. This varies from country to country. For instance, in countries where wages are low, labour cost will be a small portion of total cost. Also, another factor that determines the ratio of each cost component to the total is the method of production. The wet process usually requires more fuel and therefore fuel cost is high. But the dry process economizes on fuel, but then may require expensive gadgets to ensure that the quality of cement is up to the required standard. This would then entail more maintenance costs and a higher depreciation cost. It would even mean a higher fixed cost which becomes a burden to the firm when the plant is not run to capacity.

In the case of the Nigerian Cement Company, there is an additional cost factor that does not loom high with many companies abroad. The Nigercem is involved not only in the manufacture of cement, but also, in such governmental activities as building and maintaining roads that lead to the factory, the establishment of a sixty-bed hospital for the workers, the building of residential houses and the provision of drinking water for these employees. There is a plan to build a modern market with stalls and shops where the employees can buy their provisions. In other words, the factory in addition to its cement manufacture is engaged in the creation and maintenance of a new town—a responsibility that is usually assumed by local governments in other countries. These quasi-governmental responsibilities swell the costs of the Nigerian Cement Company.

The breakdown of the costs of the company for 1962–63 financial year is as follows:*

	%
Coal, electricity and gypsum	40
Administration, welfare services and plant maintenance	30
Depreciation	20
Labour	10
	—
Total	100
	—

The fact that labour costs form only 10 per cent of total costs is quite understandable. As stated earlier, the manufacture of cement is capital intensive and therefore labour cost is not usually a very high element in total cost. But in the case of Nigercem, labour cost is much smaller than it is in companies abroad because of the fact that wages are low in Nigeria. This is true even though Nigercem pays higher daily wages than the governments.

Another interesting thing about the breakdown of the costs is that one can easily see that much of the cost in the Cement Company

---

* The secretary-accountant of the company could not give me the breakdown of the costs in the categories that I had requested. The above breakdown is not too useful because a lot of things are lumped together. Also, note that these percentages are mere approximations.

is fixed. Unfortunately, the breakdown given here does not lend itself easily to such an analysis. However, some rough estimates can be made from the figures at our disposal. The depreciation is calculated on a straight line basis. This makes the depreciation cost a fixed cost since a constant percentage of the equipment would be written off no matter the level of output. Also all the cost of administration, the welfare services, and some part of the plant maintenance costs are fixed. All cost of plant maintenance cannot be fixed because the more intensively the plant is used, the more frequent will be the maintenance. Also, some labour cost is fixed. But coal, electricity, and gypsum cost is certainly variable. We find then that between 35 to 50 per cent of the total cost in Nigercem is fixed. Such a high percentage of fixed cost to total cost is a factor that companies usually take into account in making their pricing policy. We shall return to this later.

But another question that crops up at this stage is: 'How does the unit cost in cement production generally, and at Nkalagu in particular, behave as the capacity of the plant is increased?' We have already pointed out that doubling the capacity at Nkalagu from two kilns to four, assuming there is no increase in the wage rate, will lead to an increase in labour cost of 30 per cent. It is further estimated that there will not be any increase in administrative overhead. And so, administrative cost will remain constant.

On the other hand, welfare and plant maintenance costs will increase, but it is doubtful whether they will double. It is more likely, though, that coal, electricity and gypsum costs may increase by close to 100 per cent. But all the same, it adds up to the fact that the per unit cost of cement will fall with the doubling of the present capacity.

Some rough estimates of unit cost at different levels of capacity have been made at Nkalagu. With capacity of one kiln, it is estimated that one ton of cement costs about £6 to produce. This excludes the cost of packaging. With the capacity of two kilns, the unit cost dropped to £5 per ton. And it is estimated that with a double capacity of four kilns, the unit cost will further drop to £4 per ton.

One may ask whether Nigercem can enjoy further economies of scale if the capacity is expanded beyond four kilns. The company executives are not quite sure. Assuming that the optimum capacity is four kilns, producing 500,000 tons of cement, this is much larger than what is considered the optimum capacity in the United States.

There, the optimum capacity is estimated to be about 1·5 million barrels (i.e. about 256,000 tons) of cement.*

It seems that the primary explanation for this difference in the optimum capacities of cement production at Nkalagu and in the United States is the overhead costs. Such overhead costs as welfare services are not part of the costs of companies in the U.S. But they form an important element in the total cost of Nigercem. As capacity increases and output grows, the unit cost of such overheads becomes insignificant. Another explanation for the difference, but a minor one, would be the differences in wages in Nigercem and in the U.S. But the wage differentials cannot account for much of the difference in the optimum capacity of Nigercem and the average U.S. cement company. It seems correct to maintain that the ratio of marginal output to the wage rate is higher at Nkalagu than in the average U.S. cement company. And if this is the case, then one can easily understand why the optimum capacity in the U.S. is only about 256,000 tons while it is about double at Nkalagu.

Pricing policy

The Nigerian Cement Company has a very simple pricing system. It estimates its unit cost and adds a percentage mark-up to this unit cost, and this forms its ex-factory price. The firm charges all buyers the same price, and each makes arrangements for the shipment of his cement from Nkalagu. It is the buyers, then, who pay the freight to the transport agencies.

This pricing policy departs from the established pricing system used by cement firms abroad. Both in the U.S. and the U.K., cement companies operate the 'Basing Point System' of pricing which is used to discriminate against customers that are closer to the basing points. This system of pricing which is discussed in many standard texts on price theory† requires that the firms assume the responsibility of delivering the goods from the factory to the customers. This facilitates freight absorption by the firms when that is necessary.

One may ask why the Nigerian Cement Company has not adopted this pricing system that is common among the cement industries abroad. In the cement industry, as in all other industries, the three

---

* Samuel M. Loescher, *Imperfect Collusion in the Cement Industry* (Cambridge: Harvard University Press, 1959), p. 41.

† Stephen Enke, *Intermediate Economic Theory* (New York: Prentice-Hall Inc., 1950), pp. 348–50.

most important factors that determine the price of the products are:
- (a) the cost of production,
- (b) the structure of the industry, i.e. the degree or intensity of competition within the industry, and
- (c) the condition of demand.

It has already been pointed out that in the cement industry a large percentage of the total cost is made up of fixed or overhead cost. Under such a circumstance, any disruption in production will mean a large loss to the firm. With keen competition and any threats of excess capacity, there is a greater possibility of firms running into more losses. To avert such losses the firms in the industry may devise pricing systems such as the basing-point system, that may reduce the dangers of price competition.

Such a price competition is more disastrous in cases where a commodity is standardized. And cement is a good example of a standardized product. Cut-throat price competition tends to develop most in buyers' markets. In such circumstances, producers try to reduce their losses by lowering their prices. If all of them do this, none gains. But the cement case is aggravated by the fact that the demand for cement in any region depends on the rate of development in that region. And not only do various regions develop at different rates, but also, construction activities within the various regions fluctuate rather capriciously. To counteract the consequent fluctuations in demand for their product, cement manufacturers have tended to sell in a wider market. 'The short-run fluctuations in geographic demand in the cement industry, conditioned as it is by the mobility of construction activity, encourage freight absorption as a flexible technique for promoting greater short-run stability in the level of sales of every firm.'*

It follows that the factors that make the basing-point pricing system most necessary are:
- (a) the presence of a large number of firms producing a standardized product,
- (b) the existence of excess capacity in the industry,
- (c) a cost structure where fixed costs form a large percentage of total cost, and
- (d) that transportation cost forms a large percentage of delivered price.

* Samual M. Loescher, *Imperfect Collusion in the Cement Industry* (Cambridge: Harvard University Press, 1959), p. 41.

It seems that the first two factors are the most important. It is, in fact, their absence in Nigeria that has not created the need for the Nigerian Cement Company to adopt the basing-point pricing system.

Although there is another cement manufacturing company in the Western Region, there is hardly any competition between these two. The Nigerian Cement Company enjoys a virtual monopoly in its natural market which is all Eastern Nigeria north of Aba, and some parts of the Northern Region. Initially, the company had to break into the market that was dominated by imported cement. But through price cutting and other sales promotion techniques, the company has captured most of the Eastern Region and made it its natural market.

But the basing-point system and freight absorption would have been necessary if the demand for cement within the natural market of the company were not enough to clear all the cement produced. In other words, if there were any danger of excess capacity existing in the company, it would have been necessary for it to absorb some freight in its shipments to the Northern Region or other distant markets in order to increase its sales. But since the demand for cement in its natural market is so much that it cannot satisfy all of it, the company can afford to sell at a uniform ex-factory price that avoids all discrimination.

It may be necessary to ask whether the company will continue this pricing policy indefinitely. It seems that this will continue so long as there are no changes in the existing market conditions. Should the competition grow keener, and demand fall, it will be difficult for it to continue its present pricing policy, for such might entail great losses.

Sales promotion and product distribution

Companies have found it necessary to use some advertising technique to increase their sales. In the case of the Nigerian Cement Company, this was very necessary since it had to make its existence known and the quality of its product appreciated.

Advertising could be of two types. A firm could, in its advertising, try to build up the qualities of the product it manufactures. Using cement as an example, a cement company could try to build up in the public eye the qualities of cement generally and not the particular brand of cement it produces. This could, of course, increase the demand for the product of the industry, and, although the expenditure for the advertising is borne by one firm, most of the others in the industry could gain from it.

On the other hand, a firm could, in its advertising, try to extol the qualities of its own particular brand of a product. In this case, such a firm would have to build up the demand for its own product primarily at the expense of other firms in the industry. If the other firms do not advertise as vigorously as this particular firm, or if the latter has a special quality which the others lack, this type of advertising will pay off much more easily than the other type. In the case of cement, the first type of advertising is meant to win people away from the use of burnt bricks, or mud blocks in building construction. But the second type of advertising is directed primarily, though not wholly, to people who are already using cement in their building activities, but they are being asked to shift from one brand to another.

It is in the second type of advertising that the Nigerian Cement Company was engaged. There was already a market for cement in the country when the company started to operate. But this market had been created by, and up till then was the preserve of, foreign cement manufacturers. The Nigerian Cement Company had to advertise vigorously in order to capture some part of the existing market.

Knowing our colonial past, we can easily appreciate the difficulty that Nigercem had in breaking into the market. There was a great resistance to its product. People tended to doubt the ability of Nigeria to manufacture cement that is comparable to imported cement. Moreover, there is some lethargy in people changing from a tried and familar brand of a product to a new and untried one. This resistance to locally manufactured cement is not peculiar to Nigerians alone. Alderfer and Michl discuss the same problem in the United States in these words: '. . . after information of the new cement spread to this country and its qualities were appreciated, there was a marked preference for European cements. The popularity of the foreign cements over the domestic product was so great that many of the early manufacturers were compelled by dealers to market their cement under foreign brand names.'* It would seem that the resistance in the United States in the last century was,

---

* E. B. Alderfer and H. E. Michl, *Economies of American Industry* (3rd ed., New York: McGraw-Hill Book Co., 1957), p. 182.

perhaps, stronger than the resistance which Nigercem experienced recently.

To combat this resistance the company devised some selling gimmicks. Nigercem uses such slogans as 'Fresh from the Packer'; 'Nigeria's own Cement'. While the first emphasizes the freshness of the product, the second appeals to the nationalistic instincts of the prospective buyers. These have, of course, worked successfully.

The company has now passed the stage of trying to introduce its product to the market. Its product is now accepted and respected. It has therefore had to change its advertising tactics. It now does prestige advertising which is meant to keep it in the public eye. This it does by occasional advertising through the radio, and feature articles in the national press. It makes business gifts to people. Currently, the demand for its products far exceeds the supply. It is not necessary, then, to create new demand through excessive advertising, except, of course, when the new units are ready to go into operation.

In distributing its product the Nigerian Cement Company could have chosen to deal directly with its customers by operating shops in the different parts of its natural market. But instead the company chose to reach the consumers through dealers who buy directly from the mill and then go to retail. These dealers are regular customers of the company and no person but they can buy cement from the company.

The sale through dealers has got some advantages. The company does not have to go into retail marketing with which it is not familiar. Moreover, it reduces its cost of book-keeping which would have increased with a larger number of buyers. And further still, if the company were selling to every person who comes to buy cement, it would mean that the company would not have many regular customers. Many people buy cement to build a house, and once the house is finished they stop buying cement. If such people were to buy directly from the company it would mean that as soon as they complete their buildings the company would start looking for new customers and open new books for these new customers. These would increase the cost of distribution. And it is to avoid all these difficulties and reduce the cost of distribution that the company chose to deal with only a few regular customers.

Those who buy directly from the company do not enjoy some of the facilities that are usually accorded to dealers by manufacturing companies abroad. For instance, no credit facility is accorded to them by the company, and so they have to pay cash for all their purchases before these are delivered. On the other hand, and surely because of the above, they did not have to pay any initial deposits as securities before becoming dealers. This is an unusual arrangement which is a result of the interaction of at least two factors, the monopolistic position of the company and the buoyancy of the demand for cement.

When the company started to operate, it was the first cement manufacturing company in the country. And although there is another now in production, still, Nigercem is a monopolist within its own natural market. The foreign exporters have had to absorb a lot of the freight cost to retain the market in Port Harcourt. And it is Nigercem that sets the price of cement in the Eastern Region. Moreover, since there is much demand for cement in the country, any dealers who buy cement from Nigercem for retailing are bound to make profits. And because this enterprise assures quick profits and little or no risk, people who have money are willing to accept the terms laid down by the company. Any prospective dealers have no other choice. If there had been, or were to be, a keen competition between Nigercem and other cement companies, and if the market had been, or were to be, a buyers' market, then cement retailing would involve more risks of losses and its attraction would fall. Moreover, prospective retailers would have a choice of dealing with one company or another. And then these companies, including Nigercem, would offer some attractions to these prospective dealers. Then the dealers would receive some of the facilities which are accorded to their counterparts overseas.

Profitability of the company

The profitability of any enterprise usually depends on the state of the demand for its products and the nature of its costs. Nigercem has available to it the latest technology in cement manufacturing. Moreover, its raw materials are easily available. Its costs are therefore comparable to costs of similar companies abroad, although it has a higher overhead cost because it has had to provide social amenities that are elsewhere the responsibility of local governments.

On the other hand, its demand has been more buoyant than that of similar companies abroad. The reasons for this are several. First, it has a monopoly position in all Eastern Nigeria, except for Port Harcourt, some parts of Northern Nigeria and the Mid-West. The imported cement has been driven out of the natural market of Nigercem simply because Nigercem can afford to offer a lower delivered price in these areas than the overseas exporters. This also applies to competition between Nigercem and the West African Portland Cement Company Ltd. at Ewekoro. Since cement is a standardized product, price is more important than product differentiation as a factor of competition. And because cement is a heavy product, and cheap per unit of weight, transportation cost is an important element in delivered price. It is only natural, therefore, that since Nigercem's unit cost is comparable to that of other companies, it will enjoy a monopoly position within its natural market because the cost of transportation will make the delivered prices of other companies much higher than that of Nigercem. And furthermore, there is a limit beyond which these other companies cannot absorb freight costs.

Secondly, the country is in a period of construction boom. The demand for cement is growing year by year. Nigercem enjoys a seller's market. It satisfies only a fraction of the demand for cement. In fact, the Port Harcourt market is still retained by overseas exporters mainly because Nigercem does not produce enough cement for that area. The table below shows the quantity of cement used in Nigeria, and the distribution of this between domestic production and imports for some recent years.

	A Cement consumption	B Domestic cement production[1]	C Cement imports	B as a % of A
1958	588,055 tons	110,936 tons	477,199 tons	18·8
1959	649,452 ,,	118,644 ,,	530,808 ,,	18·2
1960	781,486 ,,	155,160 ,,	626,486 ,,	19·1

[1] The figures are contained in an unpublished work of Wolfgang F. Stolper in which he brings up to 1960 the Jackson-Okigbo national income figures 1950–7.

(These figures are got from the *Nigeria Trade Summary* for the different years.)

The domestic production, up to 1960, was the same as Nigercem production. And up to 1960 Nigercem produced less than 20 per cent of the cement demanded in the country.

Under these circumstances it is bound to make a lot of profits. But there is another reason why profits, especially net profits, have been quite high. The company enjoyed up to 9 December 1962 the

111

benefit from the Industrial (Income Tax Relief) Ordinance which gave it a five-year tax-free period. We can appreciate the importance of this when we realize that the Federal Government tax rate of company profits is 40 per cent. If Nigercem had been paying the tax, its profits after tax would have been only 60 per cent of the net profits as shown in the Table below.

Profitability figures for 1957/8–1961/2[1]

1	2	3	4	5	6	7
			Profit on trading as % of			Net profit as % of
Year	Profit on trading £	Total asset £	total asset	Net profit £	Capital issued £	capital issued
1957–8	126,680	2,669,185	4·74	15,189	1,575,102	0·96
1958–9	617,976	2,801,894	22·05	423,679	1,750,000	24·21
1959–60	634,910	3,556,390	17·85	450,380	1,750,000	25·73
1960–1	957,241	4,020,389	23·80	696,334	2,100,000	33·15
1961–2	1,289,289	4,816,211	26·80	1,021,099	2,100,000	48·60

[1] The figures are from the *Report of the Directors and Statement of Accounts* of the company for the different years.

Profit on trading is the difference between total revenue and total cost, less interest payments. To get net profit, therefore, we have to deduct depreciation allowance, interest payments, and costs of issuing new shares from the profit on trading. Total assets refers to the sum of fixed assets and current assets. The latter includes inventories, some cash, and some accounts receivable.

Profit on trading is the 'gross' profit created with the assets of the company. Some of these assets are bought with borrowed money. To find out how much profit these assets are generating, it is necessary to use the figures for profit on trading, since these include the interest payments that have to be made on loans received and used to expand total assets. If there had been no loans contracted, profit on trading would not have included any interest costs that have to be paid. The percentage of 'gross' profits to total assets (column 4) has been rising. In 1961–2, each £100 worth of assets generated £26·8 worth of profits for the company. But this figure does not reveal how the shareholders are faring as regards returns accruable to them.

The net profits are the returns that are accruable to the shareholders. But these figures in absolute amount do not reveal much to us. It is when we find the ratio of these net profits to the capital issued that we can compare earnings of one share in this business with earnings of a similar share in another business. It is the ratio between columns 6 and 7 that is of interest to the shareholders. We find that, except for the first year when the company operated for only $3\frac{2}{3}$ months, net profit as a percentage of capital issued has been quite high. Moreover, the ratio has been increasing year by year. Between 1958–9 and 1961–2 the rate of profit doubled, and net profit was almost 50 per cent of the capital issued in the latter year. For a manufacturing company that had been in operation for only about five years, this was phenomenal. Of course, this rate will likely drop when the company starts to pay company tax.

But although the rate of profits has been very high, only a small portion of this net profit has been distributed to shareholders in the form of dividends. The company has maintained a policy of paying annually as dividends 10 per cent of its capital issued. But since its net profits have up to now exceeded the dividends, the company has had reserves to plough back into the business. By paying only 10 per cent of its capital issued as dividends, even though it can afford to pay more, the company can easily continue the tradition even in bad years. And by financing its expansions through reserves instead of loans, the company is avoiding high interest costs. It may be argued, though, that the shareholders are being denied the dividends that should be paid to them. But it must be realized that the ploughing back of reserves into the business makes the shares appreciate, and therefore any shareholder who disposes of his shares will realize capital gains in compensation for the dividends he did not receive. Furthermore, the capitalization of these reserves through scrip issues has the advantage of leaving the ownership of the business undiluted. With a capital authorized and issued for £4·2 million, only £2·8 million or two-thirds of this was paid in cash by the shareholders. Through ploughing back of profits and capitalization of reserves the other one-third of the £4·2 million capital issued was financed. This means that any shareholder who now has £300 ordinary shares in the company paid only £200 in cash, the other £100 was scrip issues made to him by the company. This £100 is dividends he would have received but which the company chose to reinvest in the business. . . .

113

11. START-UP OF A TEXTILE INDUSTRY: COSTS AND BENEFITS TO THE ECONOMY OF AN UNDERDEVELOPED COUNTRY

S. WILLIAMS

In every country where industrialization is a basic part of economic planning, the establishment of textile and related industries, e.g. apparel manufacture, is liable to be given high priority. This is the natural result of a variety of factors:

(a) Textile imports are generally relatively high, resulting in a significant outflow of scarce foreign exchange.

(b) The internal market often seems large enough to support local production on an import substitution basis.

(c) Often the potential exists for producing or increasing existing production of raw textile fibre from vegetable, animal, or chemically derived sources, e.g. cellulose from wood for rayon, as part of long-range agricultural plans. Logic would seem to dictate that abundant local sources of fibre would generate significant savings in an industry where raw material costs are a high percentage of total manufacturing costs.

(d) Sometimes a glance at less favoured neighbouring countries raises the hope of an export market within a regional trade framework.

(e) Textile manufacturing is sufficiently labour intensive that the benefits to the economy of the resultant employment and training are tempting to the imagination of both planner and politician.

(f) Throughout the world there is a vast capacity to produce textile machines. As well, technical obsolescence in the advanced countries plus an abundance of excess capacity has created a huge warehouse of used machinery. From all of these sources there has emanated a steady sales pressure on the underdeveloped countries, replete with the lure of easy credit, to venture into textile production. In many instances—

some economically sound, others not—this pressure has forced textile production at a rapid rate.

(g) There is a long history of international relations in the textile industry. Manufacturers in many countries are familiar with production, financial, labour, political and trade problems in many other countries. As new nations have emerged, it has been comparatively easy for textile producers from everywhere to expand their enterprise to anywhere else, smoothly integrating operations in a new country into their corporate structure.

(h) Finally, it is to be noted that, because of the great volume of export trade to underdeveloped areas from the traditional centres of textile production, many new countries are vitally important markets for these exporting countries. In the light of political realities of the day, it has proved expedient in many cases for an exporting nation to establish manufacturing facilities in the market country as a gesture to development and to protect a market position.

It is not surprising, in view of the foregoing, that textile manufacturing has advanced rapidly in the underdeveloped countries. Taking cotton as an example, while world production of cotton fibres almost doubled between 1912 and 1958, world imports of cotton remained at about the same level and world imports of cotton fabric dropped to less than one-half their earlier volume. Analysis of these data clearly reflects the internal consumption of locally grown cotton by domestic mills in the low income countries.*

What has been learned as a result of this growth in textile and allied industry throughout the world? What procedures must be followed if further growth is to be on economically sound ground?

One thing is eminently clear. The start-up of a textile manufacturing enterprise requires the same kind of careful economic and technical feasibility analysis, prior to the commitment of capital, as does any other industry. Such feasibility studies covering textiles present no unique problems. The nature and size of the internal market and the means whereby the market is being served are readily determined, as well as are trends of consumption. The technology relevant to the manufacture of any kind of yarn, fabric

* *FAO Commodity Review*, Special Supplement, Agricultural Commodities Projections for 1970, Food and Agricultural Organization of the United Nations, Rome, 1962.

or derived product is well known and the details covering machine costs, building costs to house machines, the cost of water and power and fuel, the cost of transportation, and other items affecting production costs are also readily derived from local sources or from experienced consultants. Whether or not suitable land is available at reasonable prices on which to site a plant can quickly be assessed. The availability of labour, its level of skill, its relative efficiency, the cost and duration of training and related aspects of staffing, e.g. the cost of resident foreign technicians and management, can also be estimated based on the experience of other manufacturers (whether or not in the textile field) and from the experience of educators in the technical, commercial and management training institutions. The impact of tariffs, tax laws and other government regulations can be calculated directly; the cost of sales may be a subtle estimate, but it too is one that can be made in light of existing trading patterns in the country.

There is no need to labour the point. If every new textile factory were to come into existence solely on its ability to compete on a straight commercial basis with imports, there would be no need for articles such as this one. The elements of a good feasibility study are well known, and there are competent people who can be retained to conduct such studies anywhere in the world on any phase of textile industrial development from fibre production to finished consumer product. Promoters, machine salesmen, and experienced textile manufacturers know this, and a government can rest assured that if private capital only is to be involved such studies will be made. Too, if governments are to participate in textile ventures, with equity or loan capital or through industrial incentives provided at some cost to the economy, they too need only to ensure as a matter of policy that comprehensive feasibility studies precede a final decision to move ahead with a project, assuming that feasibility in a commercial sense, that is, the yield of profit on the original investment, is to be the keystone of textile development policy.

However, it is known and accepted that industrial development in the low income countries does not depend wholly on purely commercial considerations. Private investors will not be interested unless profit is possible, but within a developing country social and political forces accelerating industrial growth often transcend the current economics of a given manufacturing project and, even where a feasibility study demonstrates that commercial profit is possible only through some form of subsidy, a judgment is often reached to pay this price for technological advance.

The price of progress in textile manufacturing may be particularly high, and it is here that a problem is defined which is deserving of far more critical attention throughout the world than has been true heretofore; namely, is it possible to calculate the balance between the cost to a national economy of providing industrial incentives, on the one hand, to encourage new textile manufacturing investment and, on the other hand, the benefits to the economy derived from the existence of a textile mill or an integrated textile industry? Unless there is a net gain, the value of this type of industrialization is illusory.

There can be no doubt that the problem is real and significant. It would be difficult, if not impossible, to find a major textile project in an underdeveloped country wherein textile manufacturing has come into existence during the past decade which is not subsidized in some way through tariff protection, or duty relief on imported machinery and materials, or tax holidays, or import control, or some combination of these and other devices such as exchange control. This situation is the result of a number of factors which must be faced realistically:

(a) Production units have tended to be relatively small and not able to provide some of the economies of size characterizing textile mills of India, Japan, Hong Kong and the exporting countries of Europe which compete most intensely for the market in the underdeveloped countries.

(b) Certain segments of the textile industry, even when relatively small, e.g. spinning, weaving and finishing flat goods, are still large enough to require more capital than is generally available locally. In turn, risk capital from abroad requires a higher rate of return than is normal to textile manufacturing in the major exporting countries.

(c) In these major textile exporting countries, the industry plays a large and vital role in the economy. Full production, full employment, and an expanding overseas market have become both economically and politically important and are heavily subsidized when the need arises. An analysis of c.i.f. prices around the world readily verifies this fact; at Lagos, Nigeria, for example, c.i.f. prices of certain classes of print goods are

117

such that a portion of the manufacturing cost must have been subsidized. The cost of raw material, labour, chemicals, shipping, *et al.*, are too well known to accept the price as one bearing the true costs of production, sales and earnings.

(d) In the underdeveloped countries there is little, if any, background in industrial textile production. No pool of skilled labour, supervisory personnel or management generally exists. Hence labour efficiency is low, negatively affecting quality and increasing labour costs. Training costs are high. The overhead burden of foreign technicians and managers, including as it does salaries at a premium level, housing, leave time and paid travel to and from the country, may also be excessively high.

(e) All textile machinery is imported into the developing countries. This requires a large inventory of spare parts. Coincident with this is a general lack of skilled mechanical and electrical services. Maintenance costs and the cost of idle machinery tend to run higher in these countries than in the older textile centres of the world.

(f) Most basic chemicals used in textile manufacturing must be imported into the underdeveloped countries, usually at a price disadvantage despite duty relief.

(g) Power, water, transport, and often fuel costs are generally high and also penalize the local manufacturer.

While all of the foregoing factors influencing the cost of production may be transient in their effect, no one can predict with assurance or with precision how many years it will take, if ever, for local production in a given underdeveloped country to become fully competitive with imports. To be realistic, therefore, any country wishing to encourage the growth of textile manufacturing must offer incentives to ensure commercial profitability and to attract the required capital. *In so far as these incentives keep the price of textile products in the local market artificially high or reduce government revenue (actual or potential), they constitute a cost to the economy.* In effect, such incentives are a subsidy provided by the public at the expense of purchasing power and available government services.

Whether or not the benefits to an economy more than offset the cost of incentives to textile manufacture is a difficult question to answer without equivocation. Some incentives such as tariff protection and duty relief have direct effects which are readily quantified. Other incentives such as tax holidays and the freedom to repatriate profits are more complex in their effect and are more difficult to rationalize into trustworthy numerical terms. Similarly, benefits **range** over quantitative and qualitative results. Foreign exchange savings, for example, related to the real value of such exchange *vis-à-vis* the value of local currency, are specific and readily identified. On the other hand, converting the value of training the unskilled or employing the unemployed in industry to an equivalent sum of money calls for certain assumptions always subject to question.

Nonetheless, the development of a textile industry worth having, if indeed it is worth having, depends upon making the best estimates possible of the cost of incentives and the value to be placed on benefits. That this is not an impossible task may be indicated by the following examples.

The cost of tariff protection lies in the higher price paid by the ultimate consumer than would be true if no tariff were imposed on the competitive import. This cost can be reduced to quantitative terms.

Illustration (a): This proposal for a cotton fabric printing mill states that because there has been no prior experience in the country, labour inefficiency and difficulties in operation would increase production costs far above world average. To compete on the local market, therefore, request is made for an increase in tariff of 7 cents per yard on all imports which could in any way be competitive.* Although mill capacity is planned at 20 million yards annually, the imports affected cover almost 270 million yards, thus raising the price to the consuming public by $18·9 million (or decreasing purchasing power by this much if the total sale of this type of fabric remained unchanged).

The cost of duty relief is the loss of revenue to the government which either would be recovered by other taxes or would result in lowering the standards of government services. These costs become particularly significant when import duties constitute a major portion of government revenue. Whether or not a loss of revenue is actually the result of duty relief depends upon prevailing conditions.

(i) If the material for which duty relief is granted does not replace another import which yields duty revenue, there is no real cost to

---

* In all illustrations, which are taken from actual cases, money value has been converted to the equivalent in U.S. currency for convenience.

the government in the sense that no prior revenue is lost. Potential revenue might not be forthcoming, but this cannot be treated as a loss in calculating the cost of industrial development.

(ii) If duty relief is granted on a material not heretofore imported but which tends to replace a prior import, a real loss of revenue is incurred equal to the duty on what is replaced. A printing mill is proposed which requests duty relief on twenty million yards of greige goods a year. Without this plant these goods would not be imported. With this operation locally the net result will be a decrease in imports of twenty million yards of printed fabric on which the duty equals 16 cents per yard. This equals a revenue loss of $3·2 million.

(iii) If duty relief is granted on a material which would continue to be imported even if the relief were not granted, the loss in revenue is directly related to the relief granted. A shirt factory has started up within a given framework of import duties affecting shirting and affecting finished shirts. Experience indicates that while a certain limited line of shirts can be made under these conditions, profit is discouragingly small and expansion out of the question. Request is made to grant duty relief on shirting used by this factory. One hundred thousand yards of shirting a year is now consumed, involving a loss of revenue of $16,000. The request indicates that with this relief production could be quadrupled and employees doubled from forty to eighty workers. Shirting imported above and beyond the original 100,000 yards consumed would involve no real loss to the economy, since this situation would reflect that described in (i) above.

Tax holidays, if used only as an incentive to the establishment of new competitive production facilities, do not generate a cost to the economy. Rather receipt of new income taxes is merely deferred for a period of years in order to ensure the formation of additional national wealth. However, when granting or withholding a tax holiday is used to control production rather than to stimulate it, a loss to the economy may be incurred.

Illustration (b): Two manufacturers of yarn and thread had been given a tax holiday for a period to cover their infant industry status. After getting into production and in light of shifting patterns in the textile market-place, each mill decided to expand into knitting of tubular interlock fabric for sale to indigenous cutters and sewers. The tax holiday was also granted to cover the knitting operation. At the same time, tax holiday benefits were denied to two other applicants wishing to knit the same types of tubular interlock fabric, but both to produce from imported yarn. One of the two withdrew its project, eliminating an investment of roughly one-half million dollars which could have resulted in employment for several hundred people. The other proceeded into partial production in the hope of obtaining an early and favoured position in the market; this objective was achieved, but only because the output concentrated on very inexpensive styles, yielding low profit. Long-range plans to expand have been curtailed and consideration is being given to selling out and leaving the country.

Calculating the net effect of the repatriation of income in the form of foreign exchange involves a number of considerations. Surely, if the profit earned by a textile mill was wholly retained and distributed locally, the economy would benefit directly. Purchasing power would grow, savings would increase, investment capital would be formed and its use encouraged. To the extent that money which might be so used is taken out of a country, there is a net loss equal to the amount of money withdrawn or even greater if foreign exchange is scarce and in reality more valuable than the exchange rate would indicate.

On the other hand, unless there is a liberal repatriation policy, foreign investors, without whom there will be little textile industry development in the low income countries, are unlikely to risk their capital. As with all incentives, the question is whether the price paid to attract these investors, e.g. the outflow of foreign exchange in this instance, yields a sufficient return.

Pursuing the lines of thinking and analysis set out above and adding in a valuation of the major benefits resulting from a textile mill operation, a reasonable balance can be struck.

Illustration (c): This proposed cotton textile mill, to spin, weave and dye in one operation and in a separate plant to print imported greige goods, calls for an investment of roughly $5 million, $4 million to come from foreign sources and the balance from the government. In full operation, import substitution requested would result in a revenue loss of $3·2 million a year. Imports would require an outflow of foreign exchange of approximately $5·4 million a year. The final product would replace imports currently valued at about $5 million. Operation of the spinning and weaving section would require the diversion of domestic raw cotton normally exported with a foreign exchange yield of roughly $800,000. A tax holiday is requested, in line with government policy and existing legislation to encourage pioneer industries, to last five years if the letter of law is followed. Repatriation of an undefined amount of income for debt service, management fees and profit is a basic requirement of the foreign investors. The impact on the economy of having this come into existence may be calculated as follows:

(i) *Direct cost to the economy*, assuming that revenue losses will be made up from other sources, will be $3·7 million; this is the revenue which would be collected on the goods to be replaced by the product of the mill.

(ii) *Foreign exchange net deficit* would amount to $3 million resulting from these elements:

(a) Outflow for fabric, chemicals and other materials exceeds the value of import substitution by $400,000.
(b) Debt service at 10 per cent of total foreign capital equals $250,000.
(c) Management fees payable to the technical partner set at $500,000.
(d) Repatriation of 50 per cent of estimated profit equals $500,000.
(e) One-half of the estimated salaries of foreign technicians would be $175,000.
(f) One-half of estimated depreciation allowance repatriated as a means of recovering capital invested would be $250,000.
(g) Miscellaneous foreign exchange costs might come to $150,000.
(h) This mill will consume domestic cotton normally exported. This diversion will eliminate approximately $800,000 per year in foreign exchange earnings.

(iii) *Benefits to the economy* would accrue in a variety of ways:

(a) One thousand native employees, not heretofore gainfully occupied, would receive a payroll of roughly $325,000 a year.
(b) One-half of the payroll of foreign personnel to be spent in the country equals $175,000.
(c) One-half of the estimated profit to stay in the country equals $500,000.
(d) One thousand untrained people would be taught operating and maintenance skills. Assuming 20 per cent turnover a

year, over five years an average of 360 people would be trained each year. In this particular country, the cost to the government of training (exclusive of capital costs) in technical schools is roughly $560 a year per student.

Assuming an average of four years of technical schooling is normal before taking employment, it may be argued that the initial training on the job and an apprentice period equal to four years in school saves the public the cost of training in a school for four years. This would bring the value of training to 4×560 per trainee or $2,240. It may also be argued that a man trained in a factory is *not* as well trained as a graduate of a four-year technical school and therefore the value of on-the-job training is *not* as great as the cost of four years in a publicly supported school. Perhaps so. However, a man trained on the job becomes a productive unit while learning; he is also learning the ways of factory life, the meaning of performance, and for his children he becomes a symbol of an acceptable changing pattern of life—a social change of vital importance if technology is to become as natural to the way of life of a developing country as agriculture and the mores of village life. More than this, the trainee becomes a part of a growing reservoir of factory labour and as such is a factor in attracting new industry. All in all, it is the author's opinion that a conservative estimate of the value to the economy of training a heretofore unemployed factory worker may be calculated by this formula: (Cost per year of keeping a student in a technical school, exclusive of capital investment)×(number of years of technical school training which is the average for the country) plus 50 per cent of the product of the foregoing multiplication. In this case, the value per trainee would

be $(\$560)(4) + \dfrac{(560)(4)}{2} = \$3,360.$

For 360 workers trained per year during the pioneer period, the average annual gain to the economy is thus $1,209,600.

(e) Estimated purchases for fuel, water, rent, power, transportation, and miscellaneous services amount to $800,000 per year. In total, this may be thought to strengthen and perhaps contribute to the growth of these vital supporting elements in an economic development programme.

(iv) *In summary:*

(a) Direct costs, e.g. loss in government revenue	$3,700,000
(b) Net foreign exchange deficit	$3,000,000
(c) Value of benefits	$3,010,000

It should be noted that no calculation has been made to cover the so-called 'multiplier effect' of payroll and other money generated by the project. This omission is due to the fact that the loss in government revenue is assumed to be recovered by other means, at the expense of current public income, in turn withdrawing payroll and profit and local expenditures and generating a negative multiplier effect. This negative effect cancels out any positive multiplier introduced by the factory operation itself. In other words, the subsidy given to the factory in the foregoing case removes purchasing power and decreases productive enterprise in the same way that the operation of the new plant generates purchasing power and stimulates new productive activity.

Is the mill proposed in illustration (c) above worth having? For some years to come, while the debt is being paid off, while a large volume of imported materials is required, until efficiency develops making the product more competitive with imports, and if the foreign investors require a substantial and immediate return on their risk capital, the value of having this mill in the country may be seriously questioned.

Does this mean that this proposal should be rejected? At this point the decision passes out of the technical realm into the area of broader economic, social and political consideration. Is industrial development so fundamental to economic development that pioneer industry must be sponsored even at very high cost? Must industrial development planning be well advanced before a given industry is permitted to develop so that there is a clearer view of which industries are more economically viable than others? Is industry necessary for internal security?

The purpose of this paper is not to answer these questions but rather to point to the need of knowing better than has been true in the past the cost of the value of claimed benefits of any industrial project. The textile industry has served to illustrate a method of closely approximating what the costs and benefits are and what they add up to as they take effect. Whatever the final decision of the governments of underdeveloped countries to subsidize their infant industries, there are ways to quantify the impact of a given manufacturing enterprise on the national economy. This calculation should always go hand in hand with the analysis of commercial profitability upon which an investor makes his decision.

In conclusion, the foregoing illustrations and calculations are not at all inclusive. They do cover the most significant elements of cost and benefits deriving from a new industrial operation. They do carry beyond textiles to any other kind of manufacturing. Other factors may come into play and may be rationalized by the same system of thought. For example, anti-dumping legislation may be sought as well as import controls or limiting competition by prohibiting new manufacturers in given fields of production. In some way, each of these actions if taken will affect the price in the marketplace, it may affect the quality of goods sold, it may affect the rate of inflow of investment capital in a negative way. Conversely this paper has not reflected the non-recurring benefits of new industry, such as payments and employment resulting from initial construction. Nor has this paper put a value on the stimulation generated by one going manufacturer to investment by others in the field. This is particularly a factor to reckon with in the textile industry which is so varied in nature and so highly interrelated. Similarly, existing industry is a living symbol of the investment climate of a country and by demonstration does far more than speeches and promises to prove the role of government in matters such as taxes, freedom from controls, and other matters of critical concern to those who risk their capital and those who come to operate and train.

Despite these limitations, it is felt that by applying the methods of analysis suggested above governments and their advisers have a powerful tool with which to cut directly to the realities of proposed textile (and other industry) projects, including schemes to grow new fibre crops and tie agriculture and industry closer together. There is no reason for a government not to know the price of industrial development at any moment in its history.

12. THE SHORTAGE OF SKILLED LABOUR

. . . The shortage of technicians and other skilled workers is, as we have seen, one of the greatest problems which has faced the country from its very beginning; and it is still chronicled by practically every employer and in almost every report of the Federal Ministry of Labour. The reasons for this shortage are of course clear. Nigeria has always been predominantly a country of subsistence agriculture carried out under conditions and by methods which could hardly have produced any of the skills required for modern industrial activity. While the early difficulties of the Government and the commercial firms might have given an impetus to the training of technicians, the depression of the 1930s, followed immediately by World War II, interposed a long breach in the country's economic development. It seems also to be now generally accepted that the system of education in the past, which aped the British system too closely, was not suitable to the technical needs of an underdeveloped country in the twentieth century. In any case much of that education was carried out by missionaries whose interests were primarily religious. As Dr. Adam Skapski, Technical Education Adviser to the Western Regional Government, pointed out in April 1959, the old system of education in Nigeria tended to 'make education bookish and not practical', and had produced mainly 'pen-pushers'.* In fact, much more than the physically arduous and often dirty work of the skilled craftsmen, a higher social status was for long attached to the white-collar jobs such as clerical work in the civil service, or book-keeping in the commercial firms, because these latter occupations brought the workers concerned into closer contact with the white bosses, who were themselves mainly administrators and managers: masters who were office bound and were never to be seen touching anything that required physical effort, or was dirty. Moreover, the cost of acquiring industrial skill, both in terms of fees and of the long period required

* *Daily Times*, Lagos, 7 April 1959.

126

to attain proficiency, has often been beyond the capacity of the great majority of the population; and until after the last war the country was hardly capable of meeting the heavy expenditure required for building and equipping technical and vocational training centres, and of attracting the necessary teaching staff from overseas. The result of these facts was that as late as 1956 the Western Region, for example, had only one Government Trade Centre with ninety-four students to serve a population of six million. The Northern Region with nearly thrice that amount of population had but three Trade Centres in 1955. In the same year only 211 candidates passed out of all the Government Trade Centres and Technical Institutes in the whole country, whilst 673 others were in training.*

The shortage of skilled labour has had two main consequences for industry. Firstly, a large proportion of the work which should have been performed by skilled workers is at present undertaken by so-called 'skilled labourers', with no vocational training except that they have learned, by a process of trial and error, to handle some simple mechanical operation. Secondly, while the gap between the wages of the skilled and unskilled workers has considerably narrowed in most of the more economically advanced countries of the world, in Nigeria the gap remains relatively very wide. In London for example, the wage of an unskilled labourer in the constructional industries was 4·08 shillings per hour in October 1957 compared with 4·17 to 5 shillings per hour for the skilled workers. In Germany, unskilled workers in agriculture earned during the period 1·23 marks an hour compared with 1·33 marks an hour for skilled workers.† The comparative position in Nigeria for the same year is illustrated by Table 1, p. 128.

It is clear from Table 1 that the skilled worker (i.e. the artisan) in Nigeria earns about two and half times as much as an ordinary unskilled labourer, whilst any one of the latter who acquires a modicum of skill at all (by attaining the grade of so-called skilled labourer) can increase his wages by at least another 50 per cent. Shortage of skilled labour has meant for the Nigerian employer, therefore, both higher operating costs because of the inefficiency which often arises from having to appoint unqualified men to do skilled jobs, and the need to pay the few who are qualified relatively high wages. This

* Department of Labour, Nigeria, *Annual Report*, 1955–6, paras. 50–54 and Table VI.
† I.L.O., *Yearbook of Labour Statistics*, 1958.

explains some of the rigidity of attitudes with which some employers meet the demands of workers for higher wages and better amenities.

That the present position as regards the shortage of skilled workers is unsatisfactory, and that urgent efforts need to be made to improve it, has been frequently pointed out. Two broad types of vocational institutions have been designed by the Governments to meet the situation: namely, the Trade Centres and the Technical Institutes (excluding university courses and those offered by the Nigerian College of Arts, Science and Technology at a much higher plane).

The Trade Centres generally offer five-year courses to primary school leavers in various skills as carpenters, masons, welders, electricians, etc. On the other hand, the Technical Institutes are open to secondary school-leavers and train technicians in architecture, civil and mechanical engineering, surveying, etc. The theoretical part of

Table 1.* A. *Average monthly earnings of artisans and labourers by type of employer, Nigeria, September 1957*

Type of employer	Artisans £	Skilled labourers £	Unskilled labourers £
Federal Government	14·4	10·5	6·0
Regional Government	12·5	7·3	5·1
Local Government	10·5	6·3	4·8
Public Corporations	16·3	9·4	5·3
Commercial and other	9·7	7·9	4·7
All employers	12·1	8·3	5·0

B. *Average monthly earnings of artisans and labourers by industry group, September 1957*

Industry Group	Artisans £	Skilled labourers £	Unskilled labourers £
Agriculture, forestry, etc.	11·0	6·5	4·1
Mining and quarrying	10·5	7·7	4·5
Manufacturing	15·8	9·1	5·1
Construction	10·1	6·4	4·5
Electricity	13·1	6·4	4·7
Commerce	13·7	9·8	5·4
Transport and communications	14·6	12·0	6·8
Services	11·8	8·6	5·6
Miscellaneous	8·5	5·7	3·9

* *Employment and Earnings Returns*, September 1957.

these courses lasts two years with a period of practical work in the trades sandwiched in between. In 1958 there were ten Trade Centres in the country with one in the Southern Cameroons, and only three Technical Institutes. During the period of 1957-8, 427 persons passed out of training in the Government Trade Centres, while the total number in training was 1,300. The corresponding figures for Government Technical Institutes were 124 and 549.* These figures constituted a tremendous improvement on the position existing even in 1955. But they remain inadequate to meet the essential needs of the country.

Some employers, unable to meet their requirements from the government institutes, have established their own training schemes. The apprenticeship scheme, which the U.A.C. had for long operated at Burutu, was in 1954 converted into a full Technical Training School where five-year courses in various trades were introduced, intended to lead to standards equivalent to those of the City and Guilds of London. In 1955 a group of principal mining employers in the Plateau minefields introduced job training for their staff in the hope of raising standards of work. In 1958 a full-scale Mines School was opened to provide training in mining technology and administration. The Shell-B.P. Petroleum Development Company opened its own Trade Centre in the Eastern Region in 1958. In April 1959, the Union Trading Company opened a Technical Training Centre in Enugu to give training in engineering and other technical subjects. The Ministries of Works, the Ports Authority and the Railway have also for long operated their own internal training schemes.

These efforts certainly show some determination to cope with the problem of shortage of skills in order to raise the productive efficiency of the Nigerian worker; but on the whole they are still inadequate. The smaller employers (who in any case constitute the majority) have been particularly handicapped. This is partly because the output of the government institutions and of the bigger firms has been too small, and partly because of the high cost of establishing individual schemes. The U.A.C. stated, for instance, in their 'Statistical and Economic Review' for January 1959, that 'the annual cost to the company of each student varies slightly according to the school and the length and type of training given. In round figures it is £250. By the time an apprentice has completed his five years, therefore, the company will have spent about £1,250 on him.' Investment of

---

* Department of Labour, *Annual Report*, 1957-8, Table VI.

this order would seem to be beyond the capacity of less affluent employers, who therefore endeavour to meet the problem through training on the job. The trade-testing results of the Ministry of Labour show, however, that these schemes of training on the job are usually ill-designed and inadequate, because the workers are generally regarded as having been engaged to a do a job and not principally to be trained. Very often, indeed, candidates go for trade tests merely because they wish to earn a promotion, for the high percentage of failures (over 60 per cent in 1955–6 and nearly 50 per cent in 1957–8*) indicates that very few have been given any systematic training.

It would thus appear that there is room for employers to organize co-operative training schemes, at least, in the large towns. There is little doubt that this is one field in which the Employers Consultative Association can render very useful service to its members. Nevertheless, the Federal and Regional Governments have undertaken to do everything possible to assist in remedying the present situation, and have adopted the policy of expanding the present training facilities, and to offer full- or part-time day-and-night courses wherever possible. These would certainly be efforts in the right direction, but an important point requires to be emphasized. So far it has seemed that practically all the Governments of the Federation have been acting blindly in this matter of training; that is to say, with little real knowledge of the country's requirements. So much emphasis has, for example, been placed on Nigerianizing the top administrative posts in the civil service that the obviously more urgent need for intermediate technical and supervisory personnel of all types has received inadequate attention. This trend needs to be reversed. Moreover, there is as yet little knowledge of what the needs of the various sectors of the national economy are. It would seem clear, therefore, that a first prerequisite to overcoming the present shortage of skilled workers and of ensuring that funds are not wasted in training persons for unimportant positions is scientific and co-ordinated planning on a wide scale. On this view a comprehensive manpower survey is long overdue, together with proper estimates, industry by industry, of the requirements of trained personnel which will match the country's rate of economic growth, bearing in mind the development programmes of the various Governments and the needs of private employers. It is understandable that the cutlass and hoe economy of the past

* Department of Labour, Nigeria, *Annual Reports*, 1955–6, and 1957–8.

could not have produced the engineers and the mechanicians required in a modern economy. But in the Nigeria of today there is no doubt that an important first step towards raising productivity and labour efficiency (and thereby the standard of living) is to train adequate labour in modern techniques for every sector of the economy. The University College, Ibadan, the new University of Nigeria at Nsuka, and the Universities at Ife and in Northern Nigeria, would seem to be quite capable of meeting the country's full requirements of top administrators, and a large proportion of the requirements of professional men, within the foreseeable future. What is required now, more than anything else, is a concentration upon the training of intermediate staff in the technician and artisan grades of all types.

To sum up, there is very little evidence upon which a firm assessment of the productive efficiency of Nigerian labour can be made. Nevertheless, it is clear that whatever may be the defects of a system of labour migration, in Nigeria it constitutes very little real problem for industry, and any emphasis now placed upon it by employers is misplaced. There is perhaps more truth in the statement that the efficiency of workers is affected by poor health. In the long run an improvement here can be found only in better education of the general population, and in an improvement in medical facilities. An improvement in general education may also result in a better appreciation of a more balanced diet with a view to combating malnutrition; but it must be said that available information tends to raise the question whether inadequate feeding on the part of a majority of Nigerian workers is not, in fact, a result of inadequate wages. While this question has not been examined here, it is instructive that the urban consumer surveys carried out by the Federal Department of Statistics clearly indicate that as the wages of Nigerian workers increase, so does the proportion of earnings they spend on food.* It is an economic fact that this relation between wages and expenditure on food exists principally where wages are very low, other things being equal.

The shortage of skill is perhaps the greatest personal handicap of Nigerian workers today and, while much has been done to meet it, more emphasis needs to be placed on training schemes for intermediate industrial staff. Finally, it needs to be made clear that all the complaints by management which ascribe low productivity to

* Cf. *I.L.I. Bulletin*, No. 6 of 1 November 1959, where these surveys are summarized.

the deficient character of Nigerian labour are rapidly becoming out-moded. Most of these complaints have no basis in fact, and tend to excuse the management from playing their part in ensuring proper industrial organization, providing effective supervision and improved conditions of work, remuneration, incentives, etc., as essentials in raising the workers' efficiency and in improving industrial relations. In Nigeria, as in most parts of Africa, too much emphasis has been placed on the part of workers in raising productivity, and too little on the role of employers. It is certainly time to reverse this emphasis.

PART III

PRICES AND MARKETS

13. INTERNATIONAL COMMODITY ARRANGEMENTS AND POLICIES

G. BLAU

The main purpose of this paper is to consider the scope and limitations of international commodity arrangements as instruments for promoting economic stability and growth, particularly from the point of view of the less developed countries. In the closing years of the war and in the immediate postwar years very high hopes were entertained of the creation of a widespread network of individual commodity agreements as part of a new international economic order. Since then there has been a large number of resolutions by the United Nations, specialized agencies, and other intergovernmental organs urging the negotiation of commodity agreements; there has also been a great deal of preparatory work and discussion concerning individual commodities. Yet, in the seventeen years since the end of the war, international agreements have been concluded for only five commodities—wheat, sugar, coffee, tin, and olive oil. Of these, the only three functioning at present as producer-consumer agreements which contain some operative provisions designed to influence world trade are those for coffee, wheat, and tin.* The total value of world trade in the five commodities for which agreements have been concluded in one form or another accounts for about 10 per cent of world trade in primary products. The proportion of trade actually covered by agreement provisions is considerably less.

---

* The International Sugar Agreement continues formally in force until the end of 1965, but its operative provisions have ceased to function as from the beginning of 1962, owing to the failure of governments to reach agreement on the re-formulation of quotas. Preliminary discussions on the formulation of operative provisions for a new Sugar Agreement are in progress. The Olive Oil Agreement, although negotiated in accordance with the Havana Charter, provides only for a series of co-ordinated national measures without attempting to regulate international trade (which in the case of olive oil merely accounts for about 5 per cent of world production and consumption). Preparatory work by the FAO Cocoa Study Group led to the convening, in September/October 1963, of a negotiating United Nations Cocoa Conference which, however, had to adjourn without reaching agreement.

133

In recent years there has been a growing sense of disappointment, particularly on the part of the primary producing countries, with the limited results attained so far. Increasing attention has been paid to other techniques which could serve either as a substitute for, or as a complement to, the working of international commodity agreements. At the same time, efforts continue to be made by governments to overcome the obstacles that have hitherto frustrated the conclusion of more effective commodity agreements on standard lines and also to explore the possibilities of new types of agreements of a more comprehensive kind.

Objectives of commodity agreements

International commodity agreements can, in principle, be devised to serve one of five objectives or a combination of them:

(i) They can attempt to raise, or uphold, export earnings by means of arrangements among producers, restricting production or exports or both (the prewar commodity agreements concluded in the 1930s were mainly of this type, and their experience has illustrated some of the difficulties of such arrangements in the forms then applied).

(ii) They can try to promote economic stability, in both producing and consuming countries, by preventing undue fluctuations of prices and quantities traded but without attempting to influence long-term trends.

(iii) They can endeavour to mitigate the problems and hardships resulting from the need for long-term adjustments in cases of persistent disequilibrium between production and consumption, particularly under conditions of inelastic supply and demand.

(iv) They can try to counteract the shrinkage of markets to primary producers which results from protectionist measures or preferential arrangements in importing countries.

(v) They can be used as instruments for intergovernmental commodity programming on more comprehensive lines, taking account of trade on both commercial and concessional terms, of national policies relating to production, prices, and stocks, and of the close links between problems of commodity trade, aid, and development programmes.

One of the chief difficulties in the actual negotiation of international commodity agreements has been that the participating governments have not always been fully conscious of which of these five objectives they were mainly aiming at; nor were they fully conscious of the extent to which any one of these objectives, or a combination of them, could be successfully attained by one or the other of the standard types of agreement-techniques. The primary exporting countries have been naturally interested not just in the stability of prices but in securing reasonable returns in terms of the manufactured goods which they are buying—in much the same manner in which the primary producers of the developed countries are mainly interested in obtaining some degree of parity of purchasing power in relation to the rest of the economy. The importing countries, on the other hand, have been mainly interested in securing more stable conditions of trade and have been prepared to consider any measures influencing the levels of exporters' returns, over an average of years, only insofar as such measures formed part of a process of orderly adjustment of production to the changing conditions of the world markets. Hence the emphasis in Chapter VI of the Havana Charter (which was intended, and still serves, as a code of guiding principles governing international commodity negotiations) that no interested government should be excluded from negotiations, and further that 'participating countries which are mainly interested in imports of the commodity concerned, shall in decisions on substantive matters, have together a number of votes equal to that of those mainly interested in obtaining export markets for the commodity'. The two main objectives of international commodity agreements, as envisaged in Chapter VI of the Havana Charter, are to prevent or moderate pronounced fluctuations in prices but without interfering with long-term trends, and to provide a framework for facilitating adjustments between production and consumption, having regard in both cases to the desirability of securing long-term equilibrium between the forces of supply and demand. In other words, the main objectives are those stated under (ii) and (iii) above.

Balance of bargaining power

The provisions of the Havana Charter which prescribe that producers and consumers should have equal weight in shaping the provisions of an international agreement are obviously important

135

and commendable from the point of view of international ethics. At the same time, they have undoubtedly made the negotiation of individual commodity agreements more difficult than during the interwar period of largely unilateral approaches by producers or by their governments. For these provisions of the Charter imply that an agreement is negotiable only as regards matters on which there is an identity of interests of both parties, or on points on which a 'bargaining balance' can be reached, i.e., where the advantages of adhering to the agreement are assumed to balance its disadvantages, from the point of view of each participant.

Indeed, it is only in regard to the moderation or elimination of price fluctuations that there is a clear identity of interests between the exporting and the importing countries—though even here the interests of the exporting countries (which in typical cases derive the great bulk of their foreign income from the sale of one or a few primary commodities) are very much greater than those of the importers whose economies are not affected to a comparable extent by changes in the price of any one of these commodities.

The postulate of non-interference with long-term trends implies that prices resulting from an agreement should not differ, on the average over a number of years, from what they would have been in the absence of an agreement. Since the future is unknown, this 'neutral price' can be definitely ascertained only *ex post*, whereas the technical solution of the problem presupposes that it is known *ex ante*. In the absence of such pre-knowledge, any commodity agreement of this kind necessarily partakes of the character of a speculative deal—a deal which can be justified as a form of insurance against the risk of undue losses resulting from large and unexpected price variations. The fact that the conclusion of price-stabilizing commodity agreements has proved so difficult in practice appears to indicate that neither exporters nor importers were really prepared to pay a substantial premium for this kind of insurance. Moreover, for a number of commodities it is difficult, or impossible, to speak of a representative world price. And as to the interests of exporters, their *main* concern, of course, has been with prospects for their total export proceeds (depending on volume as well as price) and with the average level of export proceeds over a number of years, measured in terms of import purchasing power, not merely with short-term fluctuations in money terms.

Added to this is the fact that in recent years (since 1954) the primary exporting countries have been faced with a slow deterioration in their terms of trade resulting from an unfavourable trend of commodity prices in relation to the prices of manufactures. The impact of cyclical changes has become relatively less important. Yet, for a solution of the trend problem the types of commodity agreements which have been the subject of international discussion and negotiation in the 1950s are not, in themselves, a sufficient instrument. Nor did these agreement-techniques take sufficient account of the need for improved co-ordination of national policies in both developed and developing countries. . . .

Three standard types of agreements

Three types of agreements have been negotiated and their subsequent history illustrates the same fundamental difficulties.

The first of these is the *multilateral contract agreement*. The main feature of such an agreement is that it contains an obligation on importers or exporters to buy or sell certain guaranteed quantities. These guarantees have to be implemented at a stipulated maximum price, or stipulated minimum price, whenever the free-market price reaches or exceeds these limits. To be reasonably effective, such a multilateral contract agreement should cover a high proportion (say two-thirds) of the total trade of the participants and the spread of prices between the floor and the ceiling should not be too wide. It would then protect the real national income of both the importing and the exporting participants from the major ill consequences of fluctuations in the world price, while preserving the free-market price as a mechanism of adjustment for securing a balance between world production and consumption.

The only case of a multilateral contract agreement is the International Wheat Agreement. The original agreement of 1949 provided for guaranteed quantities which covered about two-thirds of world trade; the maximum price was $1.80 per bushel and the minimum price was stipulated to fall progressively from $1.50 in the first year covered by the agreement to $1.20 in the fourth and final year. During the four-year period world prices were running continuously above the stipulated maximum; importing participants availed themselves of their right to buy the agreed quantities at the stipulated maximum price, so that no less than 95 per cent of the guarantees were effective. As it turned out, therefore, the 1949 agreement operated entirely in the interests of the importers. When the agreement came up for re-negotiation in 1953, the major exporters were successful in securing a rise in the stipulated maximum price to $2.05, and of the stipulated minimum price to $1.55, throughout the subsequent three-year period. This was achieved at the expense of the withdrawal of the United Kingdom, whose representatives expected—correctly as it turned out—a decline in world prices. During the period covered by the second agreement, some other importers also withdrew. As a result, the proportion of world trade covered under the second agreement dropped to 25 per cent, as against 60 per cent in the case of the first. When the agreement was re-negotiated for the third time in 1959, the idea of guaranteed quantities was abandoned and was replaced by an undertaking of member-importing countries to purchase a minimum percentage of their commercial requirements from member-exporting countries, as long as prices moved within a stipulated range, but without any obligation to buy guaranteed quantities at the minimum price. The exporters retain the obligation to sell at the maximum price, if called upon to do so by importing countries, an amount equal to the average of importers' purchases over the previous four years (minus transactions already made within the agreement year).* This new type of agreement has made it possible to bring in the great bulk of commercial trade, but only at the expense of eliminating some of its former operative provisions concerning rights and obligations, particularly those relating to purchases of stipulated guaranteed quantities at specified minimum price levels. In any case, during the period covered by the four agreements the significance of the world price of wheat as a mechanism of adjustment has been progressively undermined, partly because it has more and more been set by the two largest exporters and partly because, faced with growing surplus supplies, the exporters have been disposing of an increasing proportion of their supplies under special arrangements on concessional terms.† New forms of regulation in importing countries have imposed further limitations on the effectiveness of the agreement, as now constituted, particularly also with respect to the inter-relations of trade in wheat and coarse grains.

The second type of agreement, on which particularly high hopes had been set in the early postwar years, consists of the institution of

---

* The latest agreement, which started operating in 1962, is similar in character to the 1950 agreement. The minimum and maximum prices have been raised to $1.62½ and $2.02½ per bushel. The U.S.S.R. is a member of the current wheat agreement.

† This point will be further considered on p. 144 below.

an *international buffer stock*, which stabilizes prices by an obligation to buy whenever the world price falls below a certain minimum and to sell when the price rises above a certain maximum (combined perhaps with a discretionary right to buy or sell between these limits). The well-known problem of a buffer stock scheme of providing adequate finance to enable the authority to carry out its functions is closely related to the difficulty of successfully forecasting the future relationship between supply and demand, and of securing international agreement on a range of prices at levels consistent with the prospective movement of the long-term price which secures a balance in the international market. Unless the trend of this long-term world price is stable or rising, a buffer stock is not likely to be successful in ironing out the fluctuations from the trend for more than a limited period of time. The reason is that with a falling trend the necessary downward adjustment of the operating range of prices cannot be secured with sufficient promptitude, even if the experts were successful in distinguishing between what is a fluctuation and what is a trend. With a rising trend the same difficulty arises, but since this does not impair the finances of the buffer stock authority (on the contrary, it tends to strengthen them), it does not prevent it from resuming operations subsequently, once agreement has been secured on the revision of the operating range of prices.

The only buffer stock scheme covered by an international agreement is the International Tin Agreement, which, however, provides for contingent export control as well as for a buffer stock. As it has turned out, this is one of the few commodities for which in recent years the relationship between world consumption and production has been favourable to producers. Nevertheless, the scheme ran into difficulties less than two years after its inception in 1956, when the price of tin fell heavily and the manager of the buffer stock used up all his cash resources (including some supplementary resources) in the purchase of tin without succeeding in stabilizing the price. Subsequently, the world price was held up by the export controls provided in the agreement. Over the first full year of control, the overall reduction of exports by participating countries was no less than 41 per cent, and over the second full year it was 36 per cent. Despite this, and owing to considerable supplies from the U.S.S.R., the price collapsed temporarily in the last quarter of 1958 but recovered rapidly in the subsequent year, aided by an arrangement with the U.S.S.R. about exports.

The third type of agreement is an *export-restriction agreement*, which makes provision for the limitation of exports insofar as this is necessary in order to secure some degree of stability of prices. The Havana Charter laid down specific conditions with which the operation of such an agreement should comply, designed mainly to protect the interests of consumers and to prevent the imposition of too rigid a pattern of production. Unlike the two types of agreements already considered, the effectiveness of an export-restriction agreement depends to a very large degree on the comprehensiveness of the agreement, i.e., on the extent to which it brings under control all important sources of export, actual and potential; on the extent to which substitutes are available; and on the importance of international trade of the commodity in relation to world production and consumption. Moreover, to be effective, an export-restriction scheme logically requires the regulation of output by *individual producers* and not only of exports by the countries as a whole. Failure to secure worldwide participation in a quota arrangement on the part of exporting countries is less serious insofar as importing countries are brought in as participants and undertake to discriminate (in one way or another) against non-participating exporters. At the same time, the very features likely to strengthen the effectiveness of a quota-restriction agreement as an instrument for raising or upholding export earnings in the short run—such as comprehensiveness of membership, stringent quota provisions, and strict adherence on the part of both exporters and importers—are also those likely to endanger the long-term prospects for the industry as a whole by impeding change, by sheltering high-cost producers, and by generating centrifugal forces which may eventually lead to the collapse of the whole arrangement. Great care must be taken, therefore, to set quotas realistically, so as to allow for sufficient flexibility and to encourage efficiency and desirable structural adjustments in the primary exporting countries, as well as expanding markets in importing countries.

Apart from the International Tin Agreement, to which reference has already been made in connection with its buffer stock features, the two postwar instances of operating agreements of this kind are those for sugar and coffee.* The International Sugar Agreement, in

---

* The new International Coffee Agreement, which replaced the earlier series of one-year producers' agreements, came into force in 1963, for a period of five years and with a wide membership, accounting for 99 per cent of world exports and 95 per cent of world imports. The Agreement attempts to regulate the market through percentage adjustments of basic export quotas. However,

the form negotiated in 1953, relied on a system of export quotas for the so-called 'free-market' sector which accounts for less than one-half of world sugar trade and provides the balance of requirements not covered by special trading arrangements. It differed from the export-quota agreements concluded before the war in that it contained automatic provisions for an increase in the quotas whenever the world price exceeded a certain maximum for thirty consecutive days and for a decrease in the quotas when it similarly fell below a certain minimum; and in that it imposed an obligation on importing countries to procure a certain part of their supplies from participating exporters. The exporting countries agreed to regulate their production so as to avoid the accumulation of stocks in excess of 20 per cent of their annual output. The initial export-quotas fixed each year in the light of estimated requirements were adjusted thereafter on the basis of price movements with the object of maintaining the price within the range of 3.25 to 4.35 cents. Prices remained fairly stable, near the minimum of the range, until 1956, when a short European crop and comparatively low levels of reserves coincided with the strong stimulation of demand caused by the Suez crisis. With prices running well above the maximum of 4.00 cents, all quotas and limitations became inoperative until late 1957, when prices again moved within the range. In the following year the original provisions were amended to allow for automatic and discretionary quota adjustments at various points within the initial price range. In more recent years the efficiency of the agreement has been impaired by the drastic changes in the pattern of trade following the cessation of arrangements between the United States and Cuba. Since January 1962 all operative provisions have been suspended owing to the in-

---

unlike the other main operating agreements, the Coffee Agreement does not operate on the basis of any agreed price range. Instead, adjustment of basic quotas is left to the discretion of the Council, which is to assure that 'the general level of coffee prices does not decline below the general level of such prices in 1962' and that 'prices to consumers are equitable and will not hamper a desirable increase in consumption'. The participating importers undertake to limit their imports from non-participants, whenever the exports of participants fall below 95 per cent of the total world exports of 1961. During the initial period of operations the new Coffee Agreement has had a succession of difficult problems to contend with, first as a result of a large number of requests for revisions of basic quotas, and more recently by adjustments in quotas required due to a sharp rise in coffee prices which was caused by a combination of factors. The period of operations has been too short for an appraisal of the record to be made at this stage.

ability of participating governments to agree on the distribution of quotas.

What the record of operations of these three types of agreements has shown is that it is extremely difficult to deal with the problem of price stability in isolation and to conclude agreements which succeed in stabilizing prices but without interfering with what the trends of prices would have been in the absence of such agreements.* The problems of trends and fluctuations, while they do logically call for different kinds of remedies, cannot, in fact, easily be separated and treated apart from each other outside the world of economic textbooks. The agreements operated in postwar years have succeeded in serving some limited objectives, but they have not proved capable of dealing with the two main sets of commodity problems which call for action: the need for some assurances, particularly to low-income exporting countries, of fairly stable and remunerative average levels of export proceeds for a number of years ahead, say for the five-year periods normally covered by national development plans; and the need for improved international co-ordination of *national* policies of both the developed and the developing countries.

Different categories of commodities

Before we can consider further the implications for postwar experience, it is necessary to look at the problem in more concrete terms, in the light of the main features of the actual patterns of world commodity trade. One of the reasons for the comparative lack of success so far has been that in many of the intergovernmental discussions of commodity questions the problem has been approached in a genera-

---

* It would, of course, be an exaggeration to say that the difficulty of securing agreement over prices or quotas was the sole, or even the main, factor responsible for the failure to reach agreement in the case of a number of commodities where a great deal of preparatory work was done to consider possible forms of regulation and where there was a clear desire on behalf of both exporting and importing countries to reach an agreement of some kind—as, for example, in the case of cotton, rubber, and rice. There are technical difficulties connected with grading, standardization, storage qualities, and limitations imposed on the effectiveness of controls due to competition from synthetic materials or other close substitutes. Account must also be taken of the structure of the market which, in the case of rice, for instance, is characterized by a network of bilateral trading arrangements that could not easily be dispensed with. All these factors add to the difficulties of formulating obligations capable of sufficiently clear interpretation for the functioning of legally binding commitments under an international contract. Nevertheless, given a strong political will to act, some of these technical difficulties should be capable of solution.

lized way without sufficient regard to the basic differences between different groups of commodities. Indeed, it is one of the merits of more recent intergovernmental consultations that they have drawn attention to (though they have far from solved) the different types of problems which need to be considered for different categories of products.

(a) *Commodity problems of developed countries*

It is not always realized that nearly one-half of the total value of world commercial exports of primary products* both originates in, and is absorbed by, the developed countries of North America, Western Europe, Oceania, and Japan. The bulk of such trade consists of temperate-zone agricultural products, mainly foodstuffs. The pattern of trade in this group of commodities is very largely influenced by the domestic agricultural stabilization and support policies of virtually all the importing countries and of the United States (which, of course, is the largest exporter). The funds required for the support of agriculture are drawn from the non-agricultural sectors of the countries concerned. This is a very important difference from the situation prevailing in underdeveloped countries, where virtually all incomes are low and where agriculture accounts for the dominant part of the national income. In such countries there are no resources available for the price support of agricultural export commodities. Indeed, the export-producing sectors of these economies are often called upon to provide economic assistance for programmes to raise productivity in the even poorer agricultural subsistence sectors and for purposes of development and diversification generally.

The existence of an extended network of domestic agricultural policies in the developed countries has important consequences. It must be recognized that a network of such measures provides an effective barrier against any sudden large-scale contraction of agricultural incomes such as occured in the great depression of the early 1930s. At the same time, the existence of independent national policies of price and output regulation has created a situation in which the patterns of production for some of the most important commodities (such as wheat) have been completely divorced from world supply and demand relationships, resulting in large and growing surplus stocks in some of the exporting countries. These policies have led to the introduction of export subsidies or of two-price systems on be-

* Including base metals.

143

half of the exporters, and of varying forms of import regulation on behalf of the importers.

The emergence of structural surpluses—a consequence of remarkable technological progress and not only of the national policies—has resulted in new forms of trade flows, on concessional terms, from the developed mainly to the underdeveloped countries.* It has not been found possible until now to bring such concessional trade within the operative provisions of the International Wheat Agreement (which is the sole international agreement in operation for a predominantly temperate-zone staple commodity). However, a beginning has been made in evolving a new code of international ethics through the acceptance, by most of the governments concerned, of a flexible set of principles† which encourages constructive use of surplus supplies, mainly in low-income food-deficit countries, and at the same time provides some safeguards for the interests of commercial exporters. It has also been found possible to secure the acceptance by a large number of governments of a set of principles concerning national price stabilization and support policies,‡ which reflects the highest common denominator of international understanding attainable so far from governments with differing and partly conflicting policies. These attempts to arrive at sets of agreed principles, which are formally accepted by governments but do not imply any contractual obligations and carry no sanctions, are nevertheless of importance, particularly in view of the fact that governments have been generally reluctant until now to accept contractual obligations that interfere with their sovereign rights in shaping domestic policies.

Thus, while the domestic agricultural policies of the developed countries have lessened their incentives, as compared with the early 1930s, to insure against violent price changes by means of international agreements, their incentives to secure access to markets have been increased as a result, and the promotion of the latter objectives requires commodity agreements of a different character. Recent discussions for some of the temperate-zone foodstuffs show an increased

---

* So far mainly from North America to the food-deficit regions of Asia and also to a number of Latin American and African countries.

† *FAO Principles of Surplus Disposal and Guiding Lines.* FAO document C55/22, Appendixes A and B, Rome, July 1955. The main feature of these principles has also been incorporated, since 1959, in the consultative provisions of the International Wheat Agreement.

‡ *National Agricultural Price Stabilization and Support Policies: Guiding Principles Recommended by FAO.* FAO, Rome, 1961.

willingness, at least in principle, to work for international agreements of a much more comprehensive type. Such agreements would comprise trade both on commercial and on concessional terms and also some guarantees of access to the European consuming markets, as well as policies concerning prices, production and stocks in the participating countries.

(b) *Commodity problems of underdeveloped countries*

With regard to the other half of world commodity trade, which comes mainly from the underdeveloped countries, the nature of the problems is different. This trade consists primarily of tropical agricultural products (though it also includes some temperate-zone agricultural exports from semi-developed countries of Latin America) and to a lesser extent, of minerals. About **three-quarters of this** trade is absorbed by the developed countries, mainly those of North America and Western Europe, which thus take about 80 per cent of the world imports on commercial terms of all primary products.* In the case of these tropical export products and minerals, in contrast to temperate-zone foodstuffs, the problem of the narrowing of markets due to protectionist measures by the importing countries exists only in relatively few cases (notably sugar),† though analogous problems arise on account of preferential arrangements which may now become more important owing to the European Common Market. On the other hand, the markets for exports of raw materials from the underdeveloped countries (with some exceptions, such as petro-

---

* The only commodity which is mainly traded *among* underdeveloped countries is rice. This accounts for a large part of their share of world imports of primary products (although not more than 4 per cent of world rice production enters into international trade). Mention should also be made of the as yet quantitatively unimportant, but expanding, flow of trade from the underdeveloped countries to the U.S.S.R. and other centrally planned economies, which might become a balancing factor of growing importance in the world trade of primary products. (Continental China exercises a rather special role as an unpredictable, but occasionally important, exporter or importer of a range of primary products from the underdeveloped countries. She has become, at least for the time being, a major importer of wheat, but these imports are drawn mainly from *developed* countries.)

† For this reason, the primary exporting countries have relatively little to gain from the usual kind of multilateral negotiations for the reciprocal reduction of tariffs and quantitative restrictions. Indeed, they may tend to lose, since their own exports are not predominantly hampered by trade restrictions, while the concessions made in return may handicap them in developing new industries.

leum) are affected by other causes: the growing use of synthetic materials of various kinds, the reduction of the amounts of raw materials required per unit of finished product, and a shift in the pattern of industrial production which has caused a decline in the relative importance of industries heavily dependent on imported materials. Added to this there is growing evidence of a structural overproduction for a large number of tropical products, owing to an increase of yields resulting from the important technological improvements of recent years, as well as the large increases in plantings (due to the high prices of the early 1950s) which are only now coming into production. Moreover, the very spread of 'development consciousness' of the underdeveloped countries has meant that increases in production have been encouraged, even of commodities whose world prospects have been known to be unfavourable, so long as they offered a promise of increased export earnings for the particular country concerned. Available projections of the main tropical products for the period up to 1970* indicate a growing excess of world production over world consumption, even on optimistic assumptions concerning the growth of demand in the high-income countries. There is scope for some increases in the relatively less prosperous areas, where the income elasticities of demand are still relatively high, and in countries where consumption is now held down by high internal revenue duties,† but, by and large, unless present trends are rapidly reversed, it is unlikely that the growth of consumption can keep pace with the projected increases in production.

The only basic long-term remedy is the economic development of the underdeveloped countries themselves. This would allow a diversification of their domestic production. They would then become less dependent on a few basic commodities for their export earnings and less dependent also on imports to cover their essential needs. On the

---

* *Agricultural Commodities—Projection for 1970*, Special Supplement to the *FAO Commodity Review 1962*. FAO, Rome, 1962.

† Recommendations for the abolition, or reduction, of revenue duties form part of the GATT Action Programme for Tropical Products and of proposals by the Commission of the European Economic Community, but action remains uncertain. The abolition of revenue duties and other fiscal charges would be of importance (particularly for Western Europe), but it could not be expected to cause any *major* changes in consumption patterns, due to the inelastic character of demand in high-income markets and wide margins of distribution and processing. Increasing interest also attaches therefore to the alternative of maintaining or even raising such charges, on the understanding that part of the proceeds be remitted to the governments of exporting countries or to an international fund.

other hand, the prospects of their economic development are greatly dependent on their ability to maintain and increase their foreign receipts, both through trade and aid. The developed countries of the world are beginning to recognize the fact that the 'commodity problem' of the underdeveloped countries is not something separate from their development problem, but that the two are intricately involved with each other. This should open the way to a new approach to international commodity arrangements—not from the narrow viewpoint of improving the functioning of particular markets, but as part of a comprehensive approach to international programming, including assistance in the form of both trade and aid for the underdeveloped areas. The provisions of the Treaty of Rome provide evidence of a certain awareness of this in that the various aspects of economic aid to underdeveloped regions—stable prices and markets, financial assistance, long-term planning of production structures—are considered together. Unfortunately, they single out a narrow group of countries—the overseas associated members of the Common Market —for such comprehensive treatment. Nonetheless, if their envisaged programmes do materialize, the need to extend the same treatment to the other underdeveloped areas of Asia, Africa, and Latin America will become the more obvious.

If one may hazard a guess as to the directions in which the thinking of the advanced countries anxious to assist the development of the poor areas of the world is likely to develop in the future, it will be in the direction of such a joint comprehensive programme. Such a programme could provide the latter not only with aid but also with longer-term contracts or other forms of market assurance for their exports. This alone would give to the less developed countries a sufficiently firm basis for the elaboration of development programmes geared to a definite knowledge of the external conditions with which they will be individually confronted.

It is obvious that it will take time in the best of circumstances before the governments of both the developed and the underdeveloped countries are prepared to face up to the need for such comprehensive long-term planning on an international scale, and before they are ready to accept its obligations. It will take years before such a joint comprehensive programme, related to both trade and aid, can be set to work effectively. In the meantime, the position of the underdeveloped countries is vulnerable and their needs are pressing. The question is what can be done *now* to alleviate the situation until such time as more comprehensive measures of world-wide programming can be made effective.

There is, of course, a great deal which the underdeveloped countries could do on their own to improve their position—as, for example, through increased efforts to raise productivity levels in their subsistence sectors, aided by land reform; the elimination of waste both in their public expenditures and in their personal consumption; fiscal reforms and the introduction of improved marketing techniques, such as marketing boards, which could serve as a means of siphoning off revenue from the exporters as well as the purpose of stabilizing producers' prices. Further consideration of these problems would, however, go beyond the scope of this paper, which is primarily concerned with international policies.

Compensatory financing

The pressing need of underdeveloped countries is for more resources, particularly of foreign exchange, to sustain their development programmes. The flow of economic aid has increased fairly rapidly, but it must be remembered that it still constitutes only a small fraction of the total foreign receipts of the underdeveloped countries. Moreover, for the period from 1954 to 1962, the rise in aid has failed to compensate for the deterioration in their terms of trade. The first objective must be seen in securing a more favourable *trend* of export earnings, aided where necessary by policies of structural adjustment in both exporting and importing countries. In addition, however, the underdeveloped countries also urgently require assistance for replenishing their liquid reserves and for moderating the impact of fluctuations in their current export receipts. This second objective could be assisted by more liberal lending policies of the International Monetary Fund* and it could also be supported by action in the field of compensatory financing, possibly on the lines of proposals

---

* Since this was written, the IMF decided to provide some added facilities for the non-automatic compensation of deficits arising from export shortfalls of a strictly temporary character. For a summary review of more recent developments, see Supplementary Note No. 1: *Proposals for Compensatory Financing— Recent Developments* (Addendum No. 1).

contained in the United Nations experts' report on the subject.*

The United Nations experts put forward a scheme for the creation of a central fund, called the Development Insurance Fund, into which all member countries would pay contributions and against which members would make financial claims which would be paid automatically in stated circumstances. Such claims would be based on the decline of export proceeds in a particular year as against the average of the three preceding years, and would cover a proportion, say 50 per cent, of the shortfall thus defined in excess of a minimum shortfall of 5 per cent for which no compensation is payable. Two alternative types were envisaged and the experts thought that there would be some merit in adopting a scheme which made use of a combination of both. Under the first type of scheme, the compensatory payments are in the nature of a cash settlement, which does not have to be repaid in the future. Under the second type of scheme, the payments take on the character of a contingent loan, which must be repaid if the export proceeds of the subsequent five years are high enough to allow it (i.e., out of the excess of export receipts over the three-year base period), but not otherwise. As regards contributions, the experts recommend that countries should contribute a percentage of their national income (possibly graduated in relation to *per caput* income), while low-income primary producing countries should contribute a fixed percentage of their export receipts. The experts estimate that the annual gross claims on the basis of a 50 per cent compensation and a 5 per cent minimum reduction would have amounted to $383 million per year on the average for the years 1953–9 for the underdeveloped countries, whereas the claims of the high-income countries would have averaged $85 million on the same basis. The necessary contributions, on the other hand, assessed on all countries' export proceeds at a standard rate, would have amounted to $326 million annually from the high-income countries and $142 million from the low-income countries; thus involving an annual net transfer of $241 million from the high-income countries to the low-income countries, on the assumption that all benefits took the form of cash settlements. The merit of this scheme is that it gives a certain insurance against hardship to the beneficiaries in return for their contri-

---

* *International Compensation for Fluctuations in Commodity Trade.* New York: United Nations, 1961. The Committee of Experts consisted of I. H. Abdel-Rahman, Antonio Carrillo Flores, Sir John G. Crawford (Chairman), Albert G. Hart, S. Posthuma, and M. L. Qureshi.

butions—in much the same way as that in which citizens of the modern state receive benefits in exchange for contributions in cases of sickness, unemployment, etc. And just as in the case of compensatory social insurance schemes, where part of the cost is borne out of general taxation, the contributions are not levied on a full actuarial basis. The adoption of such a scheme would not in itself deal with the causes of underlying problems, but it would give partial protection to underdeveloped countries against the effects of short-term fluctuations and also (though to a very much lesser extent) against an unfavourable trend of commodity prices, not only in relation to any particular commodity but to commodities in general.*

The role of commodity agreements

The adoption of a new scheme for compensatory financing would not, of course, obviate the need for a wide range of other measures of which some at least could be promoted by means of individual commodity agreements. As the United Nations experts themselves emphasized, compensatory finance is complementary to commodity agreements and not an alternative to them. But we must be clear as to the objectives which individual commodity agreements should

---

* Following the publication of the UN experts' report in 1961, the Organization of American States (OAS) published a proposal for the establishment of an international fund for the stabilization of export receipts. This was evidently influenced by the ideas of the United Nations experts. Like the UN report, the OAS proposal assumed that compensatory finance would be available to cover a proportion (two-thirds up to a maximum of 20 per cent of previous exports) of any shortfall of actual export proceeds, below their average in the previous three years. Like the UN report, the OAS proposal also envisaged that the high-income countries make a larger contribution to the fund than the low-income countries. The OAS scheme departed, however, from the recommendations of the UN experts in three respects. In the first place, compensatory finance was to be available only to low-income countries and not to all countries, as under the UN scheme—the arrangement would thus no longer have retained the character of a universal insurance scheme. In the second place, it envisaged that the fund be financed by a single once-for-all payment, of which $600 million were to be contributed by the low-income countries and $1,200 million by the high-income countries. In the third place—and this was the most important difference—the compensation payments envisaged under the OAS proposals were in the nature of loans which were to be repaid in a maximum of five years irrespective of the levels of export proceeds of the borrowing countries. The United Nations experts, on the other hand, recommended that the compensatory payments should either be outright cash settlements, or else contingent loans, which would have to be repaid only if the recipients' export earnings rose sufficiently within a specific period.

serve. In particular, it must be recognized that commodity agreements cannot be successful in securing outlets and reasonable terms, particularly over longer periods, unless they also succeed in bringing world production and consumption into balance. This naturally cannot be a matter solely of provisions relating to the international market as such, but requires a close correspondence with arrangements for the improved co-ordination of national policies. The main objective of commodity agreements should, therefore, be looked upon as an orderly method through which patterns of production, trade and demand can best be adjusted to each other over a longer period, by means which are likely to assist in securing the requirements of accelerating growth. From this point of view, quota arrangements or the multilateral contract can offer some of the elements required, for a limited range of commodities, provided that, unlike the existing agreements, they include provisions for the co-ordination of national policies of all countries concerned, and for joint programming of production patterns in both exporting and importing countries. As far as possible, they should also provide for co-ordinated measures influencing consumption, internal price levels, and related commercial and fiscal policies, not only for measures relating directly to the regulation of exports and imports.

Such co-ordination, while it could be assisted, on certain conditions, by export-restriction and multilateral contract agreements, calls in addition for a commodity-by-commodity approach of a broader kind. It is relevant here to mention that in the postwar period, in addition to commodity *agreements* which contain binding obligations between the contracting parties, international commodity *consultations* have proved of very real benefit in the actual solution of commodity problems, even when they did not eventuate in any formalized agreement. At one time commodity study groups were regarded as no more than an essential preliminary mechanism in arriving at international agreements, the tasks of which were accomplished once negotiations for a definite agreement had been opened. Experience with the Wheat Agreement and the Sugar Agreement has shown, however, that the continuing organs which were set up in connection with these agreements—the International Wheat Council and the International Sugar Council—by constituting a forum for consultations and for comprehensive annual reviews of the situation and prospects of the world market and of the plans, programmes, and policies of individual countries have provided valuable services to participating governments, quite apart from their operational functions. In addition, the intergovernmental study groups which have been set up for a wide range of commodities—grains, rice, cocoa, cotton, wool, rubber, coconut, citrus fruit, non-ferrous metals—constitute a widespread network of consultative machinery, which has undoubtedly assisted the co-ordination of national policies through the intense and mutual study of common problems. There can be no doubt that with increasing emphasis on the importance of commodity export earnings for the viability of underdeveloped countries, consultations, quite apart from more formal and mechanized arangements, will have a major role to fill. At the same time, it is essential for all such specialized commodity-by-commodity consultations to proceed in close correspondence with those on wider and related issues in international economic affairs.

Need for a concerted attack

The conclusions to be drawn from the analysis are not of the spectacular kind. There is no single panacea, no magic waving of the wand which would enable us to solve the world commodity problem in all its complexity. Indeed, an attack on any single front can reach only a limited objective. But it has perhaps been shown in this paper that there are a number of ways in which a genuine effort is likely to produce some useful results. What is needed is a concerted attack on a number of fronts—long-term lending and aid as part of a comprehensive development programme; compensatory finance; international agreements for the regulation of production, for co-ordinated planning in the creation of new capacity, and for the provision of guarantees of access to markets; long-term purchase agreements, conditional and unconditional; continuing consultations between governments, both commodity by commodity and in close link with wider discussions on trade, aid, and development planning, including also confrontations of plans of individual countries—all of which should be pursued simultaneously and with vigour.

14. POLITICS OF THE KOLA TRADE

A. COHEN

. . . The kola is a nut, the size of a Brazil-nut, with a colour ranging from dark-red to cream-white. It is consumed very widely among the savanna peoples of West Africa by men, women, and sometimes even children, is exchanged as a gift, used as a drug for certain illnesses, and is offered to guests in ceremonies. It is sustaining as food, but people derive satisfaction mainly from chewing it and from its stimulating effects. Men become addicted to it, carry it in their pockets and, in company, offer it to each other like cigarettes. The nuts are usually retailed by relatively large numbers of boys and girls, aged 7 to 14. The kola has been consumed in the Sudan for many centuries but its massive consumption is, according to the available evidence, only recent and is due partly to improved, quicker, and cheaper transport and partly to the spread of Islamic orders which strictly forbid smoking, as well as drinking alcohol.

While its major centres of consumption are in the savanna, the kola is grown only in the forest zone, where the necessary humid climatic conditions prevail. Until the end of the nineteenth century, the peoples of Northern Nigeria depended for their supplies on imports brought in very expensively operated caravans from the Gold Coast, Sierra Leone, and some other neighbouring countries. With pacification and the opening up of the Lagos–Kano railway line, an ever-increasing volume of imports from those same producing countries came by sea to Lagos and was then dispatched by train to the North. These imports, however, dwindled very rapidly as farmers in Southern Nigeria, principally those in the Western Region, with much guidance and encouragement by the authorities, greatly expanded kola cultivation along with their cocoa plants. A dramatic turning-point came with the world-wide economic crisis during the late twenties and the early thirties, when imports rapidly dwindled to a negligible quantity. The importers tried hard to persuade the Nigerian Administration to cut down the customs duties and also to reduce the railway freight charges, but were not

153

successful. Their allegations that large quantities of the nut were being smuggled into the North by land routes through French territories were investigated and found untrue. Officials who carried out the investigation in both North and South reported that the imported nut was everywhere being ousted by the Nigerian nut, whose special flavour rapidly made it more popular with the northern consumers. Today Northern Nigeria depends heavily for its supplies on the South.

During the 1930s and 1940s most of the trade was carried out by small-scale Hausa dealers and by what may be called Hausa amateurs. The kola offered, and still does, much scope and excitement to the enterprising 'wandering Hausa'. One can start business with almost any size of capital, even with as little as £5, while, in comparison, in the cattle trade one needs hundreds of pounds in order to make a start. Furthermore, the kola is comparatively easy to transport and so widely in demand that it can serve as an article of exchange for which a buyer can immediately be found nearly everywhere. Thus, almost every Hausa who was on the move between the South and the North—migrant labourers, cattle dealers, malams, beggars, porters, and petty traders of all sorts—bought kola with the money he had and took it back to the North.

That phase of adventure, however, is now over. Today one can still find non-professionals buying small quantities of kola to take back to the North, but they usually do so either for the private consumption of their families or for sale in the small immediate locality of the traders' homes. The trade has gradually fallen under the control of relatively few specialized professionals and entrepreneurs. Intense competition between traders, quicker and cheaper transport, and increasing economies resulting from widening the scale of business, have narrowed the margins of profit and the amateurs have slowly been driven out. Today almost everyone who has any connection with the kola trade—such as a carrier, packer, middleman, watchman—describes himself as a 'kola trader', but this is done mainly to claim social prestige. The number of actual traders is very small in relation to the total number of the men connected with the business.

Technical problems of the trade

The trade has always been risky and full of technical pitfalls, and even with the professionals of today it is attended by a great many uncertainties which call for the continual consultation of divining malams, since many of the ups and downs of the business are attributed to mystical forces. At almost every stage the entrepreneur is faced with the task of making decisions because the factors involved and the alternatives open for action are numerous.

To begin with, there are different types of kola. The nuts vary in size and in shade and, generally, the larger the size and the lighter the shade the higher the price. They differ also in flavour. In the major producing areas of the the Western Region of Nigeria, different areas produce different types with different flavours of nut. Also, different areas have different kola seasons. Thus, in the Shagamu area the season is October to January while in the Ibadan area, which is only about fifty miles further north, the season is January to March. Continuity of supplies for the off-season period is secured by storing the nut under special conditions. The kola is a very delicate nut and can be highly perishable, and the stored supplies have to be examined continually and tended in special ways. The storing has to be arranged in the producing areas in the South because the dry climate of the North is unfavourable to the nut. According to men in the business, stored kola greatly improves in flavour. Because of the scarcity of fresh supplies, of the expenses of storage, of the cost of expert care, and of the risks of speculation, off-season stored kola fetches nearly twice the price of fresh kola.

The business is further complicated by the fact that in the North, too, conditions vary. Different consuming areas favour different types of kola. Also, some areas can be supplied by rail and road, others only by road. Retail prices fluctuate all the time with changes in the forces of supply and demand.

It is thus essential that traders should have day-to-day knowledge about the changing conditions of supply and demand. Decisions must be taken by the trader almost every day as to what kind of kola he should buy, in which areas he can buy it, and which of these areas offer supplies at the lowest price. At the same time the trader should also know which consuming area in the North will offer him the widest margin of profit.

A second technical problem in the trade is that it is fundamental that the trader should have immediate packing services and prompt

155

transport facilities. These require the services of a large number of men in different specialized occupations.

A third problem is the necessity of securing credit and trust, without which the flow of the trade cannot be maintained. At almost every stage in the trade total strangers have to trust one another with large sums of money or quantities of goods.

Under pre-industrial conditions in West Africa, the difficulties in meeting these problems are numerous. Literacy is low, and the means of rapid communication of information not well developed. This is made the more difficult and complicated by the differences in language and cultural tradition between the centres of consumption in the North and the centres of production in the South—more specifically between Hausa and Yoruba respectively. Also, because of the lack of a high degree of effective centralization, contractual relations cannot be easily maintained or enforced by official central institutions, and modern methods of insuring goods in the various stages of transit between suppliers and retailers are not developed, though security of property is not yet very high.

The Social Organization of a Tribal Monopoly

In the course of evolving ways to meet these technical difficulties, the Hausa have managed to develop an extensive, intricate, business organization which covers every stage of the trade. A network of Hausa centres for the purchase, storing, packing, and transporting of the kola to the North sprang up all over the producing areas in Yorubaland. Hausa communities already established in connection with long-distance trade in cattle and some other commodities served as bases from which men of the kola trade operated. Those communities consequently expanded and their organization became more complex. In areas where no such Hausa communities had been in existence new communities were founded. From all these communities branched smaller Hausa communities and Hausa collecting-stations interspersed between the Yoruba farms.

The most crucial role within the structure of the organization of the kola trade, as well as within the polities of the respective local Hausa communities, is that of the kola landlord, known to all, Hausa and non-Hausa alike, by the Hausa term *mai gida*. As in the cattle trade, so in that of the kola, the landlord is a Hausa migrant who is permanently settled in Yorubaland. He plays several important roles. He runs at least one house for the accommodation of kola dealers who come on business from the North. The nine kola landlords in the Ibadan Hausa Quarter, known as Sabo,* which serves as basis for the subsequent analysis and description, run fourteen such houses. Attached to these houses they also run stores and packing yards.

The kola landlord is also the head of a commission agency which is served by several 'commission buyers' who go out daily to the outlying centres in the bush or directly to the farms, to buy supplies. Four of the nine kola landlords in Sabo act also as dealers, buying supplies regularly with their own money and sending it to agents of their own in the North. The remaining five landlords also act as dealers but do so only occasionally. For clarity of the analysis, however, it is important to separate the role of the landlord as dealer in his own right from his other roles.

Within the local Hausa community the kola landlords are usually among the biggest employers. In Sabo they have about 18 per cent of the working males of the Quarter directly under them. Apart from these employees, the kola landlords provide work for men in other occupational categories like carriers, transport commission-agents, and traders in material used in packing the nut. They also provide, in indirect ways, work for a large number of men and women who provide services of various sorts, such as cooked-food sellers, barbers, tailors, malams, and washermen.

The kola landlords are permanent settlers in the local community, while most of their clients are recent migrants. In those Hausa communities which have developed directly as a result of the development of the kola trade, like that in Shagamu, they run the Quarter politically, and the chief of the Quarter is always recruited from amongst themselves. In those communities which had been in existence before the kola business in the region developed, they share political power with the landlords of other trades. Together with the other landlords, they maintain the various institutions which give the community the social stability and cultural continuity which keep it running, despite the continual mobility and change of some of its personnel.

The principal task of the landlord in the kola business is to buy kola for northern dealers. A few of these dealers come down to Ibadan themselves, bring their money with them, and lodge with a landlord. They will then go in the company of a commission-buyer,

* Short for *Sabon Gari*.

157

who is attached to that landlord, to the sources of supply, buy the quantity they need, return back to the Quarter with the goods, supervise the packing, and then dispatch the bundles or actually accompany them on the journey to the North. But these are relatively small-scale dealers. A few other dealers send a permanent representative, who is usually a relative, to lodge with the landlord and conduct the dealer's business with the help of the landlord.

The majority of the dealers, however, trust the local landlord to act as their agent, sending him orders and money, and leaving the conduct of the business at the supplying end to his honesty and discretion. The dealer will merely send an amount of money with a simple request to 'buy good kola' of a certain type. There is no question of specifying the exact quantity of the consignment or the price at which it should be bought. Conditions change from day to day and it is not possible to exchange correspondence and quote exact prices. The whole job is left entirely in the hands of the landlord and it is he who decides on the spot what to buy with the money, where to buy it, and at what price.

This means that the landlord must enjoy the full confidence of the dealer. Such a high degree of trust is achieved by the landlord after many years of business during which he proves his honesty and his wisdom in buying. His position, reputation, and connections within the local community are equally important in building up his business trustworthiness. Sometimes he sends to the dealer, along with the dealer's order, a consignment of his own, which he buys with his own money, and entrusts its sale to the northern dealer. He does so only partly for profit, his main purpose being to gain the confidence of the dealer by showing mutual trust. The landlord's commission is not fixed. He is in fact at liberty to fix his own, but in order to retain the dealer's confidence he usually cuts that commission to a minimum. The landlord's commission is nearly always in the form of a lump sum, deducted from the amount sent to him, and not a percentage.

In addition to his roles as chief commission-buyer, innkeeper, and dealer, the landlord also runs a packing service. The kola is packed in a special way, in basket-like bundles, about 4 feet in height and 2 feet in diameter. The main packing material is rope imported from the North and special fresh green leaves brought from the forest. The packing is done by skilled workers. Usually three men work as a team on each package. One of them is the chief packer, the second his assistant, and the third is a 'measurer' who ascertains the exact quantity of kola in the package by bringing the nut to the packers from a large heap in a special standard-sized basket. A bundle will usually take about twenty minutes to finish. The chief packer gets two shillings for each bundle and out of this he pays sixpence to his assistant. The measurer is paid separately by the landlord. Usually there are, in each packing yard, several teams of packers. In addition to packers and measurers, the yard is also served by several carriers whose sole job is to carry the nut from the lorries to the yard and to carry bundles from the yard to the lorries.

The transport of the goods to the North is arranged by the land-lord, who maintains for this purpose connections with transport commission agents who are Hausa living within the Quarter. If the consignment is to be sent by rail, it is taken by lorry to the railway station where it is immediately entrusted to a 'porters' supervisor' under whom work a number of porters. In the Ibadan railway station there are between 200 and 300 (depending on the season) Hausa porters, who are organized within four business houses under four landlords in the Quarter. Under each landlord work a number of supervisors whose task is to receive the goods from the lorries and to make all the paper arrangements with the railway authorities and, finally, to supervise the loading on the wagons.

If the consignment is to be sent by lorry, then the arrangements are made in one of the two lorry parks* of the Quarter. Business in these lorry parks is dominated by two transport landlords who have under them several commission agents, each of whom is aided by a number of 'boys'. One of these two landlords bears the title 'Chief of the Transporters', after nomination by the men in the business and after official installation† by the Chief of the Quarter. The transporters of the Quarter are commission agents who negotiate business for lorry owners and lorry drivers who regularly call at the Quarter's two lorry parks. The transport landlords also run houses for the accommoda-tion of lorry drivers and lorry owners as well as of passengers in transit.

In recent years more kola has been sent by lorry than by train. The railway authorities are trying to lure back the traffic by offering

---

* One is known as the Kano Lorry Park and the other, a much smaller one, as the Sokoto Lorry Park.

† The official ceremony is referred to as 'turbanning', as it involves putting a white turban by the Chief of the Quarter on the head of the man on whom the title is conferred.

cheaper freight charges and by providing lorry services between kola yards and stations. But the advantages of the lorries are still numerous. Lorry service is more personal than that of the railway; the trader entrusts his goods to a responsible transport landlord who is permanently settled within the Quarter, and is a reputedly trustworthy person who undertakes to compensate the owner of the dispatched goods for any loss incurred in transit. The transport landlord and his agents, in their turn, are personally acquainted with the lorry owners and drivers. Lorry transport is also faster than rail transport and more convenient, in that the goods are taken straight from the yard in the South to the dealer's place in the North. Those northern kola dealers who travel south themselves to supervise the purchase of a consignment usually travel back to the North in the same lorry that carries their kola. Some of these dealers even manage to sell all or some of their consignment on the way, towards the end of the journey. Sometimes, the consignment is redirected at the last moment to another destination, still in the North, where sale conditions are known to have become more favourable.*

Contact and The Moral Community†

One significant aspect of all these arrangements for the purchase, packing, and dispatching of the kola is that they involve a large number of men in different occupational specializations which are functionally interdependent. A second aspect is that these men live in spatial proximity, within the same Quarter, and can thus co-operate promptly and efficiently. Thirdly, all these men are Hausa who share the same language and the same cultural tradition. Among other things, these conditions contribute greatly towards solving the problem of speed which is so crucial in the long-distance trade in a perishable commodity. . . .

In 1934, after the steady increase in the volume of kola exported to the North during the preceding few years, the Ibadan Native Authority Council decided to establish a kola market on a plot

---

* The discussion in this paper covers the organization of the trade only at the exporting end in the South.

† The paragraphs on 'The Moral Community' and on other sociological aspects of this trade have been omitted here (Editors).

adjacent to the Hausa Quarter, Sabo, in order to facilitate the trade, assuming that supplies would be brought to the market by enterprising Yoruba traders who would buy the kola from the farmers and sell it to the Hausa. The all-Yoruba Council were enthusiastic and hopeful. They decided that the market, which was to be called 'Aleshinloye', would be opened by an official ceremony and that notices about its opening should be put in railway stations 'as far as Kano and in all the principal towns'. They instructed the Chief of Sabo to send his messengers to the northern provinces in order to announce the establishment of the market to the great merchants in the major towns and to see to it that those merchants should attend the opening ceremony.

From the records of a few years later one learns that the market was a complete failure. The Hausa kola traders were not in attendance there. Fighting shy of the Yoruba kola traders, they continued to go to the sources of the kola, penetrating deeply into the forest, and buying their supplies straight from the farmers. When export from this area had begun, the Hausa traders had operated from the already existing Hausa communities as bases, leaving these communities in the morning and returning to them later in the day with the purchased supplies. But within a short period they had established Hausa stations, within Yoruba settlements near the farms, which served as outposts from which Hausa commission buyers operated, with the help of locally stationed Hausa guides and brokers. In a few years' time these outposts turned into fully fledged and well-organized Hausa communities. . . .

By means of these processes the Hausa have established an elaborate, large-scale, complex organization by which they have managed to control the kola trade, to overcome the difficulties involved in achieving this control, and even to dictate prices to the farmers.

As Hausa monopoly over the trade tightened up, the Yoruba kola traders organized their efforts for counter-action. As from the early 1930s they began to submit one petition after another to the Administration and to the local Yoruba chiefs demanding that the Hausa 'strangers' should be prevented from going direct to the farms and should be forced to buy their supplies from the formally established markets. In 1940 the Council of the Chiefs of Ibadan discussed the matter in a number of its meetings and resolved that a rule should be officially laid down 'that no one other than a native of Ibadan

161

and its villages should buy kola in the Ibadan District except in the kola markets'. But the Resident vetoed the decision on the ground that it would be a direct interference with the freedom of trade. . . .

The dispute continued for years and has been recently carried over to the post-independence period. The restraining influence of the former Administration has been replaced by that of the Federal Government and federal party politics. The Hausa kola landlords continue to manœuvre their way by repeatedly accommodating their tactics to changes in party politics on the local, regional, and federal levels.

Today some kola is sold in a number of markets in the Region. In Ibadan there is a special section for the sale of kola in the King's Market (*Oja-Oba*). Also, some Yoruba farmers and traders occasionally load lorries with kola and go direct to the Hausa Quarter to offer the nut for sale to the kola landlords. But the quantity of kola involved in all this is only a small fraction of the total volume of export to the North. The bulk is still bought by the Hausa straight from the farms.

Struggle over the commission

The dispute between Hausa and Yoruba was not confined to the question of the collection of supplies. At some stages, both Yoruba farmers and Yoruba kola traders joined forces against the Hausa over the payment of commission, known by the Hausa term *lāda*. From the beginning the Hausa claimed that it was only proper and 'in accordance with the accepted custom' that the Yoruba sellers should pay the commission, amounting to 10 per cent of the purchase price, to the Hausa commission buyers. When a Yoruba seller refused to comply with this demand, the Hausa boycotted him until he was forced to pay. What has angered the Yoruba most is that while the commission in the case of the kola is taken from the seller, it is taken from the buyer in the case of cattle—the payer in both cases being Yoruba.

The Yoruba have not stopped agitating against this apparent 'injustice' and at some stages they tried to hit back. In 1950 the Hausa kola landlords throughout the region declared a boycott of the kola farmers from Agege who had refused *en masse* to pay the commission to the Hausa agents. The Nigerian *Daily Times* wrote (on 13 May 1950) that kola planters from Remo, Ijebo-Ode, Ifo, Attan, Otta, Abeokutta, Ojokoro, and other centres, had resolved to

162

give the Hausa kola traders a one and a half month ultimatum to reconsider their decision of boycotting the Agege sellers, and to stop the collection of *lāda* in all kola-producing areas. At the expiration of the period of the ultimatum, if the Hausa traders remained unyielding, the planters would start direct dealings with consumers in the North. The paper mentioned that the decision had been taken at a meeting held at the 'Headquarters Store of the Nigerian Farmers' Union', Agege, at which representatives were present. In their speeches the delegates were reported to have urged all kola planters to stand firm and to endeavour to put an end to what they called 'bad practice' of the Hausa traders.

But the odds against the farmers' stand have been many. They are numerous and are scattered over a wide region with few occasions on which they can interact. They have made many attempts to organize effectively, but their associations have been mainly local and ephemeral. These associations have come into being only during a particular, immediate crisis, at the end of which they have disintegrated.

In contrast, the kola landlords are much fewer in number, possibly not exceeding 200 (in 1963) over the whole Region. Although they are based in particular localities, they regularly and frequently meet together. As different areas have different types and different seasons of kola, a landlord buys supplies from different areas. His business interests are thus not confined to his local settlement but cover a very large part of the Region. They often meet at the kola sheds of the railway stations and in the lorry parks. In addition to this interaction between the landlords, thousands of Hausa commission buyers, carriers, packers, and porters circulate, in accordance with the seasons, between the various centres and are also followed in this movement by men and women from different occupational categories to provide the necessary services for them. For all these the kola is a fundamental vested interest and their moral and political support of the stand of their patrons, the landlords, is unquestionably given. For these Hausa men, kola is their life, and is a tribal political issue of the first order. . . .

15. COMPETITION IN THE NIGERIAN BREAD INDUSTRY

P. KILBY

Development of competition: Lagos and Ibadan

. . . We may begin by reviewing the salient features of the evolution of the baking industry in Lagos. . . . During the two decades preceding 1946 the profit margin on bread sales was very high—a result of modest flour prices, relatively low wages, and but 5 per cent commission.* For most of the city's bakers operating, on a small scale, total entrepreneurial earnings were not excessive. Only in the case of the four mechanized firms enjoying large volume sales were absolute profits of a truly large magnitude. The sixtyfold increase in Schackleford's equity shares (£50 to £3,000) testifies to the uniquely favourable position of the mechanized producer during this period. In the Schumpeterian framework, such producers were enjoying transitional monopoly as the reward for their innovation.

The situation altered radically with World War II. The phenomenal upsurge in demand, resulting in bread shortages and inflated prices, attracted the attention of large segments of the Lagos commercial community and other prospective entrepreneurs to the possibilities of the baking industry. (It was this perception which sparked the migration abroad for technical training.) On the basis of a moderately large pool of baker-journeymen trained during the preceding twenty years, there was a very rapid expansion between 1946 and 1952 in the number of hand bakeries owned and operated by Nigerians. Profit margins narrowed with rising materials and wage costs on the production side, and with augmented commission rates imposed by intensifying competition.

The year 1948 witnessed the establishment of the city's first postwar mechanized bakery. The following year the total number of such firms grew from five to fifteen. In 1951 the commission rose from a

* Commission paid by bakers to retailers (Editors).

164

shilling on the pound sterling to one shilling and sixpence. As the number of dough brake users increased, the commission continued to rise, reaching four shillings and sixpence in 1957. The outcome of this rapid growth of competition among mechanized producers was a limited number of closures, substantial reductions in the sales volume of the original 'four' (in the neighbourhood of 40 per cent), and the emergence of some ten to twelve new firms equal in size to the 'four'. After 1957, efforts of the individual firm to expand its sales were directed to the development of external markets.

By the establishment of Firm B in 1951 Ibadan got its first mechanized bakery, some twenty-five years after Schackleford's introduction of the dough brake in Lagos. By 1952 Firm B was converting 4,000 lb of flour per day and selling its product at a commission rate of one shilling and sixpence on the pound. The next year Firm E obtained a dough brake and, in order to build up custom quickly, increased the commission by a half. In 1954 four more dough-brake users, including Firms A, C, and D, entered the market. The following year the number of mechanized producers swelled to eight. Intense rivalry which developed between the firms of Arabia and Ibukun-Olu soon escalated into a general price war. In nine months the commission rate had jumped from three shillings to five. Then in 1956 the struggle shifted to product improvement: sweeter bread formulas, wax wrappers, slicing, credit, and in-town deliveries.

By 1957 the 'war' had run its course: all the participants were financially exhausted, the original instigator had gone bankrupt, and Firm B had virtually closed down. Firm C emerged as Ibadan's largest producer. Within twelve months the commission rate had dropped to four shillings.

The number of mechanized producers in Ibadan continued to increase. After 1955, however, new entrants established on a relatively small scale; most of them operated locally made dough brakes and produced Senegar and other unwrapped bread. Among the seven 'quality' producers, all further attempts to expand output were directed to the opening up of external markets. By 1960 it is estimated that 40 per cent of production of all mechanized bakeries was being sold outside Ibadan.

The absence of overt price competition after 1957 does not mean that the relative positions of the five firms remained unaltered. In 1959 the entrepreneur of Firm E secured a loan of £15,000 which he used to purchase a fleet of vans and expand his plant, enabling him to increase production from a flour equivalent of 1,500 lb to 4,000 lb. Difficulties in maintaining the new level induced Firm E in mid-1960 to wrap threepenny bread as well as the sixpenny and shilling. In addition, rebates and payment of vendors' taxi fares added another 'hidden' 5 per cent to the discount rate. Frequent auctioning became necessary. This pressure to maintain sales derived from debt servicing and heavy depreciation charges.

Firm A baked approximately 500 lb of flour daily from 1957 until June of 1960, when . . . acquisition of a van enabled it to undertake distribution to the rural areas. During the subsequent two years flour consumption ranged from 700 to 1,000 lb. Firm B staged a gradual recovery beginning in 1960 and by 1962 had attained a flour intake level of 1,500 lb. Firm C enjoyed moderate growth in output over the period and by 1962 was converting approximately 2,700 lb of flour per day.

Of all the Ibadan producers, it is the performance of Firm D which is most significant. During the time of severe competition Firm D was able to maintain sales, 1,000 lb of flour equivalent, without raising its commission above four shillings and without in-town deliveries, wrapping, or credit. It was not until 1958 that Firm D first used wrappers and not until 1959 that it used wax wrappers. At the time of the productivity study it was noted that the demand for 'Lion' bread exceeded existing capacity. Earlier in the same year a branch plant converting 1,200 lb of flour was opened in Oshogbo.

The very limited degree of management control . . . had been developing with the growth in output. Repeated labour troubles* and discovered pilferage persuaded the entrepreneur, himself only semiliterate, to employ an experienced bookkeeper-supervisor. The latter, beginning in August 1960, took over employment responsibilities and introduced an effective control system which, in conjunction with the new cash register and oil-fired oven, raised the per cent of optimum revenue realized to the 85 percentile range. The profit margin was thus greatly widened.

On 5 July 1961, Firm D, in an unaccompanied move, reduced its commission from the prevailing rate of 16⅔ per cent to 12½ per cent.

---

* In April and August 1960 the bakers of Firm D went on strike in unsuccessful bids to have the month's wages paid on the last day of the month instead of the third day of the following month. The existing system insured that the employer would see any departing baker after the individual had actually left the job and thus provided protection against theft from this quarter.

The following month sales reached £9,000, or an average flour intake of 4,500 lb per day, double the figure of twelve months earlier. Once again, this was achieved without increasing the proportion of sales in outlying markets, without extending credit, and without delivery to the vendors.

The marked consumer popularity of 'Lion' bread which made such a move possible has already been traced to the qualitative characteristics of Firm D's product. This product quality does not refer to the kinds of ingredients: Firm A, which found it necessary to cut all loaves heavy, used the same ingredients. Bread quality as we have used the term in this study refers to fine variation in ingredients proportion, fermentation, and baking procedures which are determined by reference to local consumer tastes. The owner of Firm D, a baker by occupation, sampled all of Ibadan's brands and experimented for several years in the early 1950s before settling on his present techniques. By mixing the condiments himself, the entrepreneur is able to protect his formula.

Forms of competition

We shall pause briefly at this point in our narrative and, using the Ibadan market as our example, single out the three major ways in which a firm can increase its sales in a given market. These forms of competition are but another expression, formulated from the producers' viewpoint, of the considerations influencing the vendors' choice of suppliers treated.

The first and most important way a firm can increase its share of the market is to develop the appropriate product quality in the manner just described. Interestingly, it appears that only a small minority of bakers are aware of this qualitative factor and the potentialities of experimentation. Not unexpectedly, this lack of awareness is most marked among those entrepreneurs who are not themselves bakers. In the case of Firm D and in similar instances in the Eastern Region, competitors typically attributed their success to a lucky choice of wrapper design and colour, secret concessions to the hawkers, or some inexplicable public whim.

When no seller enjoys a decisive qualitative advantage, which is most often the case, competition for market share will take the form of price reduction and product improvement. Over the last three decades standard retail prices have become so ingrained in the public mind that no reduction or augmentation in the traditional price long persists. In contrast, covert price changes in the form of varying loaf weights have occurred historically in response to changes in cost and intensity of competition. The second instrument of price competition consists in raising the discount rate to the hawker. In the first instance competition results in a gain to the customer; in the second, the benefit accrues to the vendor.

Varying loaf weights is most prevalent form of price competition because it is difficult to detect and less automatic in provoking retaliation. . . . Heavy cuttings are the norm for the unwrapped, undifferentiated, 'economy' loaf. For wrapped bread, all else being equal, heavier cuttings will tend after about a month's time to result in increased sales. In actual practice 'all else' is never 'equal,' and competitors cannot be sure which factors—wrapper design, credit, sales organization, hidden rebates, loaf weights, etc.—are responsible for the changed market situation.

An increase in the discount rate by a major producer, on the other hand, leads to an immediate and massive response from the hawkers, whose profits stand to increase by an amount equal to the increment in the commission. Retaliation is swift: the competitive advantage is lost after a day or two and all producers thereafter suffer from a reduced margin. Apparently, only the hawkers have gained. Consequently, in most markets there has been open price war in the early stages of competition between mechanized producers, followed thereafter by more moderate, less open forms of competition.

The third method for increasing market share is product improvement. In this category we include all product embellishments and ancillary services not encompassed in price or quality competition as defined above. Thus wrapping, slicing, enriching ingredients, delivery, and credit fall into this residual classification. Of these improvements, only the use of wax wrappers has the same force as an increase in the discount rate: a baker either wraps his bread or cuts the heavier 'economy' loaf. Owing to the time lag in designing and ordering the imported wrappers, the first firm to introduce this improvement enjoys a once-and-for-all advantage over its competitors. Sales response to any other single form of product improvement tends to be slight. Each producer will usually arrive at some combination of product improvements and, possibly, heavier cuttings, on the basis of his competitive position, the size of his realized margin (i.e. his ability to bear increased costs), and his personal predilections.

Implicit in the foregoing analysis of methods of competition is the unreal assumption that the entrepreneur's decisions are taken with reference to a single market. In fact the alternative of selling some part of his production in less competitive outlying markets will always substantially modify decisions on price, product improvement and loaf weights. . . .

Barriers to entry

The changing pattern of competition in the baking industry from 1920 to 1962 can be explained largely in terms of the barriers to entry. In the prewar period the paucity of technical knowledge, including the 'secret' of the dough brake, constituted a barrier to the prospective Nigerian investor virtually prohibitive for mechanized production and only slightly less so in the case of hand baking. This was the period of 'monopolistic' profits for established producers.

The second phase was precipitated by the war. By this time the availability of technical skills had greatly increased and demand was expanding so rapidly that even the poorest quality bread found a ready market. As a consequence the technological barrier was greatly lowered. Thus from 1946 to 1952 there was a sharp increase in the number of hand-operated bakeries.

A reduction in the number of baking establishments marks the third phase as machine-made bread sweeps the market. Capital requirements, and hence the financial barrier to entry, rise substantially. Entrepreneurial profits increase with the expansion of sales volume per firm. In the fourth phase, when the locally made dough brake begins to make itself felt, the investment barrier is eroded and a new burst of entrants and intensifying competition follow.

The fifth phase, which can be said to have started around 1958–60, coincides with the catching up of the supply of machine-made bread with demand and the development of product improvement (with the consequence of narrowing profit margins) as the principal technique of competition. Investment, technical skill, and organizational ability requirements combine to raise, once again, the barriers to entry.

The optimum-size firm: some theoretical considerations

How far is the present tendency toward concentration of output among a limited number of large firms likely to proceed? Before a direct answer to this question is attempted, it will be helpful if we break down the operations of a baking enterprise into its component functions and consider at what scale of production each of these functions can be performed most efficiently.* Such an analysis will, *de minimum*, define the range of possible outcomes—the lower limit of competitive atomism, on the one hand, and the upper boundary of monopolistic concentration, on the other.

The first aspect we shall consider is the technological: what is the optimum technical unit for baking bread? It was pointed out [earlier] . . . that the larger firm enjoys a fuller division of labour than does the small.† The greater the emphasis on product improvement, the greater the advantage to the large producer who can more fully utilize the larger, more economical ovens and specialized wrapping and slicing equipment. Nevertheless, the cost comparisons showed that the net savings were of a very small order.

Far more favourable to the large concern are the financial economies of scale. Of prime importance are the substantial savings which accrue from bulk flour purchasing. The large firm can usually obtain most of its working capital requirements through credit from its suppliers and bank overdrafts. Lumpy purchases, such as imported wax wrappers, do not entail the same dangerous degree of illiquidity that they do for the small firm. In the sphere of marketing, the scale of operations and access to short-term loan capital enables the larger enterprise to extend credit to vendors. Finally, greater financial resources endow it with greater staying power during periods of severe price-cutting. The small firm, however, is usually able to suspend production temporarily at little cost and without prejudicing future operations, i.e. without difficulty in regaining its market share.

From the viewpoint of managerial efficiency, it is clear that the small producer will have the advantage. A relatively simple recording system and the entrepreneur's personal supervision is sufficient to ensure reasonable efficiency in scaling and baking and to avoid major theft. For the larger firm the control of production and distribution

---

* Following E. A. G. Robinson, *The Structure of Competitive Industry* (4th ed., Chicago, 1962), chaps. ii–vi.

† In the following discussion 'large' applies to all producers converting 2,000 lb of flour per day and above, while 'small' refers to those converting 800 lb or less.

demands scarce organizational skills and continuous management exertion.*

Finally, the optimum size in relation to the selling function would appear to favour the small firm. Although the large seller can extend credit and advertise, his distribution costs and control problems are greater. On the other hand, given the 'convenience' patronage of hawkers in the immediate area and the importance of brand variety, it is a relatively easy matter to sell a daily bread equivalent of 500 to 600 lb of flour.

The preceding analysis implies that small mechanized producers are likely to retain a significant place in the over-all bread market. The existence of market segmentation, in particular the demand for the 'economy' loaf, reinforces this conclusion. On the other hand, the analysis would seem to suggest that the future is much less bright for the medium-sized firm, falling in the intermediate flour consumption range of 800 to 1,900 lb. Enjoying neither the financial advantages of the large enterprise nor the organizational simplicity or marketing ease of the small producer, and yet possessing the liabilities of both, it seems probable that the medium-sized firm will eventually give way to the encroachments of its larger competitor.

Future patterns of competition

In the preceding discussion the theoretical and *a priori* nature of the argument was underlined. The introduction of the empirical findings ... fundamentally qualifies the conclusions based on such structural deductions. In particular, variations in managerial ability and technical skill can be so great as to override almost all advantages and disadvantages of scale. In like manner, unique consumer preference modifies and postpones increasing marginal costs imposed by distribution. Indeed, it is conceivable that two or three multiplant producers who stood out from all others in being 100 per cent efficient, supremely quality conscious, and ruthlessly aggressive in selling could drive all competitors to the wall and effectively monopolize Nigeria's entire bread market. Such talent, however, does not exist in the required diversity and excellence in Europe or America, much less in a developing country such as Nigeria.

The more likely pattern of development, given the industry's past

---

* To some extent management requirements represent a threshold that the large firm has already achieved, rather than an operational liability. But, of course, the potential for 'slippage' is always present.

performance and current state of technical and managerial skills, is that a number of firms from among those enjoying some degree of consumer preference will expand, at the expense of their medium-sized competitors, up to a limit of about 15,000 lb daily intake of flour.* The growth firms will be distinguished by the organizing powers of their entrepreneurs. A three-plant limit to the size of the individual firm, or a maximum flour consumption of 15,000 lb, is imposed by the complexity of management control and problems of delegation.†

In general, with the slowing down in the rate of growth of bread consumption as a result of the exhaustion of market-widening possibilities, competition may be expected to intensify. In the United States during the pre-1920 market-widening phase the baking industry's margin on sales was 15 to 20 per cent, whereas in 1953 the figure had dropped to less than 5 per cent;‡ the rate of return on investment declined from more than double the national average to some 10 per cent below the average. Likewise, increased competition reduced the number of firms from 24,500 in 1919 to 6,000 in 1947.§

The major force influencing the geographic distribution of the baking industry is the locus of demand. Bread consumption tends to be concentrated in the towns. The number of towns which comprise the market for any given baking plant will depend upon how centrally it is located. In this respect producers in Onitsha and Ibadan enjoy the country's largest natural markets. Locational advantages may be modified by unevenness in the supply of entrepreneurship. Thus Lagos, Ibadan, and Onitsha are net exporters, while many other towns tend to be substantial importers. Owing to sheer distances in the north and lack of road connections between east and west, bread markets are likely to remain regional and (in the north and west) subregional.

* This would include such firms as Onitsha I, which enjoy a lesser degree of consumer preference than the outstanding cases cited.

† There are some ten firms operating two plants; none as of 1962 operate more than two. It is interesting to note that the tri-plant, 15,000-lb limit was the ceiling to Schackleford's expansion in the Gold Coast.

‡ Between 1870 and 1920 bread production grew fortyfold, based primarily upon the housewives' shift from homemade to store-bought bread. From 1920 to 1950 there was a mere threefold increase.

§ H. Kyrk and J. S. Davis, *The American Baking Industry, 1849–1923*. Miscellaneous Publication No. 2, Food Research Institute (Stanford University, 1925), and C. C. Slater, *Baking in America* (Easton, 1956), II, 40, 377. See also C. L. Alsberg, *Combination in the American Bread-Baking Industry*, Food Research Institute (Stanford University, 1926).

16. THE MARKETS FOR FOODS IN GHANA

R. M. LAWSON

... There are three main reasons why the price of local foodstuffs has increased and these are discussed below:

1. The movement of agricultural manpower into other sectors.

(a) There has been a continuous movement of labour from rural to urban areas over the last ten years, which was accentuated in 1963–5 by the accelerated demand for labour in new industrial and construction projects. In addition to those actually employed there are many more who come hoping for work. Between 1961 and early 1965 possibly some 100,000 persons or more had left the rural areas. This may be a conservative estimate. A more knowledgeable source has put it at 400,000, but statistics to support these figures are not yet available.

(b) There has been a fall in the size of immigrant labour force engaged in agriculture. In 1960, 17 per cent of Ghana's male labour force was made up of international migrants about 10,000 of whom were employed in the agricultural sector.* Since the Census was taken at a time which is fairly inactive in agriculture, it is likely that the participation of immigrants in agriculture was more than this. Immigrant labour force has decreased considerably in the last two years.† A variety of reasons are given, some political, some economic, including more strict customs and exchange control regulations. Another reason may be that in some of the neighbouring African countries there is now an increased demand for this sort of labour at home.

(c) Agricultural manpower has been drawn into state farms and the Workers Brigade and probably some 50,000 to 60,000 are now involved in this. The 1965 target for labour in the State Farms was given at 197,810‡ but this was by no means

---

* Census of Population, 1960. Government Printer, Accra.
† Unpublished data from Central Bureau of Statistics.
‡ Annual Plan for the Second Plan Year—1965 Financial Year. Appendix I.

achieved. The latest available statistics show that in 1963–4 some 51,226 acres were under cultivation by the State Farms, but only 20,000 acres were producing food crops. During this period some 15,000 men were employed and this gives a land/labour ratio which is lower than that of the small-scale private farming sector.* Another serious factor reducing the agricultural labour force is the loss of child labour, now taken off into education. This is mentioned in the Malpractices Report.† What is not mentioned is that the shape of population distribution gives a pyramid so that today more children have to be supported by fewer adult producers than was hitherto the case. Before compulsory education a child of about 12 was able to support himself in food. There are today probably 0·3 million children above the age of 12 still undergoing education. A child of this age could probably support himself in food.

Further, the education of children affects the labour supply position for two or three years after they leave school. Half-educated teenagers are not satisfied to go back to the land, and though many of them may ultimately do so they seem to spend one year or more looking around elsewhere for work, doing casual labour in the towns, sometimes spending a year as messengers or in other semi-menial work and after a time many drift back to rural areas again. In considering the drift of agricultural manpower into other occupations one must take into account the natural increase in population. Allowing for this it is possible that the net loss in the agricultural labour force may not have been very great. But even if the agricultural labour force were static it would require an annually increasing rate of productivity to feed a growing population.

2. A second factor affecting the production and therefore the price of local foodstuffs is the increasing competition for the use of land. For example, certain crops which provide food for human consumption are increasingly used for animal and poultry food, though the phenomenal rise in the price of such foods in 1965 temporarily halted this development and a fall in poultry production followed, as for example in the Volta Resettlement Scheme. In addition the use of land for non-food crops is increasing.

---

* Agricultural Census, Phase II 1964. Vol I, *Statistics of Large Scale Specialized, Institutional and Co-operation Economy.*
† Report of the Commission of Enquiry into Trade Malpractices in Ghana, 1966 (*Editors*).

In 1963–4 some 40,000 acres were under industrial crops in large-scale farms. The growth of tobacco by the small-scale private farmer has also been encouraged by the favourable and stable price offered by the Tobacco Marketing Board. The use of land and agricultural labour for the production of non-food crops will increase as the demand for industrial raw materials to feed new processing industries develops.

3. A third reason for the increase in prices of local foodstuffs has been suggested by the Commission (para. 60), that owing to the reduction in new planting of cocoa there has been a decrease in the interplanting of food crops by cocoa farmers. This is particularly the case with plantains and cocoyams. The fall in the supply of plantains to the market, however, is far more likely to be due to the failure of the transport system to get them to market than in the failure to produce. A far more important aspect of the shortage of foodstuffs is the serious fall in the number of lorries which carry produce. Nearly the entire system of distribution depends on lorry transport. In 1965 the number of lorries newly registered probably totalled only about one-third of those of 1963.* It is possible that of those already registered a further third were off the roads for varying lengths of time due to lack of spares. The shortage of lorry transport probably also led to an increase in transport charges, though no data is available from which to make a comparative study. What about the effect of demand factors on price? Imports of the staples (maize, rice and flour) in the first quarter of 1965 fell to one-third of the comparative figures for the same period in 1964. Hitherto these provided the market with quantities equal to 5 per cent of the total quantity of locally produced staples. The withdrawal of such imports from the market thus led to an increased pressure of demand on locally produced foods.

A second influence on demand for food is of course the rise in incomes. Between 1964–5 real Gross Domestic Product rose 4·5 per cent and caused a rise in demands for food, particularly for superior local foodstuffs such as maize and yams. A further increase in demand emanated from the rural labour force which had moved from food producing to other employments, though it is difficult to estimate this influence until more statistics are processed.

Having discussed very cursorily the factors behind the demand

* *Central Bureau of Statistics Newsletter.* Motor Registration Statistics, February, 1966.

and supply situation of local foodstuffs, the methods by which these are marketed and distributed can now be examined. First—the general perspective of trade. There are some 323,900 traders in Ghana and about 83 per cent of these are women. Together they constitute one-eighth of the total labour force and there is a proportion of one trader to twenty-two head of population. In addition many farmers' wives, not necessarily recorded as traders in the Census, also undertake to trade in farm products at certain times of the year. So the number engaged in trade is likely to be a fluctuating figure, particularly with the trade in seasonal foods. For instance, the number of fish traders in the main Kumasi market varies from 400 to 700 according to the fishing seasons.* Eighty-six per cent of traders are self-employed, operating on a very small scale with low turnovers and low incomes, in a system of distribution which, generally speaking, is highly competitive, though a few pockets of controlling rings may occur in certain areas where competitive forces can be contained. These are in fact rare, though because they exist mostly in the big cities it has been easy for superficial observers to generalize on conditions in places like Accra and apply their notions to the system at large.

Trade in local foodstuffs is much greater than that of imported foods, since in value it is ten times as great and has to be collected from geographically wide sources of production. Even if we include all imported durable and non-durable consumer goods, the value of local foodstuffs is five times their total value.

The present internal trading system for both local and imported consumer goods is characterized by low labour costs, very few overheads apart from transport costs, a well-developed entrepreneurship, which operates with a great amount of mobility and flexibility. It utilizes labour which has a low opportunity cost. Trade is an employment which is adapted to the institutional framework of the economy. It economizes in capital and educated managerial ability and these are Ghana's scarcest resources.

Another aspect of the trading system is the variety of functions which each trader may undertake. She can occupy any and sometimes many positions in the long chain of distribution from producer to consumer, e.g., she may be the person who buys from the producer, she may be the wholesaler and also the retailer, or a combination of all. We can perhaps discuss this organization of trade

* Annual Report of the Fisheries Division, Ministry of Agriculture, 1961–2.

best by describing different types of markets in broad general terms. First at the level of the small village with a population less than 500. Such a village will probably not have a market. Surplus foods will be either sold immediately in the nearest market or stored for eventual sale possibly at better prices. There will be little local food for sale in the village as all farmers will use their own foods for subsistence. In such villages any foods which are sold, e.g. to non-farmers, such as teachers, are sold at a retail price higher than that of the nearest big market. Villagers bring back from the market to the village foods which they do not grow such as tomatoes and other vegetables. These too sell at a retail price much higher than at the large market since they will probably have passed through the hands of a large number of middlemen before reaching the final village consumer. (The inclusion of such items in the price index explains why the rural retail local food price index is usually higher than the urban one.) Another situation sometimes occurs in small rural villages which some people find difficult to explain—that is that there, the main product of the area is often actually in short retail supply and sells at a high retail price. This is because the farmer markets in large quantities and takes his goods to sell to wholesalers at the nearest market, thus leaving little at home. This is often the case, for example, with fish on the coast which may be scarce there compared to the nearest town.

In these rural markets farmers sell their foods in competition with farmer-traders, i.e. farmers who will have collected additional supplies from neighbouring farmers. If production in the area is highly localized then the farmers and farmer-traders have a very strong bargaining hand when selling to visiting wholesalers. This selling advantage, however, is less where the farmer is dealing in perishables for which there is no other market, or in weighty goods for which he has no storage facilities, or where he has had to headload his goods some distance to market and does not want to return home with unsold goods.

In many areas today the trader has to actually seek out supplies. Visiting wholesalers may go to farmers, sometimes before harvest, to buy crops which are still growing. When crops are harvested the trader will revisit the area, collect the produce, hire a lorry and take the food to market. Such women may operate on their own account as collectors of food and wholesalers, or they may operate as buying agents for wholesalers in the big markets. Thus a woman trader will visit maize farmers in remote areas in the south-east of the lake, collect a lorry load and return to Accra to sell to another middle-woman. Or a fish buyer will visit the Afram and buy perhaps twenty baskets of fish, hire a lorry and take them to Koforidua. In all these country markets the farmer or his wife can cut in on this trade if they find it worth while. If a farmer has only a small quantity to sell, e.g. a headload, it may not be worth while to do this since he may be unable to get enough profit on this small scale of trade to cover his transport costs to distant markets. (The incidence of rising transport costs falls heavier on the small-scale trader than the large-scale trader and in this respect the system becomes less competitive the higher transport costs rise.) So at the village level there are many types of traders buying and selling local foodstuffs and in the present situation of shortages the farmers tend to be strong sellers.

As well as traders who tend to specialize in buying one foodstuff, feeding back to a wholesaler in the big town market, there are also thousands of itinerant traders who rove round from market to market, probably visiting five markets a week. Such a trader may take fish from Tema to Koforidua one day, take plantain to Soga-kope another day, take groundnuts from Sogakope to Accra the next day, and take vegetables to another market the following day. These traders watch the markets carefully and move goods around from where prices are low to where prices are high. Sometimes this sort of trade is undertaken by farmers' wives who, having taken their foods to a large market, have enough capital to buy other foods for resale in their own local market. But most is done by professional traders who thus perform a valuable function in stabilizing prices and evening out local shortages.

Small local markets will be visited by itinerant traders in imported goods, mostly selling cloth and canned foods, who peddle their wares from market to market probably in a regular weekly routine. Most villages with a population of over 500 will have at least one store, the national ratio in this respect being about one store to 200–300 population. A small store will probably have a monthly turnover of about £50–£70 on which a profit of about £5–£10 will be made.* The typical village storekeeper will have other sources of income, he will spend part of the day on his farm or fishing, he will open his store casually to fit in with other work, with visiting relatives, tending his farm, getting supplies from the big town. He

* Nypan, A., 'Market Trade in Accra', *Economic Bulletin*, vol. 4, 3, 1960.

will be illiterate. His store will probably be open only at certain hours of the day, such as the evening, or, if it is open at other times, it may be tended by a daughter or wife. Such a store will sell imported food. To meet the demands of low incomes he will sell cigarettes by the stick, soap in thin slices for 3*d*, sugar by the lump, four for 1*d*, and so on. More durable consumer goods, such as torches, razors, haberdashery, cosmetics and medicines, will be sold by itinerant Hausa traders who ply their wares usually round a weekly circuit of villages.

We now come to consider the main large markets of Ghana, in Accra and Kumasi. A notable characteristic of such markets in these two towns is the failure of the number of large markets to keep pace with the rapid rise in urban population over the last ten years. For instance, though there are more small markets, the main markets in Accra are no larger than they were thirty years ago. This is ideal breeding ground for monopoly, price rings and restrictive trade practices of all kinds, and these no doubt occur to a certain extent in the trade in certain foodstuffs in Kumasi and Accra. Increased pressure has been placed on markets by the prohibition of itinerant traders who plied their trade on the sidewalks.

In Accra markets there is a daily attendance of over 25,000 traders, of whom 85 per cent are women. Only about 5,500 of these have stalls for which they pay a rent.* Sixty per cent of all traders deal in local foodstuffs and fuel, 15 per cent are craft workers (dressmakers and tailors), and only 25 per cent handle imported goods. Most started business with a capital of less than £20.† In 1959 the mean average daily turnover of traders in Accra markets was 76*s* but over half had a turnover of less than 40*s* with the highest turnover in meat and the next highest in imported cloth. Profit margins were probably in the region of 20–30 per cent of turnover, so the mean gross profit would have been in 1959 in the region of 15*s* to 22*s* per day, though 35 per cent would have had less than 6*s*. (Not all traders enter the market every day, so this calculation cannot be used to calculate *per capita* annual income.) It should be noted, however, that prices, and therefore profits, have probably gone up by some 50 per cent over the 1959 level. Goods are sold at both retail and wholesale levels. In 1959 in the Accra markets about 2 per cent of

---

* Information taken from records kept by Town Clerk's Department, Accra-Tema City Council, March 1966.
† Nypan, A., *op. cit.*

the total number of traders were pure wholesalers; many more operated at both wholesale and retail levels.

One aspect of market organization about which much has been said recently, but little on the basis of careful study, is the organization of 'queen mothers'. 'Queen mothers' exist in all but the smallest markets of Ghana and in the main markets there is one for the trade in each locally produced foodstuff or commodity, though in less specialized markets, however, commodities such as tomatoes, onions and peppers may be taken together under the supervision of one 'queen mother'.

'Queen mothers' perform many functions, but not the same in all markets. One can list some of their functions:

1. In the city markets they are the elected representatives of all retailers selling the same commodity. Thus there is a 'queen mother' for the yam sellers, the cassava sellers, the corn sellers, and so on. Their main function in these markets is to protect the sectional interests of the retailers whom they represent. If they fail in this, or exploit their position to their own advantage, they may be 'destooled' in the traditionally democratic Ghanaian manner. Over recent years however, the 'queen mother' has been strongly supported by the disbanded C.P.P.* in an effort to obtain political control over this highly influential sector of the community. In some cases the C.P.P. appears to have come to some understanding with certain 'queen mothers', no doubt to their mutual advantage. Some 'queen mothers' have, for instance, collected a fee from retailers, either on a weekly or monthly basis or on the size of turnover. The exact purpose of these funds has not yet been revealed.†

2. In rural areas where the market functions partly to collect locally produced food to sell to visiting wholesalers, the 'queen mother' will be the elected representative of the supplying farmers and farmer-traders. Her duties will largely be concerned with giving bargaining strength to the farmers who otherwise would be exploited as weak sellers by the visiting large-scale middlemen.

* Convention People's Party (*Editors*).

† Case before the Kumasi High Court, February, March and April 1966, involving five Malian fishmongers who sued the Kumasi City Council for unlawfully destroying 650 bags of fish on the grounds that the fish was rotten, after they had refused to pay 12 pesewas per bag to the 'queen mother' of the fishmongers. Hearing still in process at the time of writing.

3. In city and large town markets which are limited in size and where the number of established traders is as a result restricted, an important function of 'queen mothers' is to secure an equitable division of supplies between each of the retailers. This is particularly important when supplies are scarce and when each trader wants to have at least some goods to sell. This function has been particularly important in 1965 and in recent months when certain foodstuffs have been in short supply.

4. Another function is to secure as high a selling price as possible. Traders will not admit to forming price rings, but they do say, 'The "queen mother" helps us to arrange prices.' There is no compulsion to sell at such an agreed price, but the proximity in which sellers of the same produce sit in the market generally ensures that prices will be similar amongst the retailers. The ability of 'queen mothers' to form retail price rings is generally limited to the city and large town markets, for here the markets tend to be congested and their physical size limited, thus placing the relatively small number of traders in a position of power. These traders have space allocated to them by the City or Municipal Councils and because of the pressure of demand from other traders they are able to sublet their space and for this they charge a fee. Sometimes it is on a weekly or monthly basis, sometimes on the basis of turnover. Thus, for instance, a garri wholesaler will charge 1*s* for every bag sold. The regular stall holders are thus in a very strong position to control the number of traders and the size of their turnover, and this is an ideal precondition for the formation of price rings.

5. Their ability to use this power to fix prices is to a small extent limited by the presence of two other types of seller. First are the 'callers' who go round the markets shouting out their wares and prices. These traders go where they please, but as their trade is limited to what they can headload they do not have a very large turnover and thus do not constitute a serious threat to the regular traders who operate from stalls. A further threat to the power of 'queen mothers' to fix prices is that of the 'free trader'. There is a 'free market' for most commodities in the Accra markets. These are generally small spaces set aside for any 'free trader' to come and go as she wishes. Now, since these places are situated in the sun, and since the traders

181

using them are limited to handling what they can headload, prices in the 'free markets' tend to be lower than those elsewhere in the market, since the trader usually wants to make a quick sale. Again here the size of the turnover in the 'free market' is not usually enough to have much effect on the prices charged by the regular traders, though the 'queen mother' keeps an eye on the prices charged by the 'free traders' and is to some extent influenced by them. The ability of 'queen mothers' to control prices is strongest in those commodities which are brought from far distances to the market, for the wholesale trade in such goods enjoys the economies of scale and the small, single-handed trader, or farmer-trader, would not find it worth while to travel long distances to the city market. But it is just in such goods that the large-scale wholesaler may have an effective control over supplies. In times of shortage the large-scale wholesaler disposes of her goods in a sellers' market and the 'queen mothers' can do little about it. If the foods traded are not quickly perishable the wholesaler may be able to withhold stocks from the market and cause shortage and consequent price rise. This in fact happened in the Accra markets in the trade in yams, rice and maize in 1965. Some 'queen mothers' may also be wholesalers, or employ agents to visit farmers to secure supplies, but if she is to remain in her position of respect she must not make undue gain from this to the disadvantage of her supporting retailers.

6. Apart from protecting their sectional interests in securing supplies at reasonable prices and arranging selling prices, the 'queen mother' also settles disputes and arguments between traders in her group and also represents them in dealings or disputes with any other traders in the market or with lorry drivers or wholesalers.

7. One of her most useful functions is to act as guarantor for retailers. Thus when a large load of foodstuffs arrives at the market, the 'queen mother' will guarantee payment within a short time to the credit-granting wholesaler or lorry driver (who himself may be acting as agent for a trader). This may be within a few hours, at most a day. This service enables the lorries and wholesale suppliers to have a quick turn-round of goods, it saves them from wasting time in collecting debts, and it helps to establish regular channels of trade. In a few cases the

'queen mother' may, if she has sufficient capital, purchase the goods outright when they arrive and later share them between her supporters. However, she is not able to exploit this position unduly and any unreasonable profit-making would bring her into disfavour. Since she holds her position by the mutual trust of her supporting retailers she is usually unlikely to do anything to help herself at their expense.

The organization of 'queen mothers' has been derided by those who have not understood their position. Their functions are more like those of a shop steward than a capitalist and could well provide the basis for a natural evolution into a more advanced type of trading, such as co-operative marketing or an organization involving larger retailing units. Their role has in some cases been confused with those of the large-scale wholesalers (Report, para. 76) and these are the traders who are most likely to influence prices in markets. They are few in number since there is no room in the market for many such traders, and with such protection they are able to form price agreements. However, their ability to control prices is limited to within the range of transport costs to other markets, and conditions in these other markets, for example in the other big towns near Accra such as Nsawam, Koforidua, etc., are much more competitive. Thus a plaintain retailer in Accra need not buy from an Accra wholesaler if the price in Accra is higher than the price at, say, Nsawam after allowing for the added transport costs to Nsawam. The price in Nsawam is more likely to be influenced by free market forces from farmers and traders who have supplies nearby. The effect of this is to make the retail market more competitive than the wholesale market. Consequently one finds that wholesale prices have been rising faster than retail prices. This state of affairs exists because small-time retailers can enter the market to compete at retail levels but, because of the shortage of storage and marketing space, cannot compete at wholesale level. One way to reduce the price and quantity control which the large operators have in the few large markets is to provide more competitive conditions by enlarging market facilities and making stalls and storage more widely available.

An expansion of the sale of local foodstuffs through the existing large retail stores would be a natural evolution of trade, but hitherto this development has been retarded by the inability of stores to secure regular supplies of produce. Though this will no doubt solve

G   183

itself in time, a more immediate form of competition to the market traders could come from the development, already in evidence in Accra and Kumasi, of specialized traders in local foodstuffs who operate from stalls and lock-ups which they have constructed off the sidewalks in the main thoroughfares. These are situated mostly near the large department stores and main shopping centres and therefore cater for the higher income groups, selling superior fruits and vegetables. Like the trade in the markets, they are financed and organized by illiterate women traders. Where such a stall is sublet to a number of traders they too operate some sort of price agreement, but this is highly localized in its influence. This type of trade is operated from temporary structures and more capital is needed to improve standards of hygiene and handling; this probably requires a degree of ability and knowledge beyond that of the existing women traders. But such retail outlets could form the nucleus of an improved method of food marketing.

Internal marketing and distribution operate generally efficiently and equitably under normal conditions, but in conditions of scarcity and shortage the large trader who receives preferential treatment in obtaining supplies and who has facilities for storage is obviously going to gain and to use her position to her own advantage. The example of hoarding, such as existed in imported goods, can exist to a more limited degree in local foodstuffs, and to a small extent middlemen can create shortage over a short period in anticipation of a price rise. Yams, maize, and rice are particularly vulnerable since all can be stored. The trade in yams has, to a certain extent, a protection from small-scale competition because the transport cost of bringing yams from distant food-producing sources to the market in Accra yields economies of scale to the larger trader. Now the price rings in these commodities have arisen as a result of two main causes, first a long term trend due to the shortage of storage space and lack of marketing facilities in Accra and other big cities, which has considerably cut down competition, and secondly and more recently, to shortages of all foodstuffs. Price rings are not a general characteristic of the trade in local foodstuffs outside the big cities where marketing conditions are not restricted physically and where the small trader has access to the market so that conditions are highly competitive. Price rings are a threat in the urban centres where there is little subsistence farming and no important source of food supply apart from what can be bought.

The only immediate way of dealing with this situation in Accra (apart from increasing marketing facilities) is to import food on a large scale, particularly maize and rice. But this could only be a crash programme to give a little more breathing space to allow agricultural production to improve. The long-run methods of improving food production have been well documented elsewhere: better fertilizers, better storage, improved transport facilities, better roads, and most of all an extensive agricultural extension service to help the farmer. These improvements can be undertaken without altering the existing institutional framework in the farming sector. Another aspect of the shortage of foodstuffs entering the markets is the serious fall in the number of lorries which carry produce. The shortage of lorry transport probably also led to an increase in transport charges, though no data is available from which to make a comparative study. Thus in times when lorries are in short supply the lorry owner is in a strong bargaining position with the trader and farmer and his charges may rise. It is not possible to say how competitive the system of lorry transport is under normal conditions, since there are still shortages of spares and new vehicles. Further imports of such supplies would undoubtedly expand the number of lorries plying local foodstuffs and would increase the quantity of foodstuffs reaching the market. This is not sufficiently emphasized by the Report on Malpractices, which however makes two major suggestions for improving the supply of local foodstuffs: first the establishment of Produce Marketing Boards, and secondly the development of co-operatives. Both of these are ill-thought-out policies in the Ghanaian context and somewhat impracticable in the existing institutional framework of the rural sector. It is hoped that the production and distribution of foodstuffs has been well enough described here for this to be understood. It is very doubtful whether the costs of distribution and collection of foodstuffs could be any lower than those of private traders, who operate with great mobility, with low overheads, and who, because they are motivated by profit, incur minimum overheads.

In a Food Marketing Board one has to ask who would fix the prices. Given the existing great variation in producer prices of foodstuffs and in qualities of produce throughout Ghana, would local buying officials of a Marketing Board have power to fix prices locally? And as they would be employed on a salary, what could prevent them from corrupt practices? What incentive would they have to seek out the best sources of produce in the arduous way in which the highly mobile private buyer pursues her suppliers now? If food marketing centres are to be established in a number of places, how great would be the difference between them and existing free markets in terms of economic cost to the economy? And would the farmer necessarily gain if he had to take time off from his farming to bring his produce to marketing centres? One should take a long cool look at other state organizations which are supposed to operate on commercial lines, before involving the taxpayer in further subsidies.

One marketing board is often held up to be a model on which others should be formulated. This is the Tobacco Marketing Board which has a monopoly over the purchase of tobacco grown in Ghana. But two things should be noted. First, it has stimulated production of tobacco, because the price paid to the producer is such that it has encouraged him to divert resources from food production to tobacco production. Secondly, the Board is able to offer a regular stabilized price because it is a homogeneous product and because there is only one single consumer of tobacco. But this condition does not exist in the food producing sector, which demands a high degree of flexibility both in pricing and in regulating supplies. In fact, in spite of the simple process of buying a single product, the Tobacco Board has run into serious administrative difficulties, particularly in long delays in making payments to farmers. The problem of food marketing is too complex to discuss here, but the economic cost of a marketing board should be compared with the probably more advantageous investment of improving roads and marketing facilities in the food producing areas so as to enable the existing food production to reach the consumer more easily. The Food Marketing Board is just one other panacea imported into Ghana without reference to its suitability to local conditions.

Another popular panacea imported to Ghana relates to the use of co-operatives in stimulating agricultural production. This is another ill-thought-out idea which is repeated in the Commission's Report. Again we need to examine the evidence of success that has so far been achieved in agricultural co-operatives. In fact there are very few genuine co-operatives in Ghana and many already have a bad reputation amongst the farmers. This is partly because they have been badly explained, often by officials of the U.G.F.C.C.,* who

* United Ghana Farmers' Council Co-operatives (*Editors*).

186

themselves know little about their organization, and also because they appear to be merely extensions of the political organization and not primarily methods of increasing production in the interests of the farmer and the economy. Some co-operatives are in fact nothing more than capitalist enterprises, the members of the co-operative using the resources and facilities given to them for employing labour to work on so-called co-operative farms whilst they themselves turn to their traditional methods of farming. It would be ironical indeed if co-operatives in Ghana led to the establishment of a kulak class.

Some co-operatives, for example the GNFMC* discussed in the Report, are in fact little more than an attempt to form a marketing monopoly. It is composed of a group of traders who are trying, under the guise of the name of co-operative, to secure preferential supplies of fish for their own private trading purposes. The word co-operative is used to conceal a variety of capitalist structures; some are straightforward business enterprises using employed labour, others are commercial partnerships, others are attempts at cartelization and monopoly. Most of them are described as co-operatives in order to get preferential treatment in one way or another from official organizations, such as the advantage of securing the use of tractors, or getting credit, or securing capital loans. But no official attempt is made to see that these organizations in fact operate as co-operatives or that general co-operative aims are formulated. A thorough reappraisal of the co-operative sector needs to be undertaken before the word falls into even more disrepute in the productive sectors of the economy.

I have spent some time, possibly too much, describing the internal market system of trading in Ghana, but this has been necessary to counterbalance the impression of the importance of store trading which one gets from living in Accra and from reading the Report. Store trading in Ghana and the trade in imported consumer goods in 1964 totalled £40 million. In order to assess its importance in the economy this may be compared with the consumption of local food of £264 million, and a total GDP† of £680 million in 1964. The distribution of imported goods throughout Ghana passes along a chain of distribution from large wholesalers to small retailers, sometimes through the hands of six or seven intermediaries, before

---

* Ghana National Fish Marketing Co-operative (*Editors*).
† Gross Domestic Product (*Editors*).

reaching the dispersed and sometimes remote consumers in the small quantities in which they are only able to purchase.

Hoarding of imported goods was facilitated because, it is alleged in the Report, certain storekeepers in the state-controlled Ghana National Trading Corporation, which had the monopoly over certain types of imports, gave large and preferential allocations of certain goods to favoured wholesalers, some of whom appear to have been related to them either by family or by business connections. As most of this trade was undertaken through the credit facilities of pass-books, the report attacks the pass-book system and advocates that all pass-books and other credit customers in Ghana should be registered with the Ministry of Trade and their turnovers declared. This would be a monumental task. The G.N.T.C. alone has 20,000 pass-book holders, and the other importing organizations together probably have another 10,000. Under such conditions it would be impossible to prevent people from opening more than one account. In any case some of the purchasing by large-scale wholesalers is done for cash outside the pass-book system and it would be impossible to trace each customer.

There is nothing fundamentally wrong with the pass-book and chit system. Unfortunately the system has been associated with large profits and corrupt and irregular practices during periods of scarcity. However, in such circumstances 'special' arrangements between storekeepers and large customers would inevitably arise regardless of whether they were pass-book transactions or not.

Now, while we would all agree that the long term perspective of socialism demands that trade should operate as a state sector, it should be obvious from the description of trade given here that this could not be implemented in Ghana yet. Ghana cannot afford the managerial manpower, the capital resources, the policing controls which would be necessary to operate a nationalized trading organization. As a short term measure the existing system of distribution must be utilized. It has proved very effective hitherto and it can continue to do so. Hoarding and shortages of essential goods could be prevented by a clear-cut import policy which is linked to taxation and pricing systems. Given the availability of foreign exchange, goods should be imported and taxed in accordance with national objectives. As a first stage towards state control of trade all imports of producer goods could be imported by the state and directly allocated to the users, thus by-passing all intermediaries.

The most important function of trade in Ghana today, however, is to collect vast quantities of local foodstuffs from widely dispersed and remote rural areas and to redistribute them in small quantities to some seven million consumers. The distributive system which this demands is far too complex, non-regular and seasonal and involves too many traders to be contained within a single system. Further, under present agricultural conditions it requires a mobility and spontaneity of decision and choice which is a skill learnt by experience and which would not easily, reliably, and efficiently be undertaken by officials not motivated by private profit.

The existing system economizes in capital resources, it uses labour of which there is a plentiful supply at low opportunity cost, and is therefore productive by any rational economic criteria. It utilizes the labour of illiterate women who are insufficiently educated for other employment, women who have the valuable asset of business expertise, who are risk-taking entrepreneurs. They thus release supervisory skills, management, capital, etc., which would otherwise have to be employed in trade, for employment elsewhere. If their work were superfluous or too costly from the consumers' point of view, they would be bypassed. Such traders have a low supply price in terms of daily earnings. Any attempt to enforce a different system of trading to Ghana at the present time would be to require educated clerks, literate traders, a large managerial class and hierarchy of officials, all of whom are in very short supply and who have a high supply price.

Conclusions

1. The long chain of distribution which utilizes thousands of small-scale traders is in fact a rational use of existing economic resources.
2. We have to face the fact that many individuals, whether employed by the state or by private enterprise, will find it difficult to resist the temptation to make a profit for themselves if the opportunity arises. Since such opportunities occur most easily under conditions of shortage, the best way to prevent exploitation of consumers or taxpayers is either to prevent shortages or to devise a tax system which prevents the trader from making exorbitant profits.
3. Price control is largely ineffective in such conditions without the

189

imposition of a rationing scheme and it would be impossible to institute this in Ghana. Price control leads only to abuse. It is no answer to develop a hierarchy of police controllers since this simply gives more private individuals the chance to exploit the situation for their own ends. The only solution is to prevent shortages of essential goods.

4. The less opportunities there are for putting non-productive people in positions of control over the productive sectors of the economy the better. Supervisors, state marketing officials, so-called secretaries and organizers of co-operatives which are in fact not co-operatives, all are a great economic cost to the community. The cost lies not only in the sum of their salaries, transport costs, overheads and multifarious other charges, but in the havoc they make in the farming community. Of course there may be good political reasons why we should have a cadre of supervisors going round the country telling farmers how to do their work and supervising marketing and distribution. I am not politically qualified to discuss this, but its economic cost should be considered.

5. There is nothing fundamentally wrong with the pass-book system. Pass-book trading is in fact only a proportion of total wholesale transactions in imported goods. The evolution of large wholesalers is a natural growth process which under competitive conditions allows the economies of scale to be passed on to the consumer.

6. The system of distribution in Ghana which has evolved is a rational use of economic resources. It is only when there are shortages that those who can receive preferential favours are able to exploit the situation.

What can be done to prevent further crises in the shortages which are still to come?

First, the production of local foodstuffs is the most important single contributor to the economy, since it forms the largest item in the G.D.P. (37 per cent) and because it absorbs 53 per cent of total private consumption expenditure.* It is only by increasing the productivity of foodstuff farming that capital and labour can be released for development. Secondly, improved transport (more spares for vehicles, a decrease in tax on petrol, improvement of

* Economic Survey, 1964

roads) is urgently required. Thirdly, improved marketing facilities must be provided in large towns, e.g. Accra, and also in remoter areas where food is grown and where supplies reaching the market are restricted by lack of markets. Local foodstuff production will not increase in the short run by developing co-operatives, or by spending more money on state farms, until these institutions have proved themselves.

The method of distributing imported goods must be reconsidered. The problem of allocating funds available for imports is closely linked with the planned development of the economy, and therefore a carefully worked out policy should be followed in which the quantities of imports will be related to pricing and taxation policies.

According to the needs of the economy, imports can be divided into—

(a) Necessaries (foods such as milk, maize, sugar, flour, drugs, waxprints, baby foods, meat and fish) and also spare parts, petrol and kerosene, to maintain existing capital.

(b) Producer goods such as capital equipment, heavy vehicles, industrial raw materials, etc.

(c) Everything else.

Because it is difficult to enforce price controls and because shortages will lead to hoarding, the accumulation of large private capital, and corruption in allocation of goods, it is necessary to ensure that there are ample supplies of the necessary imports listed above.

Goods under category (b) above would have to be imported in accordance with the national plan for industrial development and be imported directly by the state for allocation to the users, thus by-passing the intermediary. This would be the logical starting-point to a nationalized trading sector.

The inflationary trends in the economy and excessive purchasing power would have to be mopped up by high prices of all other imported goods. In so far as other imported goods are concerned it would be necessary first to consider the volume of these which could be imported, given the remaining available balance of exchange. Secondly, some attempt must be made to determine the equilibrium level of prices which these would fetch on a free market, and on the basis of the difference between equilibrium prices and import prices, heavy import duties should be imposed to allow only a reasonable margin of profit to be made on these goods. Such an import policy would serve two useful purposes, non-necessaries would be allocated only to those who could pay for them, and prices of necessaries would remain within the range of all consumers.

Corruption is a problem *sui generis* and the Commission is to be commended both for exposing such corruption and insisting that the government should investigate all corrupt practices within its own state enterprises and public corporations. Public boards should be answerable to the public. The Abraham Commission has probably merely pecked at the fringe of corruption and it is of course not the first commission of enquiry to expose corruption in high places. But the decision to continue with such purges is probably of political rather than economic significance and outside my field. But if the government is serious about searching for corruption it should not have a commission of enquiry which is entirely made up of politicians. They may be too easily scared by the skeletons they find in the cupboards.

17. DISTRIBUTIVE TRADE—A CRITIQUE OF GOVERNMENT POLICY

O. OLAKANPO

. . . On the basis of the official figures in the Nigerian National Accounts, it would seem that in 1957 total personal expenditure in Nigeria on all consumer goods and services reached the record figure of £811 million. However, this sum did not pass entirely through the hands of the distributors. To know what amount passed through the distributors or the estimate of retail turnover or value, it is necessary to exclude expenditure on such items as Travel, Education, Fuel and light, and Miscellaneous Services. When this has been done it appears that in 1957 total retail sales through shops, stores, etc., amounted to £728 million compared with £560 million in 1950. This represents 30 per cent increase in retail value over the period.

Table 1

| | 1950 | | 1957 | | |
	Total retail value £m	Percentage of total	Total retail value £m	Percentage of total	1957 as % of 1950
Food	470	84	568	78	121
Drink	9	1·4	16	2·2	200
Tobacco	15	2·7	18	2·5	120
Clothing	50	8·8	77	10·5	158
Other non-durable goods	8	1·4	30	4·1	375
Durable goods	10	1·8	19	2·6	190
Total	562		728		

The rate of increase in retail sales of each class of commodity has varied. The retail sale of drink has doubled while that of 'other non-durable goods' has more than trebled. The retail turnover of

193

durable goods and clothing has risen by 90 and 58 per cent respectively. The least rate of growth has been recorded for food and tobacco, having increased by 21 and 20 per cent respectively.

How was the total amount of retail sale of £728 million shared between the expatriate and the indigenous distributors? In the absence of a Census of Distribution for Nigeria, it is difficult to calculate the volume of trade by type of shop. As expatriate shops are predominantly large-scale—chain stores and department stores —the share of expatriate firms in total retail sales could have been calculated with reasonable accuracy from such a census of distribution. Barring this, we may examine the commodity groups in which expatriate firms specialize, and relate the retail sales of these commodities to the total retail sales—thus giving us the expatriate share. In using this method one is bound to run into some difficulties. For some of the commodity groups in Table 1 are not exclusive to the expatriate or the indigenous distributors. Large-scale retail shops such as department stores sell numerous commodities ranging from groceries to durable consumer goods.

A rough idea of the share of the expatriates in total retail turnover may perhaps be obtained if we assume that expatriates have a larger share of distributive trade in imported goods than the indigenous firms, and that the indigenous distributors have a larger share of the distributive trade in locally produced goods. This appears to be a fairly accurate assumption. Given this, the share of the expatriate will depend on the import content of consumer goods, and this is estimated at 20 per cent. Thus of the total retail turnover of £728 million in 1957, the retail value of imports amounted to only £148 million.

What proportion of total imports is handled by the expatriates? In 1949 it is estimated that about 85 per cent of the import trade of Nigeria was handled by European firms, about 10 per cent by Lebanese and Indian firms, and about 5 per cent by African firms. It is reasonable to assume that the share of African firms has doubled between 1949 and 1957, thus reducing the share of expatriates to 80 per cent. On this basis, out of the total retail values of imports amounting to £148 million, expatriate firms would account for £126 million, the rest being the share of indigenous firms. However, the sum of £126 million, which is only about 17 per cent of the total retail turnover, does not represent the total retail turnover of expatriate firms. This is because both the expatriate firms and the indigenous firms participate in the distribution of locally produced goods. But it is difficult to ascertain with any precision the relative standing of each group.

Since official policy aims at eliminating the expatriate firms for the benefits of the indigenous firms, the question arises as to whether the surviving units (i.e. the indigenous units) would be able to provide, with equal efficiency, the services now provided by the expatriate firms. It may be helpful first to discuss some of the main features of these two groups—the expatriate group and the indigenous group—in distributive trade.

Table 2. *Import content of consumer goods*

	1950				1957			
	Total retail value £m	Of which imports £m	Percentage of imports	Home produced £m	Total retail value £m	Of which imports £m	Percentage of imports	Home produced £m
Food	470	7	1·5	463	568	27	4·7	541
Drink	9	3	33	6	16	7	43·7	9
Tobacco	15	7	46·6	8	18	4	22·2	14
Clothing	50	40	80	10	77	66	85·7	11
Other non-durable goods	8	6	75	2	30	25	83·3	5
Durable goods	10	10	100	—	19	19	100	—
Total	562	73		489	728			580

We can distinguish four main types of retail trading units in the country—the independent or unit shop, the chain store, the department store and the co-operative store. The first type of unit operates on a small scale, while the latter three operate on a larger scale, combining the economies of large-scale buying and selling, centralized purchases, and decentralized sales, and offering highly elaborate consumer services. Generally the indigenous trading firms are predominantly of the first type—the independent or unit shop—while the expatriate trading firms are of the large trading unit types. Thus comparison of the features of the two sectors of distributive trades largely becomes a comparison of small-scale and large-scale operations in distributive trades.

The indigenous sector

The 'unit' store which operates as an independent business, drawing customers primarily from the immediate neighbourhood, represents perhaps about 80 to 90 per cent of all shops in Nigeria. The term 'unit' shop is here used to include 'booths', 'shops', 'stores', 'stalls' and market-places. Except in some towns where Lebanese and Syrians operate small shops, this 'unit' type of trading unit is exclusive to the indigenous traders.

An important characteristic of this unit is its very low capital (fixed and working) requirements. The retailer usually obtains his goods on credit from the expatriate firms. He does not carry a stock since this is usually replenished at short intervals. Rent is usually low and in some cases may not involve a monetary cost, as when the retailer is in a position to convert a part of his dwelling into a shop. The employment of assistants, while not unusual, is not universal and may indeed be unnecessary, as assistance in the running of the shop may be forthcoming from members of the family.

Thus the overhead costs of a 'unit' shop are low. But this does not imply a low unit cost of retailing in the indigenous distributive sector and therefore a low price to the consumer. For one feature of this sector is the very low rate of turnover. It is difficult to make any accurate guess of the average daily turnover of indigenous retail trading units, for much depends on the location. But it seems plausible to assume that shops with a total daily turnover of less than £1 are distressingly numerous in the country. Hence the ratio of total cost to the rate of turnover which the custom of the unit shop permits tends to raise the average cost of retailing and therefore the retail margin.

On the level of market structure the indigenous sector exhibits the features of both monopoly and competition. This sector comprises a large number of independent units selling physically identical commodities. Entry into distributive trade in the indigenous sector is easy, because of low capital outlay. However, each unit store has an element of monopoly power. The extent of this depends on its location. Generally the unit store sells to the neighbourhood. The bulk of its customers purchase in small quantities and only as they need commodities. They also know the shopkeeper personally, and each trip is somewhat in the nature of a visit and tends to cement the bonds between buyers and sellers. This relationship ensures that each retail unit has a hard core of clientele who will buy from it irrespective of price changes. It is therefore possible for physically identical commodities to sell for different prices even in neighbouring stores.

The result of this monopolistic competition is not that profits in distribution in the indigenous sector are unusually large. This could hardly be so in view of the easy entry into the business. However, the number of units in this sector is greater than would otherwise be the case if perfect competition prevailed. As Professor Lewis has observed, a reduction in the number of units may lead to a fall in retail margins to the betterment of consumers.

Expatriate sector

In contrast to the indigenous sector of distributive trade the market structure in the expatriate sector is characterized by oligopoly. Expatriate trading firms are invariably organized on a large scale, and a large proportion of import trade is concentrated in the hands of a few firms.

This concentration in contrast to the atomistic situation in the indigenous sector points to a different market conduct among established expatriate firms. The price-calculating policies of the expatriate firms are not formulated independently, but in the light of recognizable interdependence with each other. In his study of West African Trade, Peter Bauer observed that 'Firms have been intensely preoccupied with the activities and conduct of individual competitors: they have acted in the knowledge that a price change initiated by one of their members was likely to bring about retaliation.'* This circular interdependence does not suggest collusion.

The oligopolistic structure of the expatriate sector implies that entry into this sector will not be as easy as in the atomistically organized indigenous sector. The difficulty of entry into the expatriate sector may be attributed to two special factors:

(1) Established expatriate firms have absolute cost advantages over potential entrants.
(2) Established firms enjoy certain economies of large scale.

By and large, an absolute cost advantage to established firms may exist if these firms have price and other advantages over potential entrants in securing supply of merchandise and investible funds.

* P. T. Bauer, *West African Trade* (Cambridge University Press), p. 100.

The expatriate firms usually have exclusive trading agencies with overseas manufacturers of almost all brands of consumer goods. This is especially common in trade in consumer durable goods such as refrigerators, motor vehicles, electrical and household appliances. Apart from exclusive agencies, there are few cases where expatriate firms are financially linked with overseas manufacturers. There have been instances of African traders who have travelled to Europe to negotiate for exclusive agencies only to find that Europe's exporters or manufacturers have a long established agency contract with expatriate firms in Nigeria.

A potential entrant is also at a disadvantage in securing the absolute capital requirements for efficient entry. There is often a time lag involved between the placing of orders for merchandise and its disposal, and the finance of stock requires a sizeable amount of capital.* A potential entrant firm may not be able to secure this capital or it may secure it at less favourable terms than the established firm. The established firms not only have large capital of their own, but have easier access to bank credit than potential entrants.

Because of these absolute cost advantages established firms in the expatriate sector are in a position to raise prices above the competitive level without attracting entry. They have the ability to do so by virtue of the fact that the level of their costs is lower than that of a potential entrant firm.

The advantages arising out of the economies of scale may take the form of lower operating costs expressed as a percentage of net sales, less invoice costs. There are two aspects of lower operating costs in relation to size. Firstly, the scale of operations allows for considerable specialization in function, such as specialization in buying, selling, displaying, and staff training. Secondly, the scale of operations may be accompanied by an increase in the rate of stock-turn once the need to increase the stocks held is not proportionate to the increase in the sales undertaken.

These absolute cost advantages need not, however, result in excessively high retail margin to consumers. Neither can it be used as a rational explanation of the distorted view that expatriate firms in distributive trades exploit the Africans. Indeed the early stage of growing of large-scale retailing may be marked by a low price policy, since during this process of expansion the large-scale unit would

* For other factors making for high capital requirements in West African trade, see P. T. Bauer, *op. cit.* chapter II.

aim at lowering its costs by undercutting any competitor it encounters.

The consumer derives benefits from large-scale trading units which small indigenous trading units cannot provide in equal measure. Distribution involves more than the transfer of goods from the producer to the consumer. The distributive functions for which the retailer is paid by the community include the supply of consumers with products of the *right kind* and in the *right quantities*, the assortment of commodities to be sold, the spreading of information about new products, and provision of miscellaneous services such as credit facilities, rest rooms, etc. A retailer must never be out of stock for anything he may reasonably be expected to be asked for and he must not hold more of any given stock than will prevent this from occurring, allowing a reasonable margin of error. The ability of a retailer to fulfil this optimum stock requirement depends on his working capital and his appraisal of the market conditions that affect the branches of trade in which he operates. We have already observed the limitations, with respect to capital requirements, from which the small units suffer. The large-scale unit can obtain a better knowledge of market conditions either from outside specialists or from its employees who through long years of operations in different lines are specialists in market forecasting. On the spreading of information, large-scale retail units are, through their capital resources, able to afford more on advertising than the small units.

There are also those miscellaneous services, which may be grouped together under the title 'amenities', e.g. comfortable premises, rest rooms, coffee bars, music and the like. All these are usually provided by the expatriate firms. These amenities are 'gimmicks' which expatriate trading firms can afford to offer and by their aid invoke a large body of customers.

The objective of government policy can be assumed to be the maximization of national welfare. Given this objective, the question of the relative efficiency of each of the two groups of distributive trades is an important guide to policy. The discussion so far on the organizational pattern and features of the two groups, while giving some insights into the distributive services provided by each group, does not provide us with a basis for a conclusion on the relative efficiency of one group *vis-à-vis* the other. The estimate of efficiency of the distributive trades can of course be made in the light of organizational pattern of these trades and the economies of marketing. But the conclusion thus reached may be a false guide to policy.

The mere fact of size and the economic advantages derived from it do not provide a *prima facie* evidence that the expatriate firms are more efficient than the indigenous firms. Although the organization pattern of the indigenous group, comprising, as it does, a medley of puny one-man enterprises, pedlars, stall-keepers, may be wasteful of manpower, yet this is not a *prima facie* evidence of inefficiency. Indeed Professor P. T. Bauer has written in eloquent and convincing terms of the essential and efficient services performed by these small retail units. In his opinion, the liberal use of manpower is fully offset by the economy in one of the scarce co-operating factors in retail trade—namely capital.*

A simple criterion of efficiency in distributive trades would appear to be this: can the consumer get what he wants, when he wants it, with as little call on the scarce resources of the community as possible? It does not matter on the basis of this criterion whether a trading unit operates on a small scale or on a large scale. The small shop caters to the needs of a circle of customers having different tastes and idiosyncrasies dissimilar to those possessed by those customers who prefer shopping in large-scale trading units. The small trading unit has virtues from the economic point of view which the large trading unit cannot afford in equal measure, such as proximity. A very large proportion of indigenous trading units are scattered all over the country. They sell to the neighbourhood and appeal to customers who prefer shopping around the corner to travelling to the central shops of a town or city. Further, the indigenous shop-keeper has some special interest in his customers which the customer is unlikely to sense in the large departmental store where he is one among thousands of daily customers. Similarly, the large expatriate trading units attract a given set of customers and provide a given set of services which small shops cannot afford in equal measures. Thus the two units are to a very large extent complementary rather than competitive, and may be said to exhibit features of efficiency in their respective sphere of operations.

If the services provided by the two groups are complementary, what then should be the policy of the government for increasing the indigenous share in distributive trades? Briefly, I think, the policy of the government should be such as to enable the indigenous traders to make inroads into the branches of distributive trades which are at present the exclusive preserve of the expatriate.

* P. T. Bauer, *op. cit.*, pp. 26–31.

This in turn implies the direction of policy toward the barriers to entry into the oligopolistic organized expatriate sector. As a beginning in this direction, we should perhaps start with a policy designed to reduce absolute cost barriers. This will include easing the supply of capital to potential indigenous entrants and attacks on exclusive agencies.

The first problem in the way of developing indigenous firms of comparable strength with expatriate firms is bound to be the provision of capital. The resources of African trading firms are inadequate to meet the capital requirements necessary for operating certain branches of trade. Moreover, large-scale trading requires not only capital but skilful management. Much has been written in praise of the skill of the Africans in trading. Of the initiative and skill of the African traders, it has been remarked that 'in his or her own field, the African trader does not lack initiative'. Professor P. T. Bauer has observed the exceptional effort, foresight, resourcefulness, thrift, and ability of the African trader and his ability to perceive economic opportunity.*

Can we conclude from these observations that given adequate capital, indigenous trading firms could effectively enter into different branches of trade, which are now in the expatriate sector? While admitting the qualities of enterprise possessed by the African, it would be wrong to conclude from this that Africans have the managerial experience and the technical skill required for the operation of modern large trading units. The manifestations of the qualities of the African traders which have been mentioned have indeed been on a small scale and the activities to which they give rise are also small. It would be sheer delusion to think that access to capital is the main prerequisite for the emergence of large indigenous trading units. Thus, apart from capital, the second major problem in the development of large-scale indigenous trading firms is the shortage of personnel both at managerial and technical level.

It thus appears that if indigenous commercial enterprises are to make a major inroad into the branches of trade now controlled by expatriates, the two major problems mentioned above must be tackled. There are at least three ways whereby these problems can be solved. These are:

(i) Establishment of State Trading Agency;

* P. T. Bauer, *op. cit.*, pp. 30–1.

(ii) Revitalization of Co-operative Trading Organization;

(iii) Encouragement of indigenous private commercial enterprise.

A state trading agency may well be a quick way of ousting expatriates from distributive trades. Such an agency would have the financial strength necessary to compete with expatriate firms. Insofar as management is concerned, the government may rely initially on expatriate staff, who would also train indigenous managers and technicians to take over eventually. A state trading agency would also be more able to divert business from the expatriate firms than indigenous private commercial enterprise. For apart from using the normal market mechanism to compete with the expatriate firms, the government can use legislative powers, import control, its buying power, and other techniques to ensure that a larger proportion of total imports is channelled to the consumer via the state agency.

Simple as this solution may at first sight seem, one is faced with the very serious doubt as to the efficiency of official management in commerce. State control of distribution is of no use if it is ill directed and if those responsible for leadership are not always eager to adopt new methods and to take risks. With private enterprise the incentive of profit tempts and spurs it to make experiments and take risks.

Thus the main ground for opposing state trading is that it would be most unlikely to secure the adaptability, elasticity, and enterprise that are necessary to progress. And it is putting it mildly to say that the experience of government management of existing state enterprises does not at all encourage one to expect that our government could deal with the tremendous task of managing a trading organization. However, experience must not tempt us to be too certain about future possibilities. We may be able to create some day a bureaucracy which shall be efficient, intelligent, and economical in the best sense of the word. But as things are at present, it seems most probable that it would be economically disastrous to hand over a sizeable proportion of distribution to officials.

Alternatively, the Federal Government may, with the governments of the regions, increase the indigenous share in distribution by strengthening co-operative trading units. Strictly, there is little difference between this method and the first. Under the present setup, co-operative movement in Nigeria is by and large controlled by the government and as such the government exercises as much power over it as it does in the case of public corporations. Thus whether the government enters distributive trades via a state trading agency or via co-operative trading, the implication would still be an increase in the share of the public sector in the Nigerian economy. This, however, is not a bad thing, provided the agency associated with the government is efficiently managed. It does appear that with co-operative trading the danger of red-tape, bureaucratic control, inelasticity, and unadaptability, may be less than it would be with a state trading agency. Barring the exigencies of politics, it should be possible to evolve a marriage of indigenous private enterprise and official control within a co-operative set-up. This alternative has many possibilities and its implementation should be explored.

The third alternative, which is the encouragement of indigenous private enterprise in commerce and trade, is also pregnant with difficulties. The issue involved is clear enough: how to make indigenous commercial enterprises financially viable, and managerially and technically competent enough to compete with the expatriate firms. But, as we have seen, the structure of the indigenous sector of distribution, with its medley of small firms, implies that there is no easy solution to the problem.

The government has an important part to play in the encouragement of private indigenous enterprises. The provision of capital, the training of managers and technicians, and the creation of an atmosphere conducive to effective competition with expatriate firms, are examples of the ways whereby the government can help. Yet these have long been realized by the governments, though the task has not been faced squarely. For as far back as 1958 the Federal Government appointed a Committee on Aid to African businessmen. The Report of this Committee was submitted in 1959. It is a matter of doubt whether the government has implemented the recommendations of this Committee. It may be that the Committee was rather too emotional in its approach to the problems of African businessmen. And as such, its appraisal of the problem and therefore some of its recommendations might have lacked objectivity. It appears, nevertheless, that an implementation of some of the recommendations of the Committee will be a step in the right direction.

It must however be emphasized that any measures taken by the government to encourage indigenous private enterprises in commerce and trade would take time to fructify and may thus confirm the expatriates in their entrenched position in commerce for a time. It may therefore be necessary for the government to encourage, by means of various inducements, the formation of indigenous partnerships and joint stock companies specially oriented towards commerce and trade. The government may make such combinations a pre-condition for giving financial and managerial assistance to indigenous firms. Also, if indigenous firms are to be encouraged, a review of the control of the sources of supply of imports by expatriates seems urgent. There is no doubt that the strength of expatriates derives in part from their control of the sources of supply of imports. The government could effectively undermine this source of strength to the advantage of indigenous firms.

While doing all that is necessary to strengthen indigenous private enterprise in commerce, it may still be necessary for the purpose of achieving a quick result for the government to have a stake in distribution. It is mentioned above that co-operative trading provides the government with this opportunity. Alternatively, the proposed Development Bank may launch a State Trading Corporation, with capital derived partly from shares sold to local investors, and partly from government sources. Either of these alternatives which fall short of government full monopoly of important sections of distribution should be explored.

18. AGRICULTURE IN A DEVELOPING ECONOMY

H. A. OLUWASANMI

The purpose of this paper is threefold: it is intended, first, to throw some light on the general behaviour of agriculture in a dynamic situation in which, as in Nigeria, the real product of a nation is increasing; secondly, to determine as accurately as existing statistical information will permit the pattern of expenditure on food as consumption expenditure increases; and thirdly, to judge the probable contribution of agriculture to the general growth of the Nigerian economy.

The accretion to the national product consequent upon general economic expansion will, in any given period, be used partly for building the national stock of capital, partly for the provision of social services and other services traditionally provided by government, and partly for increasing the level of consumption.

It is of vital interest to know just how the increased consumption expenditure which generally characterizes a growing economy is distributed among the goods and services produced by the various sectors of the economy because, in the long run, the changing pattern of consumption determines the allocation of productive resources to the different sectors, and, therefore, the relative contribution of each sector to the national product.

The key to the behaviour of consumer's expenditure on food products and, therefore, to an understanding of the place of agriculture in a growing economy is to be found in the expenditure elasticity of demand for food. In the present state of knowledge we can do no more than make reasoned generalizations about the long-run pattern of food consumption in Nigeria as indeed in most underdeveloped countries. Such generalizations will be based upon the available statistical evidence as well as on the evidence provided by consumer behaviour in countries that have passed the 'take-off' stage in their development. Statistical proofs for the operation of

Engel's law among consumers in the more advanced countries are so overwhelming as to render a review of them here superfluous. From these results it is tempting to want to generalize about the behaviour of consumers in less economically advanced countries without reference to such concrete proofs as are available.

Consumer surveys

In this respect the results of a number of consumer surveys, which are summarized here for the first time, are of interest to students of Nigerian agriculture and to economists interested in the overall development of such underdeveloped countries as Nigeria. The surveys were carried out by the Federal Department of Statistics among wage and salary earners in four urban areas in Nigeria at various times between 1953 and 1955. The surveyed households fall within three broad occupational groups, namely, labourers, artisans and clerks. These surveys did not cover the new urban élite composed

Table 1. *Food expenditure as percentage of monthly household expenditure in four urban areas in Nigeria by income levels.*
1953–55[1]

Income group (shillings per month).	Kaduna/ Zaria (%)	Lagos (%)	Enugu (%)	Ibadan (%)
Under 100s	61·6	—	—	—
100s to 149s	52·5	50·8	52·6	58·8
150s to 249s	46·6	45·5	45·7	45·0
250s to 349s	43·2	41·9	41·0	44·1
350s and over	43·6	—	—	—

[1] Sources: Federal Department of Statistics, *Urban Consumer Surveys in Nigeria —Lagos/Enugu/Ibadan* (Lagos, 1957); *Urban Consumer Surveys in Nigeria— Kaduna/Zaria* (Lagos, 1959). Expenditure on goods and services includes expenditure on food.

principally of higher civil servants, legislators, professionals, business men and teachers, and the vast rural population which constitutes about 75 per cent of the total population and which numbered among its members well-to-do cocoa, oil palm, and groundnut farmers. The coverage of the surveys both in terms of occupations and range of incomes necessarily limits the inference that can be drawn from them. Nevertheless, the expenditure habits of the group of wage and salary earners covered in the survey are of special significance in determining the future of agriculture in Nigeria, as these groups constitute the most numerous and thus, for the present analysis, the most vital elements in these urban areas.

For household incomes ranging between 100 shillings and 350 shillings per month the relation between total expenditure on goods and services and expenditure on food conforms to the pattern of consumer behaviour found by Engels and other workers in Western Europe and the United States. In the four urban areas shown in Table 1, food expenditure represents a declining proportion of total expenditure. In the Kaduna/Zaria area where the survey covered a wider range of incomes, the lowest income group with less than 100 shillings per month devoted 61·6 per cent of all expenditures on goods and services to food. As incomes increased from 100 shillings to 350 shillings the proportion of the increased total expenditure on food declined, reaching a low of 43·2 per cent for households earning between 250 and 350 shillings per month. With monthly incomes of 350 shillings and above the proportion of all expenditure devoted to food rose slightly to 43·6 per cent. As will be expected the absolute amount of money spent on food increased with increases in total expenditure.

Table 2. *Average monthly expenditure on goods and services per household in Kaduna/Zaria area by income levels. 1955*[1]

Income group (shillings per month).	No. of households	Average size of households	Expenditure on goods and services (shillings)	Food expenditure (shillings)
Under 100s	185	2·4	164	101
100s to 149s	123	2·8	216	113
150s to 249s	193	3·1	272	126
250s to 349s	101	2·7	321	138
350s and over	99	5·3	463	201

[1] Source: *Urban Consumer Surveys in Nigeria-Kaduna/Zaria.*

It will be observed that for all classes of incomes household expenditure exceeds household income. This is explained by the fact that the range of income in each class represents the 'basic incomes' of households in that class, that is, income derived from principal employers. As shown in Table 3, the total cash incomes of households include this basic income and cash receipts from subsidiary occupations, rents, gifts, loans and withdrawals from savings. With this all-inclusive definition of income, those households earning below 150 shillings per month were still unable to cover their monthly expenditure on goods and services from their cash earnings. They relied heavily on borrowings and credit purchases to meet their expenses on basic necessities. The higher income groups, on the other hand, particularly those earning above 250 shillings per month, were able to cover their expenses on goods and services from their cash earnings, although they too borrowed probably for dowry payments, weddings and funeral ceremonies. In fact, most households were net receivers of loans and gifts. This is a curious and interesting phenomenon. The survey expressed surprise in finding 'that in the lowest paid income group, over 40 per cent of total

Table 3. *Average monthly income and expenditure for households in Kaduna/Zaria area by income levels, 1955*[1]

Income group (shillings per month).	Cash earnings	Gifts	Savings withdrawals	Loans received	Other cash receipts	Total cash income	Credit purchases	Expenditure on goods and services
	s	*s*	*s*	*s*	*s*	*s*	*s*	*s*
Under 100*s*	128	7·8	2·5	33·0	2·5	174	15·4	164
100*s* to 149*s*	175	7·5	6·7	46·8	7·1	243	16·6	216
150*s* to 249*s*	254	12·2	23·3	35·0	6·4	331	7·3	272
250*s* to 349*s*	354	18·8	37·5	38·0	5·0	453	4·3	321
350*s* and over	542	5·5	56·5	22·0	8·6	635	7·8	463

[1] Source: *Urban Consumer Survey in Nigeria-Kaduna/Zaria.* Credit purchases included house rent not paid during the current month.

cash receipts come from sources other than the main occupation. It is also noteworthy that in the highest paid group, despite their average earnings of £27 per month, on average they borrow a further 22 shillings.'*

The distribution of food expenditure among the various food products is of equal significance for the long-run development of specific enterprises within the agricultural industry. Although consumers as a whole spend a declining proportion of their increasing expenditures on food, they spend proportionately less on certain food items and more on others as their incomes rise. Generally, the

* *Ibid.*, p. 20.
208

shift in food expenditure is from bulky and starchy products to food of high protein content.

In Table 4, columns 1, 2 and 7 are of special interest. As household incomes increased from 100 shillings to 350 shillings per month the expenditure on starchy food, that is, expenditure on gari (cassava flour), bread, rice and other grains (millet, guinea corn and maize), yams and other root crops, declined from 47·4 per cent to 40·7 per cent of the monthly average household food expenditure. In contrast, expenditure on animal proteins rose from 21·8 per cent of the

Table 4. *Expenditures on specified foods as percentage of average household expenditure on food in Kaduna/Zaria by income levels, 1955*[1]

Income group (shillings per month)	(1) Bulky foods	(2) Animal protein	(3) Oils and fats	(4) Vegetables and ground nuts	(5) Pre-serva-tives	(6) Fruits and nuts	(7) Im-ported food	(8) Bought meals[2]
	%	%	%	%	%	%	%	%
Under 100s	47·4	21·8	6·7	11·1	3·0	1·3	1·5	7·2
100s to 149s	45·7	23·2	6·9	11·2	3·4	1·0	2·4	6·2
150s to 249s	43·5	27·4	7·4	10·0	2·8	1·5	4·9	2·5
250s to 349s	44·2	28·0	6·8	8·5	2·5	1·2	6·5	2·3
350s and over	40·7	32·6	6·7	8·4	1·9	1·5	6·9	1·3

[1] Source: Ibid. Credit purchase included house rent not paid during the current month.

[2] Expenditure on 'bought meals' is determined by the relative size of the households in each income group. About 38 per cent of households with incomes lower than 100 shillings per month and 37 per cent of those earning between 100 shillings and 150 shillings consist of one person each. In contrast, 40 per cent of households with incomes of over 350 shillings per month have six persons each. The lower income groups do not have the same facilities as the higher income groups for preparing their meals at home. Hence the relatively high incidence of 'bought meals' among this class of workers.

monthly household expenditure on food to 32·6 per cent. While the expenditure on oils and fats remained almost a constant proportion of food expenditure at all levels of incomes, expenditure on imported food—largely tinned milk, food beverages, and other tinned food—rose from 1·5 per cent of the monthly food expenditure of the lowest income groups to about 7 per cent for those households having average monthly incomes of over 350 shillings. The picture in Ibadan closely parallels that for Kaduna and Zaria. The proportion of food expenditure devoted to bulky items declined from 41·8 per cent for household earnings less than 150 shillings per month to 34·7 per cent for those households with incomes of over 250 shillings per month. As was the case with the Kaduna/Zaria households, expenditure on imported food rose from 2·7 per cent of the food expenditure of Ibadan households earning below 150 shillings per month to 5·6 per cent for those households with average incomes of over 250 shillings per month.

It is to be noted, however, that money expenditure devoted to each food item rose with increases in levels of income. In the Kaduna-Zaria area monthly expenditure on starchy items, which constitute the bulk of the food consumed by lower-income households, rose from 47·6 shillings for households with less than 100 shillings per month to over 82·08 shillings for households earning more than 350 shillings per month. For animal proteins the rise was from 22 shillings per month per household to 65 shillings. The increase in the absolute amount of money expenditure by the higher-income groups on staples is accounted for by the larger households of artisans and clerks who received these higher incomes. It should be observed that the cheapening of food proteins throughout the country has much to do with improved (cheaper) transport facilities.

The Engelian pattern is clearly discernible in these surveys. It will however be hazardous to generalize about the behaviour of all classes of Nigerian consumers on the basis of the evidence reviewed here, or to argue that the expenditure elasticity of demand for food at all levels of incomes will follow the pattern in Western Europe and the United States. For one thing, the coverage of the survey is too limited. For another, with *per capita* income at approximately £30 per annum it is realistic to assume the existence of pre-Engelian conditions among large numbers of the Nigerian population and to suppose that the expenditure elasticity of demand of those whose incomes are closer to the national average will be relatively high and even positive over a certain range of income. The pattern of food expenditure in the different parts of the country will also be affected by differences in the kinds of food available to consumers and by regional differences in household or individual incomes.

Demand for food and Nigeria's agriculture

Nevertheless, these urban income surveys, covering as they do sections of the urban population whose numbers and incomes are likely to rise as the economy expands, appear to provide a valid basis for answering certain questions about the future contribution of agriculture to an expanding Nigerian economy.

At the present stage of development in Nigeria agriculture and allied industries contribute about 68 per cent of the gross domestic product* and employ more than 75 per cent of its total working population.† Given a situation of rapid economic expansion it is clear from the foregoing exposition that the proportionate contribution of agriculture to the national product will sustain a steady decline as economic development progresses. The actual rate of decline of agriculture's contribution to the national product will depend as much upon the rate of growth of non-agricultural industries as upon the rate of development within agriculture itself.

The relative decline of agriculture which inevitably follows from general economic expansion is usually accompanied by a reallocation of resources in favour of non-agricultural industries. The most important manifestation of this process is the shift of population from rural to urban occupations.‡ The shift of population from agriculture to the expanding sectors of the economy raises a problem of fundamental importance for the economy as a whole and leads us to the consideration of the second subject of this paper, namely, the probable contribution of agriculture to a growing Nigerian economy.

It is essential at this stage in the argument to restate the primary function of agriculture, which briefly put is to 'supply mankind with food and raw materials which are of animal or vegetable [origin]'.§ It follows from this that in the early stages of economic development a more realistic criterion for measuring the contribution of the agricultural industry to the national economy is the efficiency with which it performs its traditional functions of providing food and raw materials for the non-agricultural sections of the economy. Consequently, the rate at which labour can be advantageously transferred from agriculture to the expanding sectors of the economy will depend upon whether the underlying conditions of production in agriculture, that is to say, whether agricultural techniques and

---

* A. R. Prest and I. C. Stewart, *The National Income of Nigeria*, 1950–1 (London, 1953). The 1956–7 estimates of the national income put agriculture's contribution at 61¾ per cent of the gross domestic product. See *Economic Survey of Nigeria*, 1959 (Lagos, 1959), p. 16.
† *Population Censuses of Nigeria* 1952–3 (Lagos, Government Printer).
‡ Colin Clark, *The Conditions of Economic Progress* (London, 1957), p. 492 *et seq.*
§ Rene Dumont, *Types of Rural Economy* (London, 1957), pp. 1–2.

organization permit a declining agriculture to satisfy the needs of an expanding urban population for food, and of growing industries for raw materials.

To get a clearer picture of agriculture's contribution as the economy expands we will make the simplifying assumption that under existing technologies of production and distribution the output of food and raw materials from Nigerian farms is adequate for the present needs of the population. In this circumstance a given transfer of population from agriculture to other forms of economic activity without compensating changes in agricultural techniques and organization—that is, without fundamental technological changes which permit the resources left in agriculture to achieve higher productivity—will cause maladjustments throughout the economy. Such maladjustments will express themselves in a slackening in the supplies of food and raw materials relative to increase in demand, and, consequently, in relatively high cost structures for the newly established manufacturing industries.

It is possible that two objections may be raised against this line of reasoning. It may be argued firstly that in Nigeria food supplies are already adequate for the needs of the population, and secondly, that a reduction of the agricultural population will further enhance the output of food from Nigerian farms by making available to cultivators larger acreages.

In terms of total intake of calories per head of population food supplies may be said to be adequate at present levels of production. But a considerable part of the calories consumed by the average Nigerian comes from bulky and starchy food products with notable deficiencies in proteins and other essential food items.* With rising levels of incomes the first major effort of consumers is to correct any dietary imbalance by expanding the demand for certain food items while curtailing demand for others.

The Nigerian urban wage earner, as his income rises, spends a rising proportion of his food expenditure on such high-yielding protein food products as meat, fish, eggs, milk and other dairy products. Since some of these items are not readily available from domestic sources he relies on imports for his supplies of them. In this sense, if not in any other, food supplies from domestic sources

---

* The average calorie intake is estimated at about 2,250 calories per day. Except in Northern Nigeria and in urban areas of the South the intake of vegetable and animal proteins is low. See International Bank, *The Economic Development of Nigeria* (Baltimore, 1955), pp. 238–42.

are not really adequate to meet the changing pattern of food consumption in Nigeria. Even when food supply from domestic sources is adequate for the needs of the population 'it would still be true that the principal road to progress would be through intensified efforts to improve efficiency in production of food. Our concern is not with the amount of food available but with food production per person engaged in agriculture.'*

This leads us to the second objection, namely, that a reduction of the agricultural population will increase the output of food because those remaining in agriculture will now have the opportunity of increasing the size of their farms.

Implicit in this argument is the assumption that high pressures of population against land resources is the principal cause of low productivity in Nigerian agriculture. This will be the case if small size of holdings, one of the basic features of agricultural organization in Nigeria, is a consequence of population pressures on the land. Except in the overcrowded conditions of certain provinces in Eastern Nigeria there are large tracts of uncultivated farm land in many parts of the country.† Land is not the limiting factor of size in Nigerian agriculture. Primitive techniques and tools of farming and a tenure system and social organization which render it virtually impossible for farmers to move freely from regions of high population density to areas where land is in excess supply are the real factors limiting both the scale of operation and the volume of output in agriculture.

Where, as in Nigeria, technical and social conditions are the basic factors limiting the size of the operating units in agriculture, a reduction of the agricultural population may have adverse effects on the total volume of food output. Admittedly, a declining rural population will free more land for the use of the farmers left in agriculture. The consequent increase in the size of farms will, other things being equal, lead to increased output of farm products. It is, however, doubtful whether under the existing technical conditions of agricultural production any real increase in size will follow as a matter of course from a decline in the agricultural population. With his primitive hoe and cutlass it is highly unrealistic to assume that a mere increase in the cultivable area will induce the farmer to increase the size of his holdings. For example, in the less crowded areas of

* W. A. Lewis, *Report on Industrialisation and the Gold Coast* (Acra, 1953), p. 3.
† In both Northern and Western Nigeria over 50 per cent of the cultivable area is classified as 'uncultivated bush'. See *Report on the Sample Census of Agriculture 1950–1*, Federal Department of Statistics, Lagos, 1952.

H. A. Oluwasanmi

Nigeria where access to farm land is relatively easy the farmer continues to operate his three-acre holdings because of the limits imposed by his tools and techniques.

It follows therefore that a technologically stagnant agriculture in an environment of general economic expansion in which the industrial-urban population is increasing while the agricultural population is declining will cause shortages in food products from domestic sources. To make up for this deficiency it may be necessary to use part of the foreign exchange earnings, which in Nigeria derive mainly from agricultural exports, for food imports. A high propensity to import consumer goods, all things being equal, will reduce the capacity of the importing country to pay for the capital goods imports required for the expansion of the industrial sector of the economy.

In 1958, for example, a total sum of over £16 million was spent on food imports. This included import expenditure of over £900,000 on dairy products, of about £50,000 on eggs, of over £6 million on fish, and of about £2 million on wheaten flour.* Given the necessary technical conditions, the demand for these products—with the probable exception of wheaten flour—can be met more cheaply from domestic sources.

The secular decline in the agricultural population which experience has taught us to expect in a developing economy may be frustrated if the underlying techniques and organization of agricultural production are not improved at the same time that manufactures expand. The relatively high proportion of the population at present engaged in food production is a manifestation of the primitive state of agricultural arts in Nigeria. A fundamental improvement in these arts will be required before a large proportion of the agricultural population can be transferred into industry with advantage to the economy. In fact, the rapid development of manufacturing industries may be retarded if by reason of its technological backwardness agriculture is unable to provide the raw materials required by new industries. Post-war experience with industrial and semi-industrial projects tends to confirm this general observation.

Agriculture and industry in Nigeria

Since the end of the Second World War a number of processing industries, notable among which are the oil mills, the rubber and

* Federal Department of Statistics, *Nigeria Trade Report*, 1957 (Lagos).

canning factories, have suffered serious set-backs due largely to insufficient supplies of raw materials. The rubber processing factory established in Benin at a total cost of £320,324 sustained a total loss of £75,534 between 1955 and 1957; in the financial year 1955–6 alone the fruit canning factory in Ibadan with a total investment of £334,497 lost £73,839, and its cumulative losses to March 1956 amounted to £99,654. Both projects are located in Western Nigeria. Similarly, the oil mills in Eastern Nigeria have shown losses throughout their lives. The public bodies responsible for the operation of these projects have frankly traced the source of their problems to agriculture.

The Western Nigerian Development Corporation, which owns and operates the Ibadan Canning Factory, complained that because 'of inadequate supplies of grapefruits and pineapples the factory's output was low in relation to its capacity'.* With regard to the rubber-processing factory, the Corporation argued that 'until sufficient supplies of good quality latex are forthcoming the factory will be seriously handicapped and will be unable to make a contribution to the economy of the Western Region commensurate with the capital investment'.†

Apart from the dependence of these plants, which process mainly for the export market, on agriculture for their raw materials, there is also a close connection between agriculture and industries producing for the home market. Expenditure on imports provides a fair measure of the size of the internal market for industrial products. The composition of these imports also gives an indication of industries which are most likely to succeed and generate further growth throughout the economy.

In 1957 a total sum of £14·5 million was spent in importing 156·2 million square yards of cotton piece-goods into Nigeria. This is in contrast to an expenditure of £780,000 on 'tools and implements' in the same year.‡ The establishment of a textile industry on a scale large enough to satisfy the home demand for this class of textile will require a considerable expansion in the output of raw cotton from Nigeria farms. Similarly, food processing plants, like the oil mills and rubber processing factories, require an adequate flow of farm

---

* Western Nigeria Development Corporation, *Annual Report* 1955–6 (Ibadan 1957), p. 36.
† *Annual Report* 1956–7, p. 22.
‡ *Digest of Statistics* (Lagos, 1959), vol. 8, 2, April 1959.

products for efficient performance. As has been remarked, over £16 million was spent in 1958 on the importation of all classes of food. Most of these can be produced conveniently and more cheaply at home. Finally, the accumulation of internal capital for financing these industries depends to a large extent on the efficiency of the export sector of agriculture which has provided the bulk of the capital for the modest development that has taken place since the end of the Second World War.

To ensure, therefore, sustained growth in the non-agricultural sectors of the economy it is the function of the agricultural industry, as it declines in relative importance, to provide food and raw materials in adequate quantities and to facilitate a rapid rate of domestic capital accumulation. The improvement in the underlying conditions of agricultural production must be of such magnitude as to permit the resources left in agriculture to satisfy the food needs of an expanding population.

Consideration of the particular forms of improvement required before agriculture can make its proper contribution to economic expansion is beyond the scope of the present paper. It may be mentioned, however, that there are two possible lines of approach to the solution of the basic problem of low productivity in Nigerian agriculture: (a) improvement of the existing technical framework of agriculture, by which is meant a general improvement of the 3-acre farms through the use of such agricultural requisites as artificial and natural fertilizers, higher yielding strains of seeds and the adoption of a more permanent system of rotation; and (b) the modification of the existing institutional framework with particular reference to land tenure and credit institutions.

It is essential to restate and bring into clearer perspective the role of agriculture in the development of Nigeria and in the development of almost all West African countries. When emphasis on increased food production and measures designed to expand the scope of the export sector of agriculture may be viewed in 'unenlightened circles' as mere continuation of colonial economic expansion, it is especially important to stress the truth that industrialization, which is generally looked upon as the universal panacea of poverty in these countries, 'can make little progress unless agriculture is progressing vigorously at the same time, to provide both market for industry and industry's labour supply'.*

* W. A. Lewis, *op. cit.*, p. 2.